OFFSHORE

OFFSHORE
The Dark Side of the Global Economy

William Brittain-Catlin

FARRAR, STRAUS AND GIROUX • NEW YORK

Farrar, Straus and Giroux
19 Union Square West, New York 10003

Distributed in Canada by Douglas & McIntyre Ltd.
Printed in the United States of America
First edition, 2005

Grateful acknowledgment is made to the following for permission to reprint previously
published material:
Lyrics from "No Letting Go" by Charles Von Wayne and Stephen "Lenky" Marsden ©
Singso WW Music (BMI), used by arrangement with The Royalty Network, Inc., and
Greensleeves Publishing Ltd.
Translation of Altenberg, *Lieder*, V by Alban Berg © 1995 by Lionel Salter, used with per-
mission of the Estate of Lionel Salter.

Library of Congress Cataloging-in-Publication Data
Brittain-Catlin, William, 1966–
    Offshore : the dark side of the global economy / William Brittain-Catlin.—
1st ed.
        p.   cm.
    Includes index.
    ISBN-13: 978-0-374-25698-2 (hardcover : alk. paper)
    ISBN-10: 0-374-25698-5 (hardcover : alk. paper)
    1. Cayman Islands—Economic conditions.   2. Tax havens—Cayman Islands.
    3. International finance—Political aspects—Cayman Islands.   4. Commercial
crimes—Cayman Islands.   5. Transnational crime—Cayman Islands.
    I. Title: Dark side of the global economy. II. Title.

HC152.2.B75 2005
330.97292'1—dc22

                                                            2005010170

Designed by Debbie Glasserman

www.fsgbooks.com

1   3   5   7   9   10   8   6   4   2

For Omari and Rainer

And often times, to win us to our harm,
The instruments of darkness tell us truths.

—SHAKESPEARE, *MACBETH*

Contents

OFFSHORE

1. Our Offshore World

Happy does the sailor return to the bright streams
From far off islands, where he has reaped—
I too would like to return to my homeland again.
Oh, how I have woefully reaped.
Your lovely shores, which have raised me
Oh grant me, you forests of my childhood,
When I return, peace once more again.

—HÖLDERLIN, *HOMELAND*

Grand Cayman, May 2003

From the public beach off West Bay Road, you can see George Town, the capital, due south down the shoreline. I look and wait for the fireworks to start. The sun has set more than an hour ago, but there are a few people on the beach. A young couple kiss. A Honduran family, feet in the sea, eat dinner from a takeout bag. Then, a few minutes after eight, the fireworks start.

It is a night in May 2003, the eve of the five hundredth anniversary of the first sighting of the Cayman Islands by Columbus, on his fourth

Atlantic crossing in 1503. A weekend of festivities has begun. Cayman is celebrating its birthday, its origins linked to the dawn of Western enlightenment, trade, and empire. Here is the prism through which our offshore world can be glimpsed.

The fireworks are over before they get started. Perhaps it's because I am too far up Seven Mile Beach to get the full effect. I expect more, a peaking crescendo of light over George Town, some gasp of excitement from the few people around me. It feels like something is being held back. There is an ambiguity to the fireworks; an outward moment of expression has been pulled back, contained, and controlled.

Back on West Bay Road, I start the drive toward George Town. The road runs down the side of Seven Mile Beach and is Cayman's most developed thoroughfare, linking the banks, offices, and law firms of the financial center with West Bay, a residential area with the islands' greatest concentration of black Caymanians. On the way you pass Wendy's, the Holiday Inn, Coutts Bank, the Governor's House, business centers, clubs, bars, and upscale condos. The massive Ritz-Carlton hotel apartment complex, yet to be finished, shoots concrete passageways over the road, stretching toward the sea. Dotted between the hotels and resorts is an occasional wooden cabin, neat and tidy, with a TV aerial and a large house number fixed to the door. No one is walking, just cars.

George Town is quiet. A few streetlamps on the main harbor road barely reveal the water to one side, and side roads on the other are merely tracks leading into the night. The glass structures of the banks that glint and gleam by day are in the shadows, their names—Barclays, Scotiabank, Butterfield—just visible in the moonlight.

The first signs of life are two policemen in white peaked caps, manning a temporary barrier. A few steps on, some Australians pass by in high spirits; then there's a sharp turn into Cardinal Avenue. Here several hundred people are crushed up together, moving to the sounds of Krosfyah, a reggae soca band from Barbados. The music is good and loud, with a full, sharp sound. A little carnival has landed in Cayman. Bodies wind and twist, following the bandleader Edwin's taut gyrations. It's black people's night. "Don't take no video," shouts Edwin, "you just gwan rob me wi' dat." Then he makes a crazy move, and the crowd start to cheer him wildly. "Now show me some grinding," urges Edwin, "real good grinding." He moves his hips round and round and up and down.

A little girl is pushed up onto the stage to take part in the grinding contest. The people roar their approval. "What's your name?" The girl whispers back, her chin pinned to her chest, hiding her face. "Dorrit!" repeats the bandleader, and then asks her age. "Seven years old!" The soca rhythm revs up. The bandleader starts to move. Dorrit starts to grind, body jerking up and down, bonding the revelers together into a single physical mass. But the girl's chin pushes harder into her chest, her eyes turned inward, hidden in shame and embarrassment, caught at once between expressive physical joy and the authority of her mental detachment from the dance. She tires, gives up, and is passed limply back into the hands of the crowd, her sacrifice complete.

Such events make headline news in Cayman. Only a week earlier, the daily newspaper, in its coverage of the Batabano, Cayman's annual carnival, had reminded readers that a group known as the Mudders, who were "renowned for lewd behaviour," had been banned from participating in the festivities. Nevertheless, the *Caymanian Compass* was sorry to report that "a small number of individuals were openly 'grinding,' with their mid-sections glued together in a highly suggestive manner as they danced to calypso songs." The paper wasn't sure if it was possible to ban grinding altogether, though that would be preferable, as modesty was "a characteristic of Cayman's conservative heritage."

Little Dorrit was caught between freedom and control, like Cayman itself between the global market economy and colonial dependency on the United Kingdom. With this thought we can begin, if we

want to look hard enough, to glimpse the strange hidden space between capital and the state, the secret realm at the ambiguous heart of
Western modernity, the ever-kept secret contradiction between the individual and the authority of the law.

The Rhythm of the Day

Throughout the weekday mornings, huge ocean cruisers with names
like *Imagination* park just outside George Town's harbor. These
twelve-deck monsters, though offshore, dwarf any structure on the island. They jump out at you in the gaps between the beachside hotels
when you stroll down West Bay Road, and your sudden thought is that
the entire island is itself being towed away and moored elsewhere
more convenient.

The cruise-ship tourists are harmless creatures nonetheless. Mostly
Americans, earnestly taking in an island that is geographically close to
them but foreign enough, with its British Empire–era post office and
library, to make it a necessary stop-off point for a wander around the
duty-free shops of George Town, picking up Rolexes and Baccarat
crystal at Kirk Freeport on Cardinal Avenue.

Several thousand tourists will come onshore off the liners, and by
midday George Town will be thronging. By early afternoon, with the
liners gone, George Town is quiet and empty. Local people go about
doing their business, have a snack outside KFC, set off back home
with a few provisions. By the seafront, near the harbor, the town returns to its fishing-village roots. Fish are cut and cleaned on a concrete slab under the shade of an umbrella, a three-man operation
performed with exact precision. Around a tree nearby, old-timers and
shirtless young men gather close to chat and joke.

When Bill Walker first came to Cayman, in 1963, a lawyer from
Guyana, he remembered that "there were cows wandering through

George Town, only one bank, only one paved road, and no telephones." Barclays, the bank, had opened in 1953 in a couple of rooms on Harbour Road. Cayman was then a seagoing society, with a strong church and one daily paper, *The Gospel of the Kingdom*. The entire population was barely 8,000. Now it is approaching 40,000. Now there is an airport with international links and a modern communications infrastructure; some 580 bank and trust companies; and 65,000 companies registered on the island, one and a half times more than the current human population. Now Cayman could boast, in truth, that it is one of the world's biggest financial centers.

Behind the tourist front line of the harbor and duty-free shops, only seconds away from where the old men take shade, is the banking and finance center. By late afternoon, all is hush. The last BMW has left for South Sand, George Town's lush suburb.

Here are congregated the offices of all but a few of the major global banks. Large modern buildings—the newer ones, like Barclays House—are in what might be called the South Florida style: pastel colors, palm trees, pediments, and columns. The offices of the Royal Bank of Canada, HSBC, UBS, and Cayman National Bank follow suit. The Bank of Butterfield and Scotiabank are in older white slab-and-glass blocks, and Dresdner Bank and others are functional tinted glass and concrete.

Each is like an ocean liner that has come across the sea and landed on the island, flying the emblem of its brand. These are the proud monuments of Cayman. Thirty years ago the Legislative Assembly Building burned to the ground, and the banks saved it in their own image, replacing it with an impenetrable glass edifice. Revenue from the banks financed the courthouse, the police headquarters, and the offices of civil bureaucracy. All these structures combine to form what has become a national aesthetic, the bonding of the will of capital and state.

Radical Instruments

Forty years ago the Cayman Islands were on the verge of economic extinction. There was no room in the modern world for an island that made rope and caught turtles and whose wetlands prevented any agriculture. Today the standard of living is the highest in the Caribbean, surpassing the United States and Britain. There is virtually no unemployment. Only the beautiful alliance of capital and state has made this possible.

It is well known in financial circles that the Cayman Islands is the fifth-largest banking center in the world, holding external assets of more than 700 billion U.S. dollars. In terms of the capital that moves across its shores, Cayman is in a league with New York, London, and Hong Kong. Most of the banking business is institutional, not private, and consists of vast overnight checking accounts for banks and corporations gaining tax-free interest on capital, a million-dollar-a-day advantage that would be impossible at home. But there are no vast reserves stashed away in George Town safes: money is "booked" in Cayman, having merely a virtual presence, similar to the tourists who pass through the island like daylight ghosts.

Cayman's role in mobilizing global capital and turning it offshore goes back to the creation of the Eurodollar market in the 1960s. At that time, the United States had a barrage of regulations and restrictions placed on the export of the dollar, policies designed to keep the U.S. external trade deficit from overheating. But this did not stop foreign, particularly European, demand for the dollar, and it led to the currency being hotly traded outside the United States. Thus the Eurodollar market was born, with dollars going offshore, where they could be bought, sold, lent, and deposited, free from U.S. regulations.

U.S. banks met the huge international demand for dollars by opening up in countries that permitted trade in Eurodollars. The City of London became a prime location and soon dominated the trade in dollars cut loose from U.S. control, turning the city into the world's largest finance center. The banks also found a welcome in the tax havens of Cayman, the Bahamas, the Netherlands Antilles, and Panama. The proximity of these countries to the United States, along with tax advantages that discounted Eurodollar deals, ease of incorporation, and the low overheads of a brass-plate operation—not much more than a telex machine and a desk in George Town or elsewhere—led to a dramatic growth in the level of deposits offshore. By the end of the 1970s, 385 billion Eurodollars were booked offshore in total, with $30 billion of that booked through tiny Cayman.

Banks today in Cayman are dealing with an amount nearly double the total offshore assets of two decades ago. This is what pushes the Cayman Islands into the premier league and sets it apart from other tax havens. Cayman is at the forefront of global capital—not marginal, but central to its all-embracing but often hidden power.

But this is not enough to survive. Cayman has to be at the cutting edge of what can be done with capital if it wants to keep on top. So it invents. It sells new financial products, offers new services that become the radical instruments of capital: mutual funds, venture capital funds, fixed-income medical receivables, structured finance, special purpose vehicles. Cayman is not merely a depository for global capital, but a business-backed state with a mission to increase the flow of capital toward its shores. It is a seller of novelties on the financial market, a sweetshop for capitalism, developing new flavors and recipes for increased returns.

Close collaboration between the private sector and government in Cayman is paramount. In committees hosted by the islands' financial secretary, bankers and financiers pitch bold ideas for attracting finance to Cayman. New laws are quickly drafted, and no one gets in the way, for business knows what it wants, and the government is heavily dependent on business for revenue. The islands' financial associations play a key role, dining and socializing with government officials and legislative members. "It's a great business situation—it's who you know," confirmed Mike Gibbs, chairman of the captive insurers association, whose members have seen a boom in the underwriting of terrorist risk in Cayman since the attacks on New York and Washington in September 2001.

There is an evangelical spirit to capitalism in Cayman, an evocation that only here, on these small islands, can the real thing be found. The spokesman for the chamber of commerce makes it plain: "Capital comes to Cayman because onshore jurisdictions don't meet the needs of entrepreneurs. They have too many regulations and restrictions. We have the instruments to raise and maximize capital, do deals, and take risks. Business wants control—and freedom—and that's why it comes to Cayman."

The Law of the Land

George Town Public Library, on dusty Edward Street, is just a step away from the radiator-grill-style facade of CIBC Bank and Trust Company Limited. The old stone library is a good retreat from the heat, and inside, young Caymanians, preparing for exams, coach each other in whispers.

On two short shelves in the library's reference section is the complete body of Cayman law, filed into twenty small folders. Like the wooden vaulted ceiling above, Cayman law is straightforward, rigid, and uncompromising. Its statutes have provided for the perfect marriage of an ultraconservative society to a radical liberal economy, and have been the foundation of Cayman's success as an offshore finance center.

The Poor Persons Law, the Public Order Law, and the Education Law are all short, sharp, and authoritative, with no more than a dozen sections each. Children shall go to school: if they don't, parents will be fined. Children shall behave: if they don't, they will be beaten. People shall not demonstrate without permission: if they do, they will be sent to prison. There are no opt-outs or exceptions for special cases. The death penalty for murder is still in force, but the last time two men were sentenced to the gallows, the United Kingdom stopped the hanging at the last hour. Cayman was not pleased. They had spent $300,000 and three months' work designing the gallows.

Company and business law takes up the bulk of Cayman legislation. There are eleven Companies Laws, and it is the only area of law where there are numerous amendments. But compared with the volumes of bankruptcy and insolvency law in the United States, there are just a few pages in Cayman. Again by comparison, labor and trade-union law is virtually nonexistent.

Henry Harford, of Maples and Calder law firm in George Town, explained that Cayman law was stuck in a kind of time warp. "It's as if the clock was stopped on English law some time in the nineteenth century—certainly before the dawn of the welfare state. Cayman law is simple and clear—what might be called a classical liberal body of law." Indeed, there is little difference between the law today and that watched over by an English colonial administrator in the mid-nineteenth century.

"There's no expectation that someone else is going to take the strain," said Harford. "In Cayman it's sink or swim. There's no consumer law, no social welfare, no endless reams of employment law. You're responsible for yourself. In business, contract law rules. You shake hands and keep your word. If something goes wrong, you are either right or wrong in law. It's there in black and white."

Perhaps because of its robust laws, Cayman is not a litigious society. In fact, it underwrites the risk of litigation elsewhere, particularly the United States. The captive insurance market—where offshore companies cover their owners' hard-to-insure onshore risks such as pollution or product liability—has grown here in direct proportion to the rising obsession with litigation in the United States. Hundreds of companies insure themselves through Cayman subsidiaries to take advantage of the islands' liberal underwriting environment. The move started back in the 1970s, when the Harvard Medical Group went to the Bahamas looking to insure themselves against medical malpractice suits. The Bahamas said no, so Harvard came to Cayman and drafted an insurance law with the government. Today, about half of the captive insurers in Cayman are U.S. health-care companies, and by tailoring their laws to business, the islands amass further revenue.

Cayman's rigid body of law has matched social order with a liberal, laissez-faire economy, directed by a minimal state. The islands have seen growth, foreign investment, and a decent standard of living, but what is striking is the complete absence of a public, political dimension to Cayman's affairs. There are elections, but not one man one vote. Political parties are only in their infancy. Elected members form teams once they are in government and then parcel out political and civil service jobs to friends and colleagues.

It is not without good reason that democracy is underdeveloped in Cayman. For some three hundred years the Cayman Islands were twice removed from political autonomy. From the seventeenth century until the late 1950s Cayman had been a dependency of Jamaica, itself under the yoke of Britain. Cayman did not prosper in this period. It was a forgotten backwater, neglected and isolated by Jamaica. In 1959 Cayman gained a measure of freedom from Jamaica with its own constitution. But the real battle came a few years later: Should Cayman break away from Britain completely by affiliating to a newly independent Jamaica, or should it choose to be a British Crown Colony? It chose the latter.

Cayman's separation from Jamaica was its moment of liberation, its historic political moment. Paradoxically, though, liberation put it under the direct control of Britain, the ultimate power, and removed any political basis to its new freedom. A political sacrifice was made, but now Cayman could exploit a body of classical law to its own advantage as a tax haven, an opportunity denied them under their tutelage to Jamaica. It would take old minds to play new tricks.

Meanwhile, Jamaica's political path from independence moved it increasingly away from a position where a tax haven could have developed. Talk in the 1960s of a planned economy for Jamaica unnerved hopes that international capital might find a refuge there, a situation confirmed in the early 1970s with the formation of the island's first socialist administration. Thereafter, Jamaica would become embroiled in political and economic crises, problems that prevent any country, let alone poor islands in the Caribbean, from becoming successful offshore finance centers.

Politics is a dirty word in Cayman. Mere mention of independence is foul. Cayman's political battles were won many years ago, and nothing must upset the perfect state of nature that the fine balance between freedom and control brings. Cayman's fear of chaos runs very deep. That is why the authoritarian strain in Cayman society is so powerful. It is but one short step back to the poverty from which the islands escaped.

"Economically, we are very liberal," says Wil Pineau, a former journalist turned businessman on Cayman. "Socially, far from it. We're conservative with a strong Christian heritage. We're skeptical of human rights and homosexuality. The constitution may not be so far advanced as other Caribbean states—but look at how bad their economies are!"

Tax Haven Nature

The natural beauty of the Cayman Islands is submerged, offshore. The islands are mere tips of underwater mountains that rise up from thousands of feet below. Shallow reefs of stony coral lead down to cavernous mountain walls, where, in and out of tunnels, schools of horse-eye jacks and manta rays glide past. Sea sponges of platinum yellow and strawberry red waft like an apparatus of tubes and fans, subaquatic machines giving hideout for neon sea creatures three feet long.

The islands hardly rise above sea level, and by comparison to what is hidden beneath, the land is unremarkable, flat, and marshy. It is as though abundance ran out of steam when it came to the matter of surface topography. Yet there is a wonder to match what is down below, its origin so drenched in myth that it has now become second nature. This is the wonder of Cayman as a tax haven.

An old Cayman folktale tells of the "Wreck of the Ten Sail." In 1794, a frigate, HMS *Convert*, leading nine merchant ships from Jamaica bound for England, struck the reef off East End, over on the far eastern side of Grand Cayman. The merchant ships, confused by the *Convert*'s warning signals, crashed against the reef too, and all the ships were wrecked. The brave inhabitants of East End set off to rescue the seamen and recover what cargo they could. The seamen were saved, but many Caymanians lost their lives. The old tale has it that among the saved was an English prince, a cousin of George III. An admiral too was said to have been brought back onshore alive. And so, as a reward for their heroic sacrifice, the king declared that Caymanians would be forever granted freedom from taxation.

Not until the late 1960s, with the abolition of tax treaties with the United States—and, with that, the power to establish complete confidentiality in its financial affairs—did Cayman become a full-fledged tax haven. However, it is doubtful that Cayman ever had any form of direct taxation. As far as anyone knows, there has never been income tax, corporation tax, capital gains tax, sales tax, inheritance tax, or death duties: the lot that generally befalls people living in the developed world.

Local revenues are maintained by import duties (Cayman imports 90 percent of its goods), the sale of postage stamps, and, since the emergence of an offshore finance center, company fees and the sale of bank licenses. But at the end of the day, if you work and live in Cayman, you take home your pay gross. This is how it has always been.

Mythology knows Cayman as "the island that time forgot." This is true, to the extent that while Cayman's development as a global financial center puts it at the center of Western modernity, it has preserved, in its political and social existence, forms of life that are—as a historical outpost of European empire—closer to the first struggles for Western control and domination of the world. This is the case with Cayman's origin as a tax haven. In the echo of the current situation one detects fragments of a time prior to the nation-state. From its mythical vantage point outside history, Cayman casts its secret spell on the modern world, compelling the latter to a freedom that demands of us a ransom for a sacrifice once and forever made.

Survival

Cayman is entwined with the sea as much as with capital. Both are molded into men like Harry Chisholm, the great-great-grandson of a navigator from Aberdeen who was shipwrecked off the south side of Cuba in 1850. The Scotsman made it to Cayman, and his descendants stayed on the islands thereafter. Today Mr. Chisholm is the managing director of the Royal Bank of Canada and presides over one of Cayman's local banks from a glass-walled corner office that surveys central George Town. His face is rugged and tanned; deep furrows across a broad, strong brow; hair jet-black with a slight kink. A face that bears the mark of survival, and a handshake that would crack the fingers of your hand.

Four generations of the Chisholm family went to sea, but not Harry. His brothers turned him against it. It was a rough life out there, a lonely life on the freight ships that crossed the Atlantic or transported iron ore from South to North America. So Harry stayed on-shore and noticed that the seamen would send their earnings home to save up for a piece of land. They would come home once in a while to build a house, then go to sea again, saving up all the while. In 1965 the Royal Bank set up in competition with Barclays to get the sea-farers' business and help them save their hard-earned money.

Harry got a job with Royal Bank. He noticed how the seamen ven-tured out into borrowing money from the bank, a practice long seen as shameful. Then young lawyers arrived on the island and found out how Cayman could be used by foreign banks and companies to make business confidential. By the early 1970s, banks big and small, mostly from the United States, moved onto Cayman to compete for institu-tional business, using the island as a deposit-gathering station. The days of seamen sending money home were long gone, but it was their descendants who were now, in 2003, in the banking hall of the Royal Bank, below Harry Chisholm in his bright corner office, paying their bills at the counter, arranging mortgages, and taking money out of cash machines.

Before finance, it was the sea. From the time of the first permanent settlements on Cayman in the early eighteenth century, people would survive by building ships and sailing out to fishing grounds hundreds of miles from home, with nothing to guide their return home but the stars. Columbus had called Cayman "Las Tortugas," after the turtles that swarmed the sea around the small islands he first sighted in May 1503. In the 1600s, English, Dutch, and French ships came to Cay-man to catch the turtles and salt them up for long-lasting rations on their colonial raiding tours of the Caribbean. Records show that Blackbeard the Pirate kept a "small turtler" at Grand Cayman. The turtles would remain a prime source of sustenance for Cayman's first few hundred settlers and then later become a means of trade with neighboring islands.

In the early twentieth century Cayman was renowned for building its own wooden vessels, but men soon began to leave shipbuilding to work on the merchant ships that carried trade to the United States and around Central America. Cayman's highly valued export labor in the shipping industry meant that new income came into the islands and supported the thousand or so families who lived there. By 1937, half of the islands' manpower aged between eighteen and sixty worked in shipping.

Cayman society, with a population of six thousand by World War II, revolved around the demands of the shipping industry. With most husbands and fathers away at sea so much of the time, island society endured a kind of permanent self-detachment, though there was comfort in the knowledge that menfolk would not always be at sea and would return one day, a fact that gave collective emotional security to family life. A strong church-based matriarchy developed onshore to withstand the realities of detachment. Divorce was rare.

Yet the men sacrificed much in their profitable isolation at sea, away for an average eighteen months at a time. Tradition instructed that one did as one's father did, and a boy "most likely left school as a 12 year old and probably covered more than five thousand miles of open water under sail" by the time he started work in the industry. He would know how to hold a sextant, understand the basics of celestial navigation, and be trained in the art of weather forecasting. Above all, he respected authority.

A career of loneliness beckoned, which, though it gave much opportunity and advantage, took men away from home, family, and children. But as it was the means to economic independence and survival, seafaring became the expected way of life. Captain John Hurlston worked for the Insco Shipping Company, and he missed his children terribly. "That's how it was in those days, you see, because if you had a job you had to try to keep it . . . there was always someone ready to take it." If Captain Hurlston was coming down from Jamaica en route to Florida, he would steer his ship within spitting distance of the south coast of Cayman, right by where his family lived on the shore. "Many times I would just come close in and blow the whistle, and the kids would run out and they'd wave. We'd wave back and forth at one another. I did that many times, but I wouldn't stop because I didn't have permission."

Cayman's seamen were renowned for their courage and independence, and their golden age was to come in the 1950s and '60s. A Michigan shipping tycoon, Daniel K. Ludwig, so-called father of the supertanker, was looking for seamen to man what would grow to be a fleet of sixty huge vessels, moving oil, iron ore, and other raw materials around the world in record amounts and at far cheaper rates than had ever before been possible. Hundreds of seamen from all over Cayman went to work for Ludwig's Liberian-registered ships on an enterprise that marked the beginning of postwar economic internationalization, transporting materials that were a prerequisite for the global industrial growth to come.

In return, seamen would remit wages of up to £225 sterling home per month, fueling, according to Colonial Reports of the time, "quite extraordinary material development and economic progress" on Cayman. The business of Cayman was exclusively the export of seamen, and no longer turtle fishing, rope making, and shipbuilding. The standard of living improved year on year, and the Colonial Report for 1955–56 stated that it was "fair to say there is no poverty in the Cayman Islands today . . . this is a statement which it would have been impossible to make even three years ago." Society began to change as the money came in. Wives took credit in shops and paid it off when their husbands' remittances arrived. Homemade porridge gave way to cornflakes as expensive imported foodstuffs from the United States replaced cheaper traditional forms of nourishment.

Benson Ebanks worked behind the counter at George Town's newly opened Barclays Bank in the early 1950s. He was the first Caymanian employed in banking on the island. Ebanks's older brother went to sea, but he told Benson of his loneliness away from home. There had to be another way to make a living, he said. Now there was, and the younger Ebanks got in near the start with Barclays. In the early days of Cayman's future financial cavalcade, Ebanks heard seafarers' wives ask each other in the banking hall: "You got yours?" or "I see you got yours." The *yours* being the monthly check sent from far away to be saved at home.

But as the first wheels of contemporary economic globalization turned in Cayman's favor, some few more revolutions later the great enterprise left Cayman behind as quickly as it had arrived. Men who had spent all their working lives at sea could now be seen hanging around in George Town with nothing to do. The thousand or so men who labored, and were rewarded, for capital's latest trading adventure had returned home, their detachment now not compensated for financially. These men were too expensive compared with the new recruits from East Asia who replaced them as globalization's laborers on the supertankers. New automated technology on the latest merchant vessels cut demand for labor even further. By the mid-1960s it was officially recognized in Cayman that the great seafaring age, which had brought prosperity and stability to the islands, was over.

Then young lawyers from the United States and elsewhere arrived in Cayman with the dream of turning the country into the new Bahamas. Banking and financial services up until this time had grown only in relation to domestic demand sparked by seamen's income. It had not occurred to Caymanians themselves that the island could develop as a financial center in its own right. Tourism, agriculture, and light industry were regarded as the way forward.

Yet lawyers like Bill Walker discovered on Cayman a class of men who, with their strong, independent-minded seafaring backgrounds, had a ready talent for and interest in finance and business. Men like Benson Ebanks and Lem Hurlston, who were both to play prominent roles in Cayman's transition to a tax haven, had each been warned

away from going to sea for fear of the loneliness and separation they
would encounter. But these were states of detachment that they had
grown up with all their lives and could now naturally employ in the
realm of finance. Others, like Thomas Jefferson, who was to become
Cayman's financial secretary, had actually worked on the oil tanker
routes up and down the Americas, transporting crude. He had been
canny enough to learn accounting on the side at night school in New
York, so when the world shipping recession hit Cayman, he had alternative opportunities to aim for. He quickly slotted into the emerging
tax haven infrastructure.

The seafaring spirit of Cayman quite naturally found its home in finance, and it welcomed with open arms the outsiders who wanted to
turn Cayman into a tax haven. By this route it was believed that prosperity could be won again. The individualism and detachment that
the seafarers had needed as a means to an end—to survive the ordeal
at sea until that time when they returned home to society—now became an end in its own right, as something to find a basis in at home
from which to profit. Onshore, there was to be no return from detachment; rather, it was to become the condition of society itself. The seafarers' sacrifice of attachment would now become society's sacrifice as
well. In this transition is found the origin of what we might call an
"offshore consciousness" in modern Cayman. It is this consciousness
and its affinity with financial globalization that keeps Cayman buoy-
ant, but like this affinity elsewhere in the world, there comes with it
fear and insecurity.

Freedom

The bureaucratic apparatus of Cayman is housed in the Tower Building, just off the beaten track into George Town. Here in a 1970s gray
concrete block are based the police, the islands' legal department, the

housing board, and social services. On the ground floor, in a little warren of offices with interconnecting doors and windows, is the General Registry. This is where births, marriages, and deaths are registered. And companies too, for in Cayman, companies are like people; they are born and attach themselves to others. But unlike people, Cayman's companies can last forever.

These offshore companies are bred as artificial humans, extraordinary in their freedom and in the protective secrecy that is the bedrock of that freedom. Within the shell of the Cayman company lies the power of political and economic individualism, a creature that hides from the outside world in order to attack it. Only a state of nature comparable to Cayman can breed such forms; only a night-watchman state admixed with the freedom of capital can make this experiment come alive.

The Cayman company is a separate legal being from its founder and shareholders. It trades as a separate person from its members. It can own property and open bank accounts—assets that belong to it alone and not to shareholders. It is free to do any kind of business it wants to, with anyone it chooses, in any transaction undertaken by a natural person. In short, Cayman companies are creatures endowed with quite incredible rights that make them equivalent to, but distinct from, real, living people. And its special rights are protected indefinitely, regardless of who owns or runs the company at any given time.

On Cayman there are more artificial people than real people, and like the real people, most of the artificial ones pay no tax. The formation of "exempt" companies has always been Cayman's main attraction, and most of the companies registered on the island pay no tax, as long as they conduct business outside Cayman. Tax-exemption certificates provide companies with a twenty-year renewable guarantee against any taxes that might be imposed in the future. As a result, all profits, income, and gains are tax-exempt.

It is not surprising that capitalism sailed to Cayman to breed offshore creatures. The creature can operate a bank account. It can enter into contracts anywhere in the world. It can store untaxed profits and use them to finance ventures elsewhere. It can act as a tax-exempt intermediary for deals and trade between other companies. It can acquire shares and bonds and resell them tax free. It can hold patents and insure risks. It can be used as a vehicle for investment funds, buying and selling its own shares, tax free. It can be exported to other states to do business there. This is a creature that can change form, mutate, and return as something else, a radical conduit for capital at its most adaptive, flexible, and plastic. Of course, this creature is the essence of any company found almost anywhere in the modern world. But only in the radical companies of Cayman does capitalism find true freedom and power.

The former head of Dow Chemical remarked in 1972, "I have long dreamed of buying an island owned by no nation and of putting the World Headquarters of the Dow Company on the truly neutral ground of such an island, beholden to no nation or society." One year later, Dow was beholden no more. Dow Banking Corporation, the multinational's very own captive bank, arrived in Cayman to handle the company's worldwide operations. The company could now raise its own capital and directly finance international production at a cost far less than if an ordinary bank were involved. Profits made overseas could be transferred back to and then recycled through Cayman rather than the United States, cutting the tax bill right down and allowing for greater capital accumulation in a central pool to be used for further overseas financing. With its own private bank in Cayman, the multinational could also become a serious player in the global financial market, raising and selling bonds, trading currencies, and hedging stock exchanges. *Beholden to no nation or society.*

Capitalism's dream has always been total detachment from the social world. It is no surprise that the vision of an "offshore republic" emerged in the 1970s, for then the burdens imposed on capital by the industrialized nations had never been higher. Tax rates soared throughout the member states of the Organisation for Economic Co-operation and Development (OECD). National restrictions and regulations on the movement and exchange of money kept capital locked into individual states, hobbled by fiscal and monetary instability, rocketing inflation, and political crises.

Yet despite state control and regulation, banks and multinationals had begun to cut across national boundaries, slowly forming new sovereignties of international capital and production. From 1950 to 1975 the number of U.S. multinationals operating in more than five countries increased from 43 to 128. At the beginning of the 1950s there was not one U.S. multinational that operated in more than twenty countries. A quarter of a century later, there were more than forty.

Capital's desire for absolute global freedom was now a distinct possibility, not a distant hope. A top executive at the Bank of America wanted to build "an international corporation that has shed all national identity." By the 1970s, capital's call to arms spoke a language that began to appeal to mainstream national politics, desperate to dig itself out of the hole of economic depression. Tax haven expert Richard Allen, an aide to Henry Kissinger when the latter was national security advisor, recognized the power of the offshore world, with its citizen multinational corporations detached and free from what he perceived as their oppression and overregulation by onshore states.

The offshore illuminati had long known the survival value to capitalism of the secret haven, safe from the rest of the world, where fortunes could be hidden and business turned around free from state diktat. The ancient order of capital had long known Switzerland. They had known Cuba until the revolution in 1959. They had known the Bahamas until there, too, political strife—or socialism—got in the way. But new islands and enclaves availed themselves and offered capital the absolute detachment it craved. "No taxes of any kind in

Cayman. No reports to any government. Confidential accounts with complete privacy." So ran the slogan for Cayman's absurdly named but nonetheless apt International Monetary Bank. Cayman opened its virtual deposit box and became host to a thousand radical agents engaged in a world revolution that would, within a decade, regenerate Western capitalism and imbue it with the revengeful spirit of a creature long repressed, sick of mere survival.

Protection

Cayman law has granted its artificial people—or offshore exempt companies—an immense freedom. In return for an annual charge of a few hundred dollars, a company can pretty well do what it wants, as long as it does it outside Cayman. But this freedom is no mere contingency. It is bestowed externally by the authority of Cayman law, which protects the company from interference within Cayman and from interference by the outside world. Therefore, for all the radical nonidentity of the ceaselessly changing form of the company in relation to capital, a distinct and permanent legal identity is attributed to it, akin to that granted an individual living person.

It is not the fact of the contract between company and state that is of most interest here. What matters is the precise observation that the realm of capital separates itself from the realm of the state at every moment a new company is formed in Cayman. In fundamental terms, the Cayman company is a cover or front for real flesh-and-blood individuals elsewhere, who have no connection to Cayman as an actual country, but who nonetheless "inhabit" Cayman exclusively for the purposes of doing business *outside* Cayman. Thus Cayman wills itself as a mere instrument of capital and private ownership, disconnecting itself as a state from its own people, and sells itself on the market to others who have no interest other than protecting the freedom of their capital in—for them—blessed secrecy.

Cayman provides the precise technology to distill capital from the state, to completely remove any link or bond between money and people and real places where people live and work and raise families. The distillation process at work in Cayman, and in other offshore finance centers, extends into the giant automaton of the global financial system with its immense and random capital flows, coldly separating people from their societies, overturning long connections between individuals and their habitats, taking control of their material well-being, and increasingly determining their political destiny. We have long pondered the phenomenon of footloose, stateless capital, free from political and state control, but our search for causes, and hence solutions, is often confused with the supposed consequences—the relentless rise of multinational corporations taking over the nation-state, for example.

We need a new way into the question, a way of thinking that captures and understands the split between capital and state, between people and their social livelihoods, at the smallest point where the split actually occurs—like that of the investigation into the atom—for only then can we begin to think about a form of politics that aims at reattaching our individual lives to society to take us back home onshore. We live in the era of offshore capitalism—where no one or nothing can remain rooted to its government except through force of war and violence, total sacrifice to the market, and the dehumanizing hunt for ever more extreme forms of self-protection that war and the market impose on us.

In our offshore world, secrecy has become the new freedom, a matter of preservation that has run away from the painful pursuit of freedom in the public realm. Freedom as secrecy is a retreat from political engagement except insofar as that engagement is determined by economic motive. It is the linchpin on which the split between capital and state, and our detachment, now turns. In Cayman we can discover a threshold, on the other side of which we observe a secret realm that proudly and staunchly defends itself against global insecurity and fear, and prospers at their—and therefore our—expense. Our task must be to relentlessly approach this secret realm, face up to it, and size it up until it is exhausted and gives away the nature of its own secret. Then we can turn against it.

Mirrors

A long counter runs across the reception area at the General Registry in the Tower Building. The office behind the counter has desks against the wall on the left- and right-hand side, each with an identical layout of computer, telephone, and neat bundle of yellow folders positioned by the keyboard. Family snapshots and little Christian homilies about perseverance and patience, belonging to the receptionists, are pinned to the wall. Between the desks, there is a doorway framing part of an anteroom, of which all that can be seen are shelves on which are stacked a dozen varieties of files, some boxed, some loose, arranged in perfect rows, numbered and lettered appropriately. On either side of the doorway, above each desk, are a pair of "Cayman sunset" photographs, in matching ornate gold frames.

I want to do a search on some Cayman-registered companies, so I write a few names down on a piece of paper and hand it to the receptionist. The receptionist disappears into the anteroom. After five minutes she comes back and hands me some computer printouts, for which I pay 54 Cayman dollars. Not surprisingly, Brazauto Trading (Cayman) Limited is a Cayman-registered company. It was formed on August 22, 1990, and was registered two days later. It is an exempt company. The company's registered agent is CIBC Bank & Trust Company (Cayman) Limited, two minutes down the road in the ugly radiator-grill building by the public library. Finally, the printout tells me that the company has been in voluntary liquidation since December 1996.

I turn the page over to see if there is anything printed on the other side. Nothing. No names of directors. No indication of what the company does or, in this case, did. No mention of who owns the company, who the shareholders are, or of anything that can tell me a little more about this mysterious artificial person. Nothing.

The receptionist has seen the same puzzled reaction on every face that comes in to find out about Cayman companies for the first time. There's a slight feeling of embarrassment as the great drama and expectation of ordering company information has, as usual, turned into a rather bathetic swap of expensive Cayman dollars for a minimal, nondescript half-page printout from a database. As one turns to leave, a small sign pinned to the wall is designed to catch your eye. It reads:

Company Information
Complete Name
Registration State
Registration/File No.
Registered Office/Agent
Type of Company
Status of Company

This is the only information we provide on company search.

I now understand the hall of mirrors that is the company search at the Tower Building, where what you see is never deeper than the surface, just a reflection of what is already barely there. I leave the counter and mumble a good-bye to the receptionists, who are now at their desks, making phone calls and tapping into their computers, like two suspiciously well-behaved twins. But at least we are at the threshold.

Secrecy

Mr. Cayman of George Town is a very secret man. No one knows who the directors of his many companies are. No one knows who owns them. Sometimes you think you've got the names of his shareholders, but then it turns out that they are only nominees and not the actual owners. No one directly involved with his companies need ever set foot in George Town. Local stand-ins will do for a de facto annual meeting. And no offshore company belonging to Mr. Cayman need ever file any financial statements or accounts.

Secrecy is the offshore world's great protector, preserving ownership, private property, and the free accumulation of capital. Secrecy is the essential correlate of modern economic freedom. It has come to be regarded as a good, a natural right, an elemental point of law, the copestone of the individual, isolate human being against whom no external authority can lay claim. These so-called values are taken up and adopted by corporations large and small. All propose to themselves the ideal of the unencumbered individual and pull down the veil of secrecy where there is advantage to be had.

Tax is the key battleground in the secret pursuit of freedom. When tax is regarded, in principle, as anathema to privacy, secrecy flourishes. The institution of taxation demands individual attachment to state and society and therefore implies some minimum relationship between the state and the financial affairs of the individual.

Release from taxation provides for detachment from the state and freedom from its external control over individual financial affairs. Secrecy is the mode by which this release is obtained. Individuals who resist taxation on grounds of principle always regard themselves as embattled men under threat, taking a great stand of right against wrong. In this way they justify secrecy as legitimate. But this principle is a cover for the entirely pragmatic aspect of secrecy: larger profit and capital accumulation for corporations and the wealthy. At the end of the day, secrecy provides a competitive advantage.

Secrecy is an exaggerated, embattled form of privacy. It is what happens to privacy when it reacts to a certain external threat. It is true that privacy has had more than enough to contend with in the era of the superstate. The history of the state shows us that the will to detach oneself from its dictates is entirely justified when these dictates are all-encompassing. But where this reaction leads us when embattled privacy becomes a political form of life is no less a problem, particularly when this reaction is pathologically obsessed by threats to individual freedom, where every nook and cranny of the state is characterized as a totalitarian affront to liberty.

Secrecy is the radical arm of privacy. It is what privacy becomes when it seeks a haven or refuge from the state to preserve itself. It speaks strongly about freedom, rights, and the individual, but it is of course a front for capital, for private ownership and its control of resources, and for corporations that secure immense profits offshore. The state has come to terms and taken on board the ideological traits of secrecy. As secrecy manifested itself in the dynamism of modern capital to outrun and outreach the state, the state had no choice but to settle up with and adapt to the secret realm, to make amends for its own past abuses of privacy and capital, and to play the game on capital's terms. Both capital and state appear to have found their compromise in the secret realm. They will remain there even as liberal society dissolves around them.

In Cayman, the protected freedom of the individual in the secret realm is put into law. Like all tax havens, Cayman is a refuge from political state intervention. Only here can the homeless, offshore individual prosper in a jurisdiction that satisfies his ego and permits him his so-called natural liberty without constraint or bind. It is the secrecy chamber from inside which the individual withstands the conflict between his own desire for freedom and the external authority of the state. Where once he was caught between obeying his own rules and those of others he despised, here he can find reconciliation in detachment, in separation from the common herd, offshore, in what he believes is true freedom. In this he is utterly wrong; for in the secret realm, freedom, like the world, is snuffed out.

What is said for the individual follows entirely for the global corporation. The model of the unencumbered individual is what these huge corporations organize themselves around in practice and the yardstick by which they measure their freedom in theory. It is the very reason and calculation why refuge is sought in offshore tax havens like Cayman.

Cayman defends its natural history of secrecy as enlightened society protects an endangered species: diligently and honorably. What is at stake in Cayman is the nimble and fast-footed spirit of material conquest, of possession, with which secrecy is allied in its tracking down of prey in the competitive ecology of capitalism. The politics of the secret realm grabs the global economy by the throat and by necessity aims to disembody its heart purely for its own consumption, lest anyone else should try and snatch it away. Cayman's history is merely the story of the human species refusing to be bound to external control— not just of the state, but of reality, time and time again.

Trust

A fellow I'll call Mike was in his early thirties. He was often at the pool bar of the Comfort Hotel on West Bay Road. Evenings and weekends he would chat with the young Australians and South Africans who passed through Cayman in the summer, working behind the hotel bars and going out on diving trips. You knew when Mike was around, and he knew too that his amplified Liverpudlian accent was a distinctive social draw.

One evening we got talking. He told me he was a trust administrator and had just moved to a Cayman bank after twelve years of setting up trusts in Canada. "I protect wealth from wives and spendthrift

kids," he said in an offhand, matter-of-fact way, secure in the knowledge that Cayman was his natural habitat. He had spent three months
already in the hotel suite, waiting for his wife to come and join him.
Mike gave the impression that he could well be in the hotel on his
own for another few months at least. Perhaps there was a problem
with his marriage, or perhaps there was no wife and Mike had just
made her up. It did not really bother him. He looked as though he
could survive perfectly well setting up trusts by day and going to the
bar every night, sipping beers in the heat, chatting to Mat from Syd-
ney about English football. "There's a kind of freedom here. It's great,
isn't it?" said Mike.

Mike is a man who can make owning something not owning something, both at the same time. Trusts are big business in Cayman, with
billions of dollars held in thousands of individual trusts—money that
is used for investing in the islands' fast-growing offshore mutual fund
industry (in which $200 billion of assets are invested), or just held
by a third party for a beneficiary whose identity is covered up and
hidden.

There is an old, dusty image of trusts, of money put away for an inheritance or passing on a family heirloom, a few deeds signed by a
family lawyer and then a cup of tea. Not so in Cayman, where trusts
are an important "wealth protection instrument" for those with money
to hold on to more money without anybody knowing about it. Every
bank on Cayman runs a large trust department, and it was trusts that
first attracted offshore business to Cayman in the 1960s. When it was
invented, the Cayman trust was a unique invention, for it combined
the traditional British common-law trust with a zero-tax regime, thus
putting wealth and assets completely beyond the reach of the state.
The Cayman trust has been much copied in the offshore financial
world.

In the offshore trust, the link between premodern forms of ownership and control and their modern equivalent is preserved. Trusts

were common in feudal England as a way in which the prohibition against the gift of land to the Church could be circumvented. As the Church was forbidden from owning land, trusts were devised in which land could be held by individuals and kept in trust for the Church. Trusts were common too during the Crusades, when they were set up to hold property for the families of knights who might never return home from wars abroad. Central to the operation of the trust is the trustee, the third party that holds legal possession of an asset for the beneficiary under terms of utter secrecy. In a sense, a trust detaches ownership from one individual and passes it off through another. Confidentiality is preserved, and the identity of any individual apart from the trustee remains unknown.

It is no accident that behind many offshore-registered companies, in Cayman and elsewhere, there lurks a trust, and behind that, there is often another. Ownership of—and even the actual nature of—an asset is successively obscured and alienated from any straightforward sense of possession in a series of Chinese boxes that give way only to further concealment. What has been grasped through the corporate front is then distanced from it and deep-frozen in layers of secret protection, all traces of human presence erased, only a series of empty shells left in its place. This web of emptiness and disconnection—formed to protect the private ownership of wealth—is what characterizes the secret realm and the freedom it expresses.

Defense of the Offshore Realm

Once upon a time, the British-appointed governor of the Cayman Islands would personally welcome new banks to the island in a quaint little ceremony. In 1973 Governor Crook opened a branch of the Bahamas-based Castle Bank & Trust Company in George Town. In his public address, the governor said that Cayman banks needed to remember that they were not the only inhabitants of Cayman, because people lived there too. "If you don't think about that," said Crook, "you might as well buy an aircraft carrier and operate from that."

Within a few years, the idea that surviving in the offshore world could be a civilized affair, concerned with the interests of people, would seem very odd indeed. Cayman's offshore exploits were about to enter the wider geopolitical realm, and to survive that permanent excursion, the islands needed to turn into a sharpshooting gunboat and fend off attack. This was a turning point in our passage into an offshore world.

In 1976 Anthony Field, the managing director of Castle Bank & Trust (Cayman) Ltd., was served with a subpoena on landing at Miami International Airport from Grand Cayman. Field was going to have to testify before a U.S. grand jury as part of an investigation into tax evasion and money laundering through offshore banks in the Caribbean. The investigation, orchestrated by the Internal Revenue Service, had been ongoing for ten years and had developed a mass of evidence in the ways and means by which the U.S. tax system had been progressively undermined by tax havens. The IRS had discovered that billions of dollars were washing through Caribbean islands, evading tax at home. An internal IRS memo noted that "taxpayers have exploited the organizational structure of the . . . service through calculated transactions which cross district, region and international boundaries." Castle Bank was considered to be the main tax evasion vehicle for wealthy Americans, so opening it up to the outside world presented the best chance yet of putting an end to U.S. tax evasion and the antisocial practices of tax havens.

The grand jury wanted Field to tell them about American clients at his bank in Cayman. For the first time, the islands' tradition of secrecy came under direct threat from a foreign power. Field's case went to appeal at the U.S. Supreme Court, but Cayman was not let off the hook: Field was ordered to stand and give evidence, something that

would effectively force him to violate Cayman's common-law obligations regarding financial confidentiality. Aside from the attack on its
legal sovereignty, there were other dangers for Cayman. If Field divulged confidential tax information before the grand jury, Cayman's
anxious private banking clients could well move their accounts to
more secretive havens, putting the islands' livelihood as an offshore
center at risk.

Cayman responded with some rapid legal drafting and produced
the Confidential Relationships (Preservation) Law. Cayman's financial secretary outlined the fundamentals of the act to the islands' ner-
vous legislative assembly: "No information relating to a customer or
client account with any institution within the local financial community can be divulged to anyone. A foreign government investigating a
case relating to a crime other than a tax offence may request this government to assist it in providing the relevant information . . . Such a
request would be examined to ensure that the purported offence
would, if committed in the Cayman Islands, be an offence under Cayman statutes." The members of the legislature roared their approval. It
would now be a crime to reveal the details of any financial or banking
arrangement made on Cayman, and drawing a further line in the
sand, it would be up to Cayman and no one else to decide what was
a crime committed on its shores.

With this new law, Cayman codified its secret realm and told the
outside world to leave it alone and mind its own business. In the face
of what it considered an attack on the convention of nations declining
to interfere with the laws of other nations, Cayman struck back with
the only means at its disposal—the law. Thus Cayman's sovereignty
was heightened and put in a state of readiness to fend off aggressors.
As a result, the offshore individual and the offshore company within
Cayman's jurisdiction were now formally protected species, untouch-
able and beyond the laws of outsiders. For capital's global offshore future, this was a significant moment. The Confidential Relationships

Law protected private ownership and money in Cayman against outside interference and control, and increased their freedom and protection relative to other states.

Cayman kept its offshore business. Indeed, it prospered, with no letup in U.S. patronage. The IRS investigation that had led to grand juries and subpoenas for tax evasion and money laundering was soon closed down, prompting allegations that Castle Bank was a front for the CIA and that many of the offshore tax evaders were in fact Republican fat cats and Nixon cronies. So it looked like the U.S. administration had discovered the utility of the offshore network for covert operations, and its financial and corporate elite had seen well the advantages of a secret space in which to protect their wealth through tax fraud. The free world was becoming an offshore world, sanctioned by the elite.

As a result, hundreds of accounts at Castle Bank, which had branches in other Caribbean tax havens, were left untouched for tax evasion, including shelters reportedly for *Playboy* publisher Hugh Hefner, actor Tony Curtis, and the owners of the Hyatt hotel chain. Castle Bank's own bankers devised schemes for clients to evade tax on U.S. property transactions; California tax attorneys used Castle and other offshore banks to generate sham loans to assist wealthy clients in evading $1.4 million in taxes by allowing them to claim back tax deductions on loan interest that was never paid.

Multinational companies tapped into the offshore network too. Toyota in the United States was investigated for allegedly accepting kickbacks in return for auto distributorships, hiding money in offshore banks and then reinvesting it in the United States. Organized crime groups set up offshore corporations to launder cash from drug deals, gambling, and racketeering, money that was reportedly used to buy prime real estate in the United States.

In a sense, Cayman was only acting as an honest broker. Its intentions were out in the open. It knew what it stood for and what it wanted to protect. There was a kind of black-and-white moral ideal-ism in its position. As far as Cayman was concerned, it was entirely a matter of individual conscience about the rights and wrongs of using the islands as a base to protect an individual's or a company's financial activities. If the individual or company concerned was responsible, de-cent, and upstanding, thought Cayman's authorities, why should free-dom be denied them offshore? Just a short flight from Miami, and any individual or company would have the secret protection to break on-shore laws that they—and crucially Cayman—regarded as illegiti-mate. In a perverse inversion of the old nation-state, a new home and dominion would be found offshore.

Cayman offered individuals and companies an escape from the state control faced in the onshore world. As long as every free con-science played by the same rules on this little Caribbean island, there would be a harmonious expression of liberty in an otherwise unfree world. This, it was claimed by the supporters of tax havens, was for the good.

Floating Free

Cayman and its offshore brethren in the Caribbean pulled up anchor and floated free. "You might as well buy an aircraft carrier and operate from that," Governor Crook had warned new banks setting up in George Town, lest they forget that Cayman had a society apart from fi-nance and capital. But banks, criminals, companies, and the rich did not want to know about society—on Cayman or anywhere else for that matter—for society imposed a burden, and they wanted none of that. They wanted to do as they pleased and live apart if necessary, a sacri-fice worth making, they thought, to rid one of the responsibility of attachment.

A U.S. investigation into offshore tax evasion backfired as its revelations got too close to the bone, too close to revealing just how far the U.S. elite had gone offshore. As a result, the tax haven network gained legitimacy in the United States, and Cayman strengthened its tradition of secrecy with new laws, sealing itself off from the outside world and asserting legal sovereignty. It now fulfilled the role of the governor's much maligned aircraft carrier, a territory open to the offshore elite, where they could land and take advantage of its freedoms, then fly away again with no regard for society. The islands' offshore detachment was complete, and with that, capital and crime defaulted to the secret realm of their freedom.

Cayman defended its tax haven business as an act of political realism in the interests of economic survival. It tried to stand on principle too: if the new Confidentiality Law was a money launderers' charter, well, so be it, for the freedom now given to respectable capital and business morally outweighed any limitation of it on account of the business of crime and corruption. What mattered in this ideal moral universe, according to Cayman, was the private ethic of autonomy and independence. As long as you were not actually aware or did not know that someone was exercising his autonomy immorally, as a criminal, you had no right turning him away. Cayman was neutral between ends, between different social outcomes or goals, because individual freedom was in itself the touchstone of morality.

Yet there was a complete blindness to the negative effects this offshore morality would have on the outside world—indeed, consequences that would conflict with what was at root valid about individual autonomy, and would undermine any trace of it through the secret legitimizing of crime, deception, and corruption. Such extreme shortsightedness was based on the firm delusion that offshore man, set apart in isolation from the common world, could forever remain protected in his sovereign bubble, untroubled.

Thus our offshore world would come to comprise a moral realm that was as ideal as it was naive, and would in time envelop us, offshore or onshore, harboring within it every concealed and corrupt intention imaginable, encouraging and reinforcing antisocial behavior of every description. The fruits of capital would grow increasingly toxic, whether through commerce or crime. In the sour taste of their flesh, the two were the same.

Offshore entities that had aspired to a kind of moral purity for the preservation of individual freedom—a release from control—were reduced in practice to the naive transport of crime and ruin, not merely because the criminal had abused them or had found a home away from home, but because the moral psychology from which these entities originated had necessarily defined freedom as a secret detachment from the world. In return, with the loss of connection to that world, and with the envelope of isolation drawn around it, freedom would descend into a horrific realm of crime and revenge. And in the midst of destruction, offshore entities would offer themselves up as allegories of a ruined, fallen freedom, their secret, terrible meaning finally revealed.

Here in Cayman, discovered on that night of celebration in May 2003, was the prism through which the detached offshore world of freedom could be glimpsed, flickering dimly in fireworks over George Town, the five-hundred-year-old memory of Cayman's original sacrifice of attachment lit up in ambivalent honor of Columbus's arrival. No amount of music and dancing into the night would recover that loss.

2. The Offshore Corporation

When the world is your financial canvas you free-think.
Boundaries disappear. Both real and perceived.
Ansbacher creates solutions free from cultural constraints.
Previously unimagined answers are presented. Problems
effectively bypassed. This is the freedom of the Ansbacher culture.
Since 1894.

—ANSBACHER BANK MARKETING BLURB

Capital Processing Plant

I could be in the library of a grand stately home. There are dark wood desks and large shaded lamps with marble bases. There is the woody smell of logs burning in a grand fireplace, but no roaring fire to be seen. One can just about hear the chink of glasses and animated chatter drifting from the dining room as the host leads the guests along to the library after dinner. But there is no one around now at Maples and Calder, the law firm located on the seafront going out of George Town toward the smart suburbs of South Sand. It is Caribbean twilight outside. Palms sway. Inside the library it feels like a comfortable winter's evening, perhaps with snow-dusted pine trees blinking in the moonlight across the fields.

What titles are on the bookshelves? *Cross-border Security*; *Aircraft Finance: Registration, Security and Enforcements*; *Delaware Limited Partnerships*; *Offshore Solvency: Security & Insolvency*. Big, heavy, dark books, their titles in gold block down the spines, authorless.

"Hello, good to see you," says Henry Harford, stepping into the room. He is a partner at the firm, and very much the lord of the manor. "Yes, here we are in the laboratory—capital's processing plant, we like to call it. You just pour in the cash flow or the asset, and out come the bonds, securities, or finance. Tax neutrality. Capital at wholesale prices."

So at Maples and Calder we find Harford and his colleagues acting for multinational companies on their finance-raising deals, raising billions of dollars in the capital markets—in the form of bonds, derivatives, and other financial instruments that will then be sliced, diced, and repackaged in Cayman and resold on the markets. The money for multibillion-dollar infrastructure projects—like transnational pipelines that run thousands of miles across continents—will be financed and executed through Cayman companies using Cayman lawyers and Cayman banks.

The latest craze in Cayman is for structured finance deals where, for example, a Japanese credit card company will sell its receivables— the income it will receive in the future as consumers pay off their credit card bills—to a Cayman company it sets up, which in turn issues a bond that it sells to investors. By securitizing future income and then selling it on the market, a company can raise thousands of millions of dollars in one swoop.

There are two main reasons for doing this kind of business in Cayman. First, regulations onshore may not permit certain types of structured finance deals at home; and second—the critical factor—finance raised in Cayman will not be taxed. Cayman's structures permit corporations to deal in and take advantage of capital undiluted, unhindered, and untaxed, free from outside interference. For multinationals, offshore centers like Cayman provide the quick and flexible route to capital at discounted, tax-free prices, whenever they want it. "What we have in Cayman is a purer, more essential form of capitalism," Harford tells me, "where business isn't distorted by tax, and the conditions for doing a deal are perfect."

Offshore Networks

Cayman has often been the capitalist's place of last resort. In 1994, Kenneth Dart, heir to the Dart Container Corporation, makers of the plastic cup, fled to Cayman. This followed a family feud in which Dart's brother Thomas accused the rest of his family of pushing him out of a family fortune worth $350 million. At one point Thomas accused his brother Kenneth of planning to convert a yacht into a mini gunship so that he could sail the world and battle off the U.S. tax authorities wherever they bothered him. A settlement was reached, and Kenneth Dart, by this time a dual citizen of Ireland and Belize, moved to Cayman, where he formed a company to manage the family's investments. On Cayman, Dart personally keeps a low profile, but his company is a high-profile sponsor of government functions and events, the Dart logo appearing on government publicity across the islands.

The day-to-day picture of multinational companies in Cayman is rather more mundane than the shenanigans of commercial buccaneers looking for a piece of freedom. It is nonetheless monumental in scale and a very deliberate and normal part of business practice for companies operating across global markets. That multinationals are, to a significant extent, "offshore" by their very nature is no euphemism. The absence of a single, fixed location defines their structure of production. Firms relocate production—or, increasingly, financial services and call-center operations—to countries with less expensive labor, *offshoring*, as it is termed. As a corollary to that, the term *offshore* defines the extent to which a company has the freedom to operate and profit outside the constraints of national boundaries. But what ultimately defines the multinational as offshore is tax. The multinational seeks to weave itself in and around the world's tax havens and offshore financial centers in its drive to remain globally competitive. The amount of tax paid can make a difference of hundreds of millions of dollars to a company's bottom line, so the extent to which tax can be minimized through offshore networks can make the difference between success and failure.

Most of the largest companies in the world are well installed in Cayman. But what you won't find there is any physical presence of an office complete with logos, staff, and a smile and a hello from a receptionist. No, in Cayman you will find blandly named companies whose names are as purely functional as the companies themselves—names that sound as bland as Russia Investments Ltd., Caribbean Holdings Inc., Britco Reinsurers LLP—for branding and image have no purpose in this closed corporate world as far away from Main Street as you can get.

Take Caymans 97 Holdings Ltd. This is a company registered with Henry Harford's law firm, Maples and Calder. Caymans 97 is based in Cayman, is tax-exempt, and was formed in 1997 as a holding company for BP—the world's second-largest oil producer. Caymans 97's innocuous name belies the fact that it is a key component of BP's corporate structure, and true to its name, it holds controlling ownership in Cayman of many of BP's worldwide operations, from drilling North Sea oil to pipelines stretching from Azerbaijan to Turkey. One of the holding company's main assets is BP Exploration, a key part of BP's worldwide oil and gas production arm, and the largest earner for the oil giant, with reported profits of more than $15 billion in 2003.

Caymans 97 will serve a variety of useful purposes for BP. It holds shares in many companies, most of them wholly BP owned, but also joint ventures with other oil firms whose operations are in politically risky or unstable countries, where keeping company ownership in Cayman gives a good measure of protection if things turn nasty on the ground. But the chief function of Caymans 97 is to pool together in one place a significant portion of the income and assets of the entire BP group. A very deep pool, in fact, worth billions of dollars. The goal is to fill the holding company pool to the brim with revenue and then keep the money in play and wash it back through the company— untaxed—only landing it onshore as income in the United States or Britain, say, when tax rates have been engineered with the rest of the company's offshore network to be most advantageous.

In any one year, BP may have up to a billion dollars' income kept in play as tax-deferred capital that can be reinvested across the company in further offshore-controlled ventures. If the game is played well, tax can be avoided pretty much indefinitely. BP will also use its accumulated offshore capital to hedge the foreign exchange and interest rate markets. In 2002 BP had more than $500 million in offshore capital invested in various financial instruments to speculate on the money markets, making it as much a bank as an oil producer. BP's ultra-private, unquoted holding company in Cayman serves as the corporation's inner sanctum of self-preservation and protection, and keeps BP competitive.

Every multinational with serious global ambitions will devise offshore instruments that help it keep millions of dollars in play, away from the heavy hand of the state. At the turn of the millennium, Apple Computer had $520 million at its disposal, pooled offshore in Cayman and other tax havens; MBNA Corporation, the credit card company, $198 million; CSX Corporation, the freight operator, $290 million; and Citigroup, the global banking firm, had $1.3 billion freed up for "indefinite" investment, permitting it, legally, to avoid paying $399 million in U.S. federal income tax. For 1999 as a whole,

U.S. multinationals had $400 billion of untaxed earnings floating around in offshore pools. By the end of 2002, the amount was about $639 billion.

Multinationals are increasingly creating their own offshore economies across the world—separate, hidden, and virtually detached from national economies—with enough combined financial power to match the very biggest states.

A quick look behind the leaders of the Fortune 500 top global corporations shows the significance of the Caribbean offshore circuitry alone. General Motors aggregates its sales and leasing revenues in Cayman and its revenues from reinsurance and finance subsidiaries in Barbados. ExxonMobil has eight holding companies in the Bahamas and Cayman alone. The Ford Motor Company's reinsurance group is split between Cayman and Bermuda, while IBM has holding companies in Bermuda, the Bahamas, the British Virgin Islands, and Barbados. These subsidiaries are not out-of-the-way entities buried deep inside an Exxon or a Ford—far from it. Each Caribbean subsidiary is essential to the competitive financial enterprise of these $100 billion corporate giants.

Global corporation number one—Wal-Mart Stores, with annual revenue in 2003 of $244 billion—conducts its global financing through three Cayman subsidiaries: Walmart Cayman (Euro) Finance Co.; Walmart Cayman (Canadian) Finance Co.; and Walmart Cayman (Sterling) Finance Co. Each will regularly issue corporate bonds out of Cayman worth anything from $500 million to $1 billion so that the parent company can purchase growth throughout the world. The cost to Wal-Mart of financing its global expansion would be much greater without the tax-free edge that Cayman provides.

Most of the global heavy hitters have offshore networks of tax-exempt and low-tax regimes, taking in a handful of the fifteen or so Caribbean tax havens and mixing them with the main European havens of Switzerland, Liechtenstein, and the Channel Islands, and perhaps even some of the remote Pacific Ocean hideaways such as Vanuatu, Nauru, and Niue. Publicly quoted companies always disclose the identities of at least a few of their offshore subsidiaries, to keep regulators off their backs, but these are merely the public froth that floats to the surface. Many thousands of others remain secret and unknown, linked up inside corporations in order to concoct and preserve financial firepower and competitive advantage.

The corporate offshore networks ease corporate access to capital. They allow capital to remain free within the company, preventing it from landing onshore, where it will be taxed. But the networks go one step further: they allow the corporation to lower overall tax rates for capital that *is* landed onshore. Multinationals can minimize their global tax liability by using offshore networks to exploit the differences between corporate tax rates in different countries. This becomes possible only when a corporation has significant global reach, like BP, with production, refining, and sales units spread across the entire globe, but it is also possible for much smaller companies—say, one with a head office in the United States, a handful of factories in China, and a back-office processing center in India. In both cases, offshore networks will shift resources around the company's international operations to eke out the best tax advantage by playing off different corporate tax rates. This practice is known as transfer pricing, which we will look at in more detail below.

Global companies constantly tinker with their offshore networks to save themselves from paying millions of dollars in tax per year. This is all mainstream, day-to-day corporate activity, but the precise offshore mechanics of transfer pricing are kept firmly under wraps by companies in order to prevent competitors from stealing their prized tax-reduction strategies. U.S. multinationals are the undisputed masters of corporate tax reduction. General Electric's financial service businesses have cut their tax rate from 27 percent in 1999 to 16 percent in 2003. Citigroup made a tax saving of $778 million in 2003 by reducing its average tax rate 3 percent on the previous year, to 31.1 percent. A *Financial Times* survey of sixty-eight top-performing U.S. multinationals showed that by bringing their tax rates down in 2003 by just 2 percent on the previous year, a total of $8.1 billion in tax was saved.

Though the tax rates of America's largest corporations decline year after year, they are by no means the lowest rates that some multinationals manage to engineer through aggressive use of their offshore networks. Rupert Murdoch's global media empire, News Corporation, is a case in point. His British holding company, Newscorp Investments, paid no U.K. taxes on £1.4 billion in profits accrued over an eleven-year period to 1999. News Corporation, the Australian parent company, paid tax at an effective rate of 6 percent from 1994 to 1998. By contrast, Murdoch's competitor Disney paid tax at 31 percent. The News Corporation corporate structure comprised a network of eight hundred subsidiaries, with sixty incorporated in tax havens, which, according to an Australian parliamentary investigation, had been used to protect all of the group's profits.

The Secret Market

The term *offshore* is a precise historical definition of U.S. corporations that tentatively established production overseas after the end of World War II. On the back of a huge growth of U.S. foreign direct investment in the 1950s, overseas subsidiaries were set up by such big American firms as Procter & Gamble, DuPont, and IBM as they first internationalized in Europe. U.S. corporations were soon faced with the problem of being taxed twice: first in the foreign countries where they operated, and second, back home in the United States. This problem could be got around by setting up in tax havens holding companies that owned the foreign subsidiaries. Tax on foreign earnings could be minimized or eliminated altogether and the savings mobilized and invested back through the holding companies in new overseas ventures.

In the early offshore period, corporations had another ace up their sleeves in the form of U.S. government tax credits for foreign subsidiaries. Corporations could get credits on foreign tax and use them to pay the tax on their domestic income in the United States. The value of these credits soared as companies engineered the revenue of foreign subsidiaries through the offshore network, then sought credit far in excess of actual liabilities. As a further government bonus, tax credit could be carried forward, allowing the company in effect a permanent interest-free loan, as well as reducing the tax burden overall.

The offshore network soon became an engine of growth and expansion for the corporation, and by extension for the U.S. economy. Without the intermediation of tax havens, and without a little help from the federal government, U.S. corporations would have found it expensive and time-consuming to internationalize, perhaps prohibitively so. The tax havens enabled companies to cut away the impediments of doing business overseas and at the same time allowed them to control foreign expansion from the U.S. corporate center, detached from the countries where operations were physically based. Variations among national tax systems could be overridden and exploited through the offshore network, as could variations among different financial and regulatory systems. From the offshore financial vantage point, local differences could be erased, and the company would be free to grow as one single U.S.-controlled entity, pursuing revenue, market share, and profits on the path of least resistance across the world.

Here was born the internal financial market of corporate capitalism — offshore and secret. The outside world of land and people, of goods and services, was now an object of that market, its fate to be determined entirely in accordance with the principles of offshore accounting, which, the corporations discovered, brought order and control to the messiness of the world where business was to be done. As the internal market of the corporation grew, distinctions among different national traditions of taxation, law, regulation, and finance became merely instruments that could be profitably played off against each other in the homogenizing advance of the corporation. Paradoxically, the more the corporation went overseas and offshore, the more internalized, private, and secret its activities became. Meanwhile, distinctive national traditions of the outside world were being challenged by the uniform identity of U.S. corporatism.

The secret trick of the corporate internal market is transfer pricing, which, as we saw above, allows global corporations to engineer lower overall tax rates by taking advantage of different national tax systems. With transfer pricing, corporations conduct intracompany business—i.e., the shifting of resources among various subsidiaries—not on an arm's-length basis where transactions between independent buyers and sellers would properly be priced externally by the market, but as transactions entirely structured within the company. The sheer size, scale, and concentration of multinationals means that they can buck external price factors and fix as they see fit the costs of the goods and services they move around the world for production and eventual sale. According to the OECD, well over half of world trade is made up of transfer pricing within corporations.

The critical element of transfer pricing for the corporation is the relative level at which it sets its prices against the tax on income derived from the sale of its products. At some point in the business cycle, the corporation has to land its product onshore—has to sell its hamburger, toothpick, or missile warhead—and when it does, it will have tax to pay on the revenue. By being able to freely engineer the price of oil, for example, before it is sold on the so-called open market, the corporation can itself control the degree to which profits and income are preserved from tax.

This is exactly what Chevron, Exxon, Mobil, and Texaco were all up to in the 1980s and early 1990s. Saudi Arabia sold crude to the American companies at below-market prices. The companies sold the crude without markup to their non-U.S. refining affiliates. The affiliates then sold the refined product at market price to foreign buyers, putting the profits beyond the reach of the U.S. tax authorities. Subsequently, and in possibly the largest-ever tax case brought by the U.S. government, the IRS claimed that the oil giants owed $6.5 billion in taxes that should have been paid had the companies properly marked up sales to their foreign affiliates, citing transfer pricing as the means by which tax had been avoided. Chevron and Mobil reportedly settled out of court, but Exxon and Texaco fought on, finally winning their cases in 1997.

The task of transfer pricing is to alter prices within the corporation as a global whole to where they will be most beneficial in terms of tax. At that maximal point, a price is set. This practice is designed to break any actual correspondence between costs, income, and production in any particular location. It is a form of bending economic reality by accounting for it in a way that takes it out of its specific local context and makes it immediately exchangeable with the bits and pieces of an entirely different context of production.

Another way of imagining this is by thinking of the entire production context of a corporation as being like a finished jigsaw puzzle picture. All the fragments fit together to complete one coherent image of production. What happens with transfer pricing is that you disassemble the jigsaw puzzle and reshape each individual piece of the puzzle—each specific part of the production process—so that it fits with the most advantageous tax arrangement. You then reassemble the newly crafted pieces to create a new image, which is the best tax deal for your corporation as a whole. The completed image, of course, does not fit together—it is meaningless and jumbled up—and bears no actual resemblance to the totality of the corporation's production.

The basic rule of thumb of transfer pricing is simple: in countries where taxes are high, corporations charge their subsidiaries more for the factors needed for production—the parts, labor costs, infrastructure, management, and transportation needed to build automobiles, for example—than they would subsidiaries in a lower-tax country or, even better, a tax-exempt country. In the higher-tax country, internal company prices are engineered to be proportionally higher than or even to exceed income, allowing tax to be offset by lots of what looks like local expenditure. In the low-tax or no-tax country, usually an offshore tax haven, the reverse is true, so prices for automobile production are structured to be as low as possible in proportion to income, creating and preserving profit.

The reality, of course, is that Ford or General Motors does not actually make anything—let alone automobiles—in offshore tax havens, but by shifting prices around the corporate offshore network, all the income and profits, and none of the actual costs of producing automobiles, can be engineered to flow through tax havens. By playing offshore against onshore, even the most marginal difference in tax rates between two jurisdictions can equate to a huge financial advantage for the tightly controlled and centralized corporation.

J. W. Smith details the mechanics of the transfer pricing merry-go-round in *The World's Wasted Wealth* in typically schematic terms:

(1) On paper [the multinational corporation will] move their head-quarters to, or establish a subsidiary in, a third country tax haven; (2) build their factory in a low-wage developing world country with a low unit cost of production, say ten dollars; (3) invoice their production to the offshore tax haven at a price that leaves no profit, that same ten-dollar production cost; (4) invoice that production from the tax haven to a high-wage country at a price that will show a profit in the paper corporation in the tax haven and none in the real corporation in the high-wage country, let's say thirty dollars per unit, ship their products direct from the low-wage developing country to

the high-wage developed country, and bank those tax-free profits in the tax haven, which is nothing more than a mailing address and a plaque on a door. No products touch that offshore entity; even the paperwork is done in the corporate home office.

One company operating a transfer pricing scheme exactly in this way—through Cayman—was Apple, the computer firm. No different from other multinationals, Apple had a complex and opaque structure of subsidiaries and holding companies, including Apple Computer Limited, an Ireland-based manufacturing company; Apple Computer Inc. Limited, an Irish company that owned the Irish manufacturing company; Apple Netherlands BV, an offshore investment company; Apple Computer Foreign Sales Corporation, a U.S. Virgin Islands corporation set up to sell to overseas markets; Apple Computer Cayman Finance Ltd., a Cayman investment company; and Apple Computer International Ltd., which Apple once described as "a Cayman Islands corporation incorporated on March 24, 1981, whose function is to conduct manufacturing operations in Singapore."

Apple did manufacture computers in Singapore. However, the purpose of the Cayman company was to pay the Singapore subsidiary, on paper, bottom dollar—say, $200—for a Singapore-produced Macintosh. The Cayman company would then sell its Singapore product to Apple in America for $900. American Apple would sell the computers to its dealers for $1,000, and the dealers would take receipt of the brand-new computers directly from the Singapore factory.

The offshore advantage was clear. Apple sold its computers in the United States, but got taxed on only $100 profit, while $700 profit was preserved tax-free in Cayman. Meanwhile, the cost of production in Singapore was inflated through the transfer to Singapore of more expensive U.S. production costs, resulting in even better savings owing to existing tax allowances for foreign corporations in Singapore. In 1992 the IRS charged Apple with avoiding corporate taxes—some

$586 million between 1984 and 1988—through transfer pricing and keeping profits offshore. The case was eventually settled out of court, leaving the precise details of Apple's schemes unclear.

A more recent case of the alleged use of transfer pricing for tax evasion involved the world's biggest watchmaker, Swatch, makers of the eponymous brand of plastic fashion watches as well as other top Swiss brands Omega and Longines. In August 2004 two former financial controllers of Swatch alleged that the company had used its offshore subsidiary in the British Virgin Islands to evade up to $180 million in taxes and customs duties by manipulating intracompany prices. After its share price dropped 10 percent on news of the allegations, Swatch was forced to admit that it was "normal practice" to make full use of transfer pricing, but only to pay no more tax than was absolutely necessary and certainly never for tax evasion. The former employees took their case to the U.S. authorities, and Swatch conducted an internal investigation. After considering the matter, Swatch declared that it "did not violate the laws" and dismissed the former employees' claims outright. Meanwhile, the United States said it had no jurisdiction over the matter.

There have been vague stabs at working out just how massive a profit machine the aggregated internal markets of global corporations are, but governments and states are generally at a loss to diagnose in detail what is really going on inside corporate internal markets and how transfer pricing works itself through the offshore network. Corporations are extremely secretive about the special tax advantages these structures give them, and they give hardly any clues about what goes on. Like the Apple case, it is only when some outlandish transfer pricing scheme or other particularly blatant bit of tax fixing goes on that even a small window is opened onto the hidden offshore world of corporations. In the case of Swatch, who admitted to transfer pricing as a matter of course, the window was opened a fraction before being fast slammed shut.

In 1990 it was estimated in a study by the U.S. House of Representatives that $35 billion a year was lost in federal taxes as a result of corporate transfer pricing. The report estimated that "more than half of almost forty foreign companies in the U.S. had paid virtually no taxes over a ten-year period." By the end of the 1990s, the loss to U.S. taxation through transfer pricing was put at nearer $50 billion a year. British and U.S. tax authorities are in constant transfer pricing disputes with firms, "but even in advanced economies . . . it is extremely difficult for the Internal Revenue Service to assess the actual extent of transfer pricing. It is even more difficult for developing countries to do so."

The hidden market inside the offshore corporation reduces the "global tax burden" or "maximizes operating performance," in today's jargon of corporate speak. This market is no more than a fix. Hidden there in the offshore network, in what Henry Harford of Maples and Calder in Cayman calls the laboratories of pure capitalism, are the treasured conceits of the corporate tax and finance men. Capital accumulating, free and uncontrolled. Taxes conjured away. Assets secured and protected. Financial power multiplied. The outside world is banished from the invisible realm of capital's processing plant, its differences and varieties an impediment to intolerant progress. In this secret empire, "in the midst of general unfreedom, men act as if they were free."

3. The Offshore Interior

> Now I look upon my desolate solitary island as the
> most pleasant place in the world, and all the happi-
> ness my heart could wish for was to be but there
> again.
>
> —DEFOE, *ROBINSON CRUSOE*

A Shell Marked Secret

Behind the doors of 75 Fort Street, George Town, lie the discreet offices of Huntlaw Corporate Services Ltd., one of the largest incorporation points for offshore companies in Cayman. In the old days, a brass
plaque of each and every company registered at Huntlaw would be
stuck up on a board outside the front door. Now, technology and the
growth in offshore registrations results in a touch screen computer system that allows you, in the cool smoked-glass and dark wood interior
of Huntlaw's reception area, to check the name of every registration at

your leisure. From 00291368 Ltd. to Zug Finanz GmbH, by way of Ultimate Joy Inc., it would take you a week to work your way through the thousands of companies that have found an offshore home at Huntlaw.

Touch the letter E on the screen, scroll up, and read the list:

> Enron Algeria
> Enron Bahamas Co. Ltd.
> Enron BPAC Ltd.
> Enron Brazil Power Holdings Ltd.

The list goes on and on, naming hundreds of Enron companies seemingly connected to activities in every corner of the globe. Bizarrely, the same company name is often listed several times over, but then you notice the addition of a Roman numeral. So you have Enron Brazil Power Investments Ltd., I through XIX—nineteen companies with virtually the same name. Why?

To knock down tax on corporate profits. Enron had 692 subsidiaries incorporated in Cayman alone in 2000, the year before it went bankrupt. It also had some 200 more companies registered in other tax havens, including 119 in the Turks and Caicos Islands (at the time one of the freest and least regulated offshore centers), with others registered in Mauritius, Bermuda, Barbados, Panama, and Guernsey. Enron's offshore network was set up with the prime intention of avoiding tax in any country where it operated. Indeed, Enron had a special unit that devised transactions that allowed the company to record the potential benefit of speculative future tax deductions as current income.

On paper, Enron made profits of nearly $2 billion between 1996 and 2000. But only in one year during that time did it pay U.S. corporate federal income tax, just $17 million in 1997. It also received net U.S. federal tax rebates of $381 million in the same period, and it picked up a rebate of $278 million in 2000 for deductions on its executive stock options. Enron pushed its tax avoidance structures to the limit. Mind you, Enron was not the only Fortune 500 company at the end of the 1990s not to pay tax. A study by Citizens for Tax Justice of half the Fortune 500 companies found that twenty-four of them owed no tax in 1998, nearly twice the number not paying any tax the year before.

Even after Enron's collapse and the revelation of its extensive offshore network, the U.S. energy sector continues to float offshore en masse to reduce its tax liabilities. Halliburton, formerly run by U.S. vice president Dick Cheney, has thirty Cayman subsidiaries. Two of its Houston, Texas, rivals—Baker Hughes Inc. and Noble Corporation—both recently moved offshore, joining Transocean Sedco Forex Inc. and GlobalSantaFe Corporation, two of the world's biggest oil drilling firms. Noble reincorporated in Cayman in 2002, saying it had no choice given the presence of its rivals in tax havens. James C. Day, Noble's CEO, explained the offshore dilemma: "I don't want a competitor to get up and say we are bringing 10 percent more to the bottom line because we have a tax structure that Noble is too stupid to take advantage of. We were caught between a rock and a hard place on it."

Within large-scale corporate capitalism, the route to expansion and growth and, at the bitter end, survival, inevitably leads offshore, for this is where the practical freedom to achieve corporate dominance resides. This has been and continues to be the reality that corporations face. The move is accompanied by the slow pulling down of the psychological drawbridge between the corporation and its object of prey—the outside world for which it competes against other corporations in the hope of turning a profit. From this stems a turning inward that is as evident on the individual psychological level of the capitalist as it is on the structural level of the corporation.

The instinct for individual self-preservation in the market and protection against competition leads to a "windowless isolation," where if—as it always does—external reality obstinately refuses to give way to corporate and individual will, the blinds are closed and external reality is blanked out. Beyond this point, strategies of deception take seed in the mind of the capitalist, whose conviction and obstinate belief in his own right to prevail, and to absolute freedom, cannot bear to be thwarted. Mastered by reality but still clinging to the belief that he is free, the individual capitalist locks himself in a tragic delusion. From there he seeks revenge for the pain that stubborn reality has made his will suffer by denying the absolute freedom he believes is rightfully his. From inside the box, the capitalist strives to dominate and control.

The Financialization of the World

Enron began life relatively out of the shell, in 1985, when it was set up as the result of a deal to combine two businesses: InterNorth, an Omaha natural gas pipeline company, and Houston Natural Gas, a Texas pipeline company. This was a regular regional operation, with real assets and a straightforward business. Under the direction of Kenneth Lay, later to become Enron's CEO and chairman, the company moved from natural gas into electricity, and then moved beyond the United States, building power stations and buying pipelines and plants overseas. From the late 1980s to the mid-1990s Enron developed interests in a whole portfolio of energy assets—electricity plants, water companies, oil tankers, and natural gas facilities—in Asia, Africa, Latin America, and Europe. During this period of global expansion, hundreds of offshore companies were set up through the good offices of Huntlaw Corporate Services to act as holding companies to control ownership of the proliferating assets.

Hunter & Hunter, the law firm of which Huntlaw is a part, advised Enron on the financing and selling of assets and on how it could structure all the parts of its corporate jigsaw into one coherent system to avoid tax. Very occasionally Enron executives would come down to Cayman to discuss what they needed, but most conversations about tax and the preparation of financial statements took place remotely, with Enron's law firm Vinson & Elkins, based in Houston.

As the 1990s progressed, Enron, it would appear, had quite taken to the aggressive reduction of corporate tax through its offshore network. As evidenced by the figures from the second half of the 1990s—where it paid tax in only one year—the offshore strategy for Enron had been a success. Within a decade of its inception, Enron had crossed the Rubicon. By craftily developing the structure of its internal market—through the aid of its offshore structures and tax avoidance schemes—it had branched out and successfully expanded and was ready to join the ranks of the global multinationals it so aspired to. But the company was radically transforming not only the way it structured its activities but the core of the business itself.

On the back of Enron's electricity interests, building on experience in trading natural gas commodities, the company's main concern by the mid-'90s was trading electricity in the United States. Contracts were bought and sold to provide electricity in the same way that raw commodities like grain and coffee were traded. Deals were done with state utility companies and industrial power users. This was the start of Enron's move away from being a primarily asset-driven utility company. From now on, *trading* energy—rather than producing or extracting it—was where Enron was heading.

To assist in pushing Enron where Lay wanted it, young and aggressive executives were recruited. Jeff Skilling joined from the consulting firm McKinsey & Company in 1990. He called the energy trading business a "once-in-a-lifetime opportunity to establish a position to last for the next hundred years." Lay became Skilling's mentor, and in 1997 Skilling was made Enron's chief operating officer. Earlier, Skilling hired Andrew Fastow, a Chicago banker with expertise in leveraged buyouts and structured finance deals. In 1998 Fastow became, at the age of thirty-six, Enron's chief financial officer, heading a finance department that had tripled in size to more than a hundred people.

Lay, Skilling, and Fastow believed in "financialization": turning electricity and gas trading into highly complex finance deals and building a market on the back of them. Lay and company were convinced that Enron could financialize anything, and so it did, by turning water, coal, newsprint, and even weather into financial instruments that could be traded. Launching Enron Online in 1999, the first global platform for commodity trading, the company invested hundreds of millions of dollars in projects whose aim was to extract exchange value from real physical assets, and then, with that value detached and separated from the asset, have it split into a myriad of financial instruments to trade on the market. The substance of the real world mattered nothing to how it could be transformed and controlled through the technical power of financialization. Enron had a gift for this kind of financial alchemy—and they made a great deal of profit from it.

Enron's most spectacular endeavor was the building of a vast coast-to-coast fiber-optic network in the United States, upon which was premised the trading of telecom network capacity in the same way that Enron traded electricity and gas. Here was to be realized a lucrative market for financialization—one that would be introduced to the world from scratch. This ambitious scheme cost Enron several hundred million dollars in investment, but the plan failed, producing losses of more than $400 million.

Enron's elite could not face the fact that its dream of turning the world into an endlessly expanding, fragmenting, complex deal market was failing. Jeff Skilling told Wall Street financial analysts that the fiber-optic project was worth $36 billion. This was just months before Enron crashed toward bankruptcy in 2001. But Skilling's brazenly upbeat assessment was what the financial world adored in Enron. It reflected Enron's culture of aggression and the ruthless ambition that had pushed the company to number seven in the Fortune 500. "They wanted to climb to the top of the mountain and pound their chest and crush anyone or anything that got in their way," recalled

John Allario, who had once worked in Enron's business development department.

Enron made U.S. capitalism feel red-hot and invincible. No one wanted failure, least of all Enron. But with their desire for market supremacy so heated, Enron's elite could not look any sort of failure in the face at all. Instead, they pushed reality away and moved deeper into themselves, further from the outside world.

By the late 1990s Enron was losing billions of dollars in the hard-asset investments it had made earlier in the decade: an electric utility in Brazil, a generating plant in India, and other various investments lost value. Another major problem was the company's investments in other companies. These investments had been made in a "sporadic fashion" over many years by an aggressive but inexperienced acquisitions force who, driven by huge incentives, imagined that they were big-time deal makers. Deals were rushed through and booked as income as soon as they were closed, well before Enron received any payment from them. No one was checking how the deals might perform in the long term. Thus senior management (or so they claimed) were shocked to discover a sprawling and chaotic investment portfolio containing poorly performing and even nonperforming assets. By mid-1999, spending in this area had gone $2.5 billion overbudget, taking Enron's total investment exposure to $3.6 billion.

Fortunately for Enron, at this stage, the financial world—none the wiser about the company's growing losses—was interested in the company's rapidly rising share price. This reflected not only general market conditions that were bullish in the extreme, but a confidence in Enron's trading wizardry to keep delivering value. To the financial world, share price was *the* measure of Enron's value, and as its share price soared in 1998 and held in 1999, Enron was considered to be in very good shape.

Thus for Enron, the key was to preserve and, if possible, leverage off the rosy picture the outside world had of it, a view determined entirely by share price. Keep the stock up, and whatever was going on inside the company could be dealt with. But how to keep the price up without delivering profits on its worsening portfolio of investments? How could this trick of the eye be done? Enron needed cash—badly—to cover its loss-making investments. It could raise cash by issuing shares on the market, but that would carry the risk of deflating the great share price. It could borrow money, but so huge a loan might jeopardize its top-grade credit rating, which in turn would lead to a dip in share price. Because Enron booked the expected future receipt of cash from its deals as current income, there was no prospect of cash coming later, so the pressure to raise instantly usable cash without issuing shares, while maintaining its credit rating, was overwhelming.

Enron was faced with a frightening contradiction between the outside view of itself in the financial markets (which was good) and the inside reality (which was bad). Apart from the truthful resolution—to declare Enron bankrupt—the only way to resolve the contradiction was to turn ever more inward, denying reality in order to wrestle free from the claims of the outside world.

The Hidden Path of Regression

In March 1998 Enron invested $10 million in Rhythms NetConnections Inc., an Internet service provider. Typical of deals in the new economy bubble, Enron made $300 million on its investment after Rhythms went public, in April 1999. The $300 million was quickly booked in Enron's accounts as income, giving the company the kind of bottom-line boost that kept its share price up. But the truth was that Enron hadn't received a dollar on its Rhythms investment: a "lockup" agreement prevented it from selling its Rhythms shares before the end of 1999. Enron had made $300 million on paper, but nothing in reality.

This $300 million was cash that Enron needed badly. An additional problem was that the Rhythms investment was "marked to market," which meant that increases and decreases in the value of the Rhythms stock would be reflected in Enron's accounts for all to see. This was fine if the stock held or increased its value, but not good if it lost value, as that would exert a downward pressure on Enron's own stock price. And given that the technology market was very volatile, the Rhythms investment had all the ingredients of yet another Enron investment going off the rails.

A few months before the Rhythms IPO, Enron's board of directors began to take notice of the fact that they had a load of risk-laden investments on their hands. In January 1999 a biweekly watch list report was produced to monitor troubled assets, and come May, with the problems with Rhythms staring the board in the face, the troubled investment was added to the list of Enron's bottom ten performing assets.

Soon after, at one of the weekly meetings to discuss the watch list report, Jeffrey Skilling expressed concern about the particular volatility of the Rhythms stock. He wanted to protect Enron against any damage that its locked-up investment might cause by suddenly crashing in value. The usual way to do this would be for Enron to cover its risk in Rhythms via a third-party investment that would hedge any losses Enron stood to sustain from Rhythms. However, this was not a viable option. The Rhythms deal was looking so bad that no third party would likely take on the risk, and why should it?

Faced with their lose-lose dilemma on Rhythms, the board asked themselves a question that would ultimately begin Enron's journey into the dark recesses of the offshore interior: Couldn't the value of Enron's own stock—still rising nicely—be used in some way to get the company the cash it needed? The question was prompted by the rising value of some forward contracts that Enron had with an investment bank to buy shares of its own stock at a fixed price. The contracts had been made to hedge against the dilution of Enron's stock value resulting from the company's employee share options. With Enron's stock well up and rising in the market, the forward contract deals had, like the Rhythms investment, a lot of locked-up value. But there was a key difference: although the return on the Rhythms deal was subject to the vagaries of a volatile tech market, the value of the forward contract deals depended only on the price of Enron shares. This meant that while Enron was doing well in the market, excellent returns would be guaranteed.

At the moment that Enron's board considered the idea of freeing up and exploiting the only asset they could lay their hands on—their tantalizing, seductively valuable stock—it began to cross the line of the generally accepted accounting principle that a company cannot recognize an increase in the value of its own stock, including forward contracts, as income. As it turned out, the line was very rapidly crossed by Enron's most senior officers.

It was Andrew Fastow who went away from the watch list meeting and put two and two together. He came up with a solution that would allow Enron to reconcile, finally, the outside world's optimistic view of the company with the embarrassing reality inside. Fastow's idea was to hedge the Rhythms investment by taking advantage of the rising value in Enron shares covered by the forward contracts. In effect, Enron would be hedging against itself: using its own stock to cover the risk in Rhythms in what was not a real hedge at all. By doing so, Enron would be breaking accepted accounting rules.

In putting together his plan, Fastow figured out the type of corporate instrument needed to activate the complex and abstract transaction he needed. The chosen instrument would have to be capitalized with the locked-up Enron stock from the forward contracts. It would then have to engage in a "hedging" transaction with Enron's stockholding in Rhythms, allowing Enron to offset losses on Rhythms if the price of Rhythms declined.

The instrument he settled on was a relatively recent invention from the Cayman Islands, one of the many offerings on the Cayman off-shore menu that finance aficionados like Fastow could taste if they needed to bend the world a little toward corporate will. The tasty dish Fastow chose was the Cayman Islands Limited Partnership.

Variously called a special purpose vehicle (SPV) or special purpose entity (SPE), the LP, as it is known, has all the benefits of a Cayman offshore company—tax exemption, secrecy, minimal registration and filing requirements—but it is quite different in one respect. Rather than taking the usual Cayman form of an artificial person free to en-gage in various transactions, the LP reduces to a transaction in itself. The partners in the LP are the investors of the transaction but have no residual corporate responsibilities or duties in the partnership. There are therefore none of the usual corporate encumbrances of directors and shareholders, company meetings, and so on.

Of course, partnerships have been around a long time and are a long-standing feature of English common law. But owing to its ex-treme flexibility, the Cayman partnership—a legal form in Cayman only since the 1990s—is quite distinct from traditional partnerships. New partners can join in the LP; old ones can leave. There are no limits to the number of partners. These changes don't affect the fun-damental transaction the LP represents, but they do of course make a difference to the pot of money that the LP can gamble with on any given transaction.

In a sense, the special purpose vehicle is financialization stripped right down to its barest, unencumbered minimum. It is the almost im-perceptible, liminal form that gives body to the hedges, swaps, op-tions, futures, and other abstract financial transactions that are traded in their thousands every day in the financial markets. For the com-plex, and secret, transaction Fastow was now contemplating, the prac-tically weightless and completely malleable Cayman SPV was the perfect instrument.

Fastow presented his plan to Lay and Skilling on June 18, 1999, and ten days later it was met with approval by Enron's board and quickly given the go-ahead. Fastow would be the general partner, or manager, of an SPV in which Enron would invest its high value stock. The selfsame SPV would then hedge Enron against any losses Enron made on Rhythms. The conjuring trick to free up and tap into Enron's own strength, in order to protect it against deals that were doing it damage, was about to begin. Fastow already had a name for his Cayman entity: LJM Cayman limited partnership—the initials LJM standing for the first names of his wife and two children.

Fastow tasked Enron's lawyers with the job of setting up LJM Cayman in George Town. But rather than use Huntlaw Corporate Services, as Enron had done with all its previous offshore incarnations, it chose Maples and Calder, across town. Henry Harford, doyen of capital processing on the island, with experience in setting up hundreds of partnerships, was their man. Harford has said he was told very little about the purpose of LJM Cayman, merely that it was going to be used as a vehicle for bringing foreign investors into Enron ventures.

The partnership structure—which consisted not only of LJM Cayman, but of Swap Sub, another Fastow-controlled SPV of which LJM Cayman itself was a partner—was fairly complex, but it met legal requirements in Cayman. Even so, Harford had a slight nagging concern. Wasn't there a conflict of interest in Fastow's dual role as both Enron's CFO and manager of what was supposed to be an independent partnership? "We said we must make sure Enron knows about it," Harford recalled thinking. "Otherwise it wouldn't be quite right." So he checked up and was told not to worry.

Of course, Enron knew well enough about the conflict of interest. Even so, it had expressly approved Fastow's central role in the transaction as the means by which it could be controlled—and kept secret. But by now Fastow was on to the next critical stage in the scheme—getting outside investors in LJM Cayman. In just a matter of days he raised a cool $15 million from Credit Suisse First Boston (CSFB) and NatWest Bank in the United Kingdom. This was just the type of hard commercial investment that would settle Enron's cash-flow problems and put the company on the road to near-term profit, preserving its place at the top of the league in the eyes of the market.

But the plan didn't resolve Enron's outside/inside contradictions; it merely deepened the falsehood through a phony offshore instrument. Enron was motivated by a will to override reality, so it set in motion the construction of ever more elaborate offshore structures that would cause the company to implode. In the process, Enron's accountants, lawyers, and investors would act no less consistently with Enron's aim of blocking out the dismal truth of its situation and, like Enron, would get sucked into a realm that had cut loose from the world and was legislated entirely by the deceptions and tricks of financial abstraction.

The complex technical structure of the Rhythms transaction, like all comparable transactions of modern finance, numbs the mind of the uninitiated. Yet the numbness must be endured, for at least a measure of the complexity needs to be grasped—albeit with a kind of dread. In evading the complexity, one becomes guilty of running away from the death's-head mask of capital's technical control, of not staring it in the face until it eventually backs away. Pain accompanies this confrontation, but avoiding reality tightens capital's grip on the world and far increases the agony.

The Rhythms transaction was concluded at the end of June 1999. Involved in the deal were Enron, LJM Cayman, Swap Sub—the other Fastow-controlled SPV in which LJM was partner—and CSFB and NatWest, the outside investors in LJM Cayman. First, Enron restructured the forward contracts and released 3.4 million shares, valued at $276 million, which it transferred to LJM. However, Enron placed restrictions on most of those shares, stipulating that they could not be sold or transferred for a certain period of time. These restrictions caused the value of the shares to be discounted by approximately $108 million. Then LJM transferred 1.6 million Enron shares to capitalize Swap Sub, along with $3.75 million in cash. With that combination of stock and cash, Swap Sub then agreed to pay Enron a fixed price of

$56 per share, or $104 million in total, for a put option on the Rhythms stock, to be redeemed when necessary.

This was not a true economic hedge. Enron was using its own stock to capitalize a partnership that hedged Enron's Rhythms investment. A real hedge would be conducted at arm's length through a third party that would take on the risk at a commercial premium and would be bound to purchase the Rhythms stock from Enron at the agreed price. In the Fastow scheme, Swap Sub's ability to meet the put option depended entirely on the price of its Enron stock. If that stock performed well, Swap Sub could meet the option even if the price of the Rhythms stock declined—that loss would be absorbed by the value gained from the forward contracts. However, if the value of Enron's stock fell to a point where Swap Sub could not afford to purchase the Rhythms stock as agreed, the hedge would fail, and disastrously so if the value of the Rhythms stock declined at the same time. Whichever way you looked at it, if share prices did not remain high enough, Enron was never going to get away from its fundamental problem: the terrible investment it had made in Rhythms and, more generally, the lack of a cash basis for any of the valuations of its worth.

But Enron was looking only at the upside—indeed, why shouldn't it? Its stock was still on the rise, so there was nothing to fear from hedging its own stock against a worthless investment. If you were smart and audacious enough to find a way, however shady, to unlock value to conjure away your problems, you deserved to get away with it. It was what made your company so valuable. This was the kind of attitude that the market hubris of the late 1990s was producing.

The same arrogance was behind one other trick Enron needed to play to make the LJM hedge work. It had to make sure that the secretive aspect of the transaction—using its own stock to hedge its own risks—was kept out of sight of the outside world and covered up. Once again, the choice of a special purpose vehicle to carry out the transaction was critical. According to SEC rules, the assets and liabilities of an SPV that a company transacted with could be legally kept off company accounts if at least 3 percent of the equity of the SPV was held by outside investors. Fastow had gone out and got CSFB and NatWest to invest in LJM—Swap Sub's limited partner—because he wanted their participation to make the transaction look like it was a bona fide SPV transaction.

On the very day the transaction was concluded, Enron's accountants, Arthur Andersen LLP, approved Swap Sub for nonconsolidation. However, Swap Sub was not merely without enough outside equity for nonconsolidation, it also had negative equity because its liability of $104 million to purchase the Rhythms stock greatly exceeded its assets of approximately $80 million in discounted Enron stock and $3.75 million cash. Later, in testimony given to Congress, Andersen's CEO explained that Andersen had made an error approving Swap Sub's nonconsolidation, blaming the mistake on "complex issues concerning the valuation of various assets and liabilities." Andersen's "error," which they never sufficiently explained, meant that Enron was able to overstate net income by $95 million in 1999 and $8 million in 2000.

By gambling its own stock to offset bad investments—and in the process boosting its income—Enron thought it could preserve its freedom as a market winner through withdrawal into the offshore interior of abstract financial instruments, secrecy, and deception. Even as this strategy unraveled for Enron, the hidden path that structured this possible freedom allowed Fastow and other Enron executives to profit personally.

As soon as the transaction was concluded, Enron's accounting staff realized that the put option from Swap Sub on Rhythms stock was not improving the stock's marked-to-market position in Enron's accounts. The whole point of the hedge had been to put a positive gloss on the Rhythms investment, and this was plainly not happening. A quick series of further derivative deals were concluded between Enron and Swap Sub to improve the hedge on Rhythms, but the situation didn't improve. Instead, the value of the Rhythms stock kept going down, bringing with it the increasing probability that Swap Sub would not be able to meet its obligations to purchase the Rhythms stock. In other words, Swap Sub faced imminent default.

Jeff Skilling took the decision to unwind the transaction and have Enron buy it out before it imploded. Fastow, meanwhile, had become a secret investor in LJM Cayman, knowing that LJM investors stood to make a quick and handsome profit if the SPV was ever wound up. He then invited a few senior Enron executives to join him in his secret get-rich-quick scheme.

A secret partnership was formed to profit from LJM's buyout: Southampton Place LP. Named after the smart suburb of Houston where some of the secret investors lived, Southampton acquired a key interest in LJM Cayman, becoming in effect the indirect owner of Swap Sub. Meanwhile, back at Enron, Fastow was engineering the windup of LJM Cayman under Skilling's direction—but on terms that were highly favorable to Southampton and above all to the Fastow Family Foundation, of which Fastow was a director. After the put option for the Rhythms stock had been terminated and the 1.6 million shares of Enron stock (which had become 3.1 million shares after a split) were returned to Enron, Swap Sub ended up receiving nearly $70 million more in assets than it had given to Enron. As for LJM Cayman, it was inexplicably allowed to keep the Enron shares it had received at the start of the transaction—a huge economic windfall. As it turned out, Southampton's investors made good returns, none more so than the Fastow Family Foundation, which—according to Enron's own investigation into the SPV transactions after the company's collapse—made $4.5 million off a $25,000 investment in LJM. However, this was just pocket change compared with the $23 million Enron paid Fastow to set up and run LJM Cayman, a figure that Fastow himself admitted to receiving when he was quizzed by the head of Enron's compensation committee in October 2001.

Toxic Death

Only a few months after the Rhythms transaction, Fastow was back at the board proposing the setting up of a second Cayman partnership, LJM2 Co-Investment LP. This was to be modeled on LJM Cayman, but on a much larger scale, seeking outside investment of more than $200 million from those willing to buy Enron's troubled assets. Again the scheme got the go-ahead, with the Enron board waiving the company's code of ethics to let Fastow proceed. The strategy of bringing outside investors was streamlined in order to get as much of their interest as possible and to iron out any difficulties meeting the SPV nonconsolidation criteria.

After Enron's lawyers had put a bit of distance between the company and the solicitation of investors in LJM2, Fastow sat back and let the big financial institutions do the marketing for his new exclusive investors club. Merrill Lynch led the sales pitch, bringing in Citigroup, JPMorganChase, CIBC, and Deutsche Bank. More diverse investors came aboard in the form of public and private pension funds, as well as a fund backed by the family that controls the Chanel fashion house. Promising a 69 percent return, LJM2 pulled in $394 million, bragging in its prospectus that it would deliver such high returns through a combination of "financial engineering," "innovative transaction structures," and rapid deal making.

The principle behind the LJM2 transactions was the same as LJM Cayman: use the "hidden" value of Enron's appreciating stock to hedge losses, but do it this time across the whole of the badly performing investment portfolio. Again, these were not to be real economic hedges, just Enron hedging risk with itself. A whole sequence of transactions was planned, using a series of partnerships set up by LJM2 that Enron would secretly do business with. These new entities, and the deals structured around them, came to be known as the Raptors. The Raptors would be nonconsolidated, off–balance sheet entities, and as long as the Enron stock price was on the up, the new raft of SPVs would be able to offset Enron's losses and pay out dividends to investors.

The Raptor transactions turned insider dealing at Enron into a new business line. With its fabricated arm's-length transactions, Enron avoided reporting losses of almost $1 billion and boosted its earnings by $1.5 billion. With the fraud stripped out, Enron's earnings would decline by 72 percent. But even the Raptors were not the end of it. Enron, it would emerge, had been contriving SPVs for the purposes of nonconsolidation since 1993, when it set up JEDI, the Joint Energy Development Investment Limited Partnership. This SPV secured $250 million from CalPERS, the California Public Employees' Retirement System. When CalPERS wanted out of JEDI, Enron needed another outside investing partner to keep the SPV nonconsolidated. So it invented one, called Chewco, to do the job, enabling Enron to cover millions of dollars of losses at JEDI and report huge profits instead.

In all, Enron used thousands of SPVs to hide loss-making assets. Of the $25 billion of debt that Enron had hidden from the world, "off–balance sheet" through nonconsolidation, approximately $14 billion was incurred through structured finance transactions using special purpose vehicles in Cayman and elsewhere in the offshore world.

Enron's offshore network had led it across the globe to expand and grow its business, but that business had been badly done, in too much of a hurry and too much under the delusion that the world could be reduced to financial abstraction. Enron continued to go deeper into the offshore network, where it regressed to contrive structures so abstract, so detached from reality that they became merely instruments of deception, which nonetheless would preserve the freedom they imagined was theirs by right and—by such deception—they hoped could be theirs again. As no deliverance ensued, cover-up compounded cover-up, until the outside world—for so long resisted and repressed by an instinct of social detachment that was at root criminal—returned to expose the tragedy of the will to absolute freedom.

The end began in 2001, when Enron's stock started to decline as the great financial bubble of the previous decade deflated. The whole strategy of offsetting losses through complex hedge and swap options was back-routed to Enron's stock price. Once the stock price started to decline, the edifice became increasingly shaky. First there were warnings that one of LJM2's Raptor investments would present a major risk if Enron stock fell below $48. At the time of the warning, the stock price was nearly double $48. By June 2001 it approached the $48 mark. There was the additional risk that a continued slide would force Enron to pay more of its stock to certain SPVs, prompting a further decline in the stock's price. In late July, with Enron stock falling and no letup in the payments to the SPVs, the downward spiral to implosion reached its finale. The SPVs, set up to rescue Enron from its cash crisis, were now triggering the complete decimation of the very stock that the rescue scheme depended on. Fastow stepped down as general manager of LJM; then, on August 14, 2001, Skilling, who had taken over as chief executive from Kenneth Lay, announced he was resigning "for personal reasons."

"Raptor looks to be a big bet. If the underlying stocks did well, then no one would be the wiser," wrote Enron whistle-blower Sherron Watkins in a letter to Kenneth Lay—who was still Enron's chairman—the day after Skilling resigned. "If the stock did well, the stock issuance to the entities would decline and the transactions would be less noticeable." However, Watkins continued, "all has gone against us." What remained, she said, was "a veil of secrecy around LJM and Raptor." An internal report in response to Watkins's concerns corroborated her view: "Within Enron there appeared to be an air of secrecy regarding the LJM partnerships and suspicions that those Enron employees acting for LJM were receiving special attention or additional compensation."

As the hedge and swap options across Enron's web of SPVs backfired, the partnerships, then Enron as a whole, imploded. Against the backdrop of a stock in free fall, Enron announced losses of $618 million and then admitted that it had overstated earnings by $586 million since 1997. In December 2001 it filed for bankruptcy, at the time the largest in U.S. history. In Cayman, looking out over George Town harbor, Henry Harford pondered the wreckage caused by the partnerships he had set up for Enron, now piled up onshore, far away in the real, visible world for all to see. He declined to go into detail. "It's the old toxic death spiral," he muttered matter-of-factly.

The Interior of Capital

In its escape into the offshore interior of secrecy and deception, Enron had blown itself apart. But this destruction did not take place in the interior. It could not be separated from the outside world that Enron had tried to master for profit and then had run away from when it resisted the company's control. Society, that public world onshore where people actually lived and worked, was not to be spared the consequences: it could not escape the fallout from Enron's secret realm as its effects fed back into a world of lost jobs, worthless stock, and vanished pensions and retirement savings. Enron's bid for freedom from externality returned a world of freedom's opposite: social destruction and the hollowing out of the public realm.

"Enron is not alone," the media reminded us constantly, reeling off the list of corporations charged with hiding this or that, with covering up and stealing. WorldCom, Tyco, Global Crossing: the billions of dollars involved in the scandals were greater than the GDP of many countries, the figures cited so huge they risked becoming meaningless and banal. Companies restated earnings after inventing reality. Hidden losses and debt, cooked books, and insider dealing were rampant. No, Enron was not alone in its aloneness, the media should have informed us, not alone in its wretched detachment from the onshore world.

Corporate America had collectively constructed an ideal of free market capitalism as a mirror against which it stroked its vanity. In the pursuit of this ideal, no conflict of interest was too great to get around. To hold on to that ideal, when reality clearly indicated that it existed no more, there were no qualms about seeking refuge in cover-ups and secrecy to try to take back control and keep on winning, as American capitalists were supposed to do. As these capitalists withdrew into their offshore interiors, the misdeeds began.

Capital in the 1990s was the freest it had ever been, the most bold and unrestrained, run riot across the world. So much was on offer and so much was up for grabs. Wall Street and the U.S. financial community pushed successive administrations—Republican and Democratic alike—to deregulate and let them capture for themselves the riches on offer. The separation of investment and commercial banks was scrapped. Accountants lobbied to be both auditors and consultants, and they succeeded. Stock options appeared on the scene as incentives for a new up-and-coming brand of ultra-ambitious—and greedy—executives. Companies operated and benefited in this freer, looser environment and became more autonomous, independent, and financially powerful.

In the process, companies were transformed, altering the way they structured themselves financially, using the offshore networks to grow, to expand, and to limit their tax bills. Into the corporate financial mix was added the micro-exchange of dealing in complex financial instruments and derivatives, currency trades and hedges. In this abstract sphere, the actual realm of production and labor became increasingly distant, the onshore public world more and more an appearance than a living reality to be grappled with. Soon the company, deluded by its detachment from the onshore world, imagined itself as merely an appearance too. This was no truer than in the dot-com boom, where the market was driven by image and appearance, not substance and reality.

It was not surprising that as the separation between onshore and offshore worlds drifted apart and the disjuncture between reality and appearance widened, the official account of companies' finances became something artificial and free-floating, detached from the real world. Accounts and audits were, after all, just another language or code among others designed to contrive the appearance of companies. Here a ready ground for lies and manipulation was prepared.

Over that possibility of deception lay the road to riches in the market. The greater the appearance of wealth and success, the better rewarded the company would be. The better the company's stock performance, the better rewarded the executives would be with their stock options. The ready ground for manipulation was quickly tilled if reality defied expectations. The market was entirely plastic, it was thought. It could be bent any which way and still go up.

Of course the contradiction between appearance and reality caught up with the market and crashed it. The weight of the collective conflict of interest could not be sustained, and the cover-ups in the secret realm to preserve the ideal of absolute freedom in the market stretched appearance too far for it to hold. The contortions were manifold: accountants covered up their clients' losses in order to gain their consultancy business; research analysts ramped up their investment bank's stock while calling it "shit" in private; IPO stocks were offered to preferred corporate clients in order to get their investment bank business; corporate stock was taken off the bottom line in order to finance outlandish rewards for executives. The market feasted off conflict of interest—conflicts that were removed from public view by the underhanded manipulation of reality, giving capital's frenzied freedom the appearance of truth.

"It is not that humans have become any more greedy than in generations past," said the Federal Reserve's chairman, Alan Greenspan, as he surveyed the wreckage of corporate America heralded by the collapse of Enron, "it is that the avenues to express greed had grown so enormously." In other words, the secret realm had manifested itself in an excess of opportunity. It had shown its anarchic face to a frenzied market. It had found its vantage point in an increasingly offshore world aided and abetted by financial and corporate deregulation bent on freeing capital from the social constraints of the onshore world.

Discipline thyself, capitalist, Greenspan intoned: "Even if the worst is over, history cautions us that memories fade. Thus it is incumbent upon us to apply the lessons of this recent period to inhibit any recurrence in the future." Keep the spirit of the secret realm alive, offshore and out of sight, but tempered, urged Greenspan, lest it destroy all us capitalists.

4. Offshore Freedom, Onshore Control

Dreaming and waking, truth and lie mingle.
Security exists nowhere.
We know nothing of others, nothing of ourselves.
We always play.
Wise the man who knows.

—SCHNITZLER, *PARACELSUS*

The Offshore Dawn of America

Enron had nearly 700 partnerships, special purpose vehicles, subsidiaries, and holding companies in Cayman. In the U.S. state of Delaware it had more than 900. Many of the Raptor and JEDI SPVs were set up in Delaware. Indeed, the majority of Enron's 3,000 corporate affiliates across the world were incorporated in America's "Corporate State." The Enron implosion was not the result of some offshore tax haven conspiracy. Enron was as much embedded, if not more so, onshore in the United States as it was in remote islands across the world.

Delaware resembles an offshore tax haven, except that it is located firmly on U.S. soil, on the ground of the first state to ratify the U.S. Constitution in 1787. The political history of the United States is as unthinkable without Delaware as is the history of American trade and commerce. Dutch, English, and Swedish trading companies battled it out from the early 1600s to establish a secure bridgehead in Delaware, for here, facing the Atlantic Ocean, was an advantageous outpost for the export of North America's abundant natural wealth to the Old World. Such trade via Delaware would contribute to the transformation of the feudal economies of old Europe into aggressive, mercantile nation-states, expanding and colonizing on the back of the rich resources of the New World.

Later, as a British colony, Delaware became a flourishing commercial center, building ships and exporting grain and wood from the American hinterland to the southern colonies, the West Indies, and Europe, constituting new networks and sinews of trade and state power. But homegrown industry took root and prospered too, with small-scale manufacturing in gun barrels and household goods, with flour mills and leather tanneries, all tapping waterpower from the streams of northern Delaware. When independence was gained, Delaware's unique combination of offshore and onshore values, of law-backed open trade and commerce, of industry and patriotism, would be forged together to become the exclusive preserve of the U.S. state and would be ideologically bound to its creation myth.

"Merchants have no country," wrote Thomas Jefferson at the dawn of the free-trade era, "the mere spot they stand on does not constitute so strong an attachment as that from which they draw their gains." This Jefferson said approvingly. For him, "the four pillars" of free America's prosperity—"agriculture, manufactures, commerce, and navigation"—"are the most thriving when left most free to individual enterprise." Here expressed is the ideal of a liberal economic utopia, free from the traditional feudal restraints of the state. But alongside the self-interested celebration of the market lies a deep attachment to the state as a realm where the material profit and gain derived from individual liberty can be lightly but ever so deliberately coaxed toward the formation of civilized society. Jefferson's statement "Government is best which governs least" is no call for the abolition of the state: it is a puzzle whose solution will eventually resolve the contradiction between the offshore and onshore values that formed Jefferson's political and social understanding.

At Home, Offshore

Though onshore, the Delaware advantage for corporations and private capital is as clear as any offshore tax haven advantage: inexpensive same-day company incorporation, low fees, minimal financial filing requirements, protection from hostile takeovers, the freedom to operate companies anonymously, no required public disclosure of accounts, shareholder secrecy, no sales or inheritance tax, tax advantages for holding companies, and a court system that is seen as having unequaled expertise in complex cases involving multinational companies. There is nothing quite comparable to Delaware in the rest of the entire onshore world, or even in most of the offshore world, for that matter.

Delaware's corporate law traditions, formed out of an era when capital and state first discovered a mutual, autonomous interest on roughly equal terms, have remained relatively uninterrupted and preserved up until the present day. Many a modern power, stricken by long bouts of state control over its national economy, is captivated in its search for economic progress by Delaware-type models of an apparently harmonious and natural relationship between capital and state, for here, they imagine correctly, the corporate and legal soul of capitalism resides.

Delaware's political economy of the freedom of capital and commerce coming together under the benign legitimacy of state authority preserves to this day the old, precisely calibrated trade-off between free capital and state control, for Delaware is modern America's onshore haven for its great corporate and financial powers. From the late nineteenth century, when Delaware liberalized its company incorporation and tax laws to attract the combined trusts and cartels of the Gilded Age, the state has led the field in bringing corporate America's holding companies to its shores.

And so Delaware remains today. America's—and the world's—largest corporations have their corporate homes in Delaware: Wal-Mart, General Motors, Ford, Boeing, Citigroup, ChevronTexaco, Coca-Cola. Neither their headquarters nor their gleaming office blocks are located in downtown Wilmington, Delaware—only their holding companies. Every single factory, shop, bottle, oil rig, bank, supermarket, and airplane part—in fact, every single asset anywhere in the world that belongs to these companies, right down to the screw used to hold a desk drawer together—is ultimately owned and controlled by their Delaware-incorporated holding companies. Ownership and control can extend no further back. It is the beginning, and the end, of the multinationals' agglomerated financial power, the starting point for the multinationals' material possession of the world, and the place where that web of possession is drawn together, contained, and compressed for capital accumulation. And all this power is translated into one single legal document of incorporation drawn up in Delaware, the home state of some 60 percent of the companies listed on the New York Stock Exchange and other U.S. exchanges. More than half of the Fortune 500 firms are there too. In all, over half a million companies are registered in Delaware.

A large corporation's main Delaware holding company stands at the apex of a pyramid of many subsidiaries. The first layer under the main holding company is often composed of subsidiary holding companies incorporated offshore, but Delaware is a favored incorporation point for these prime subsidiaries too. Boeing, for example, has, besides its main holding company, some 150 subsidiaries in Delaware—including holding companies for its operations in the United Kingdom, Australia, China, and the Middle East. Under the first level of subsidiary holding companies, the layers of the pyramid descend to their subsidiaries, and so on in turn to theirs, multiplying in quantity down to the onshore base of the pyramid, where, finally, hundreds of the company's smallest assets, the otherwise familiar topographical face of the multinational giant—the local supermarket, gas station, or fast-food restaurant—are found. The whole structure, comprising thousands of companies, is connected, right through from top to bottom and up again, to the Delaware holding company at the top. This is where the entire control and ownership of the business empire is vested.

Even if U.S. multinationals are incorporated elsewhere in the United States—for example, New York (where ExxonMobil, IBM, and General Electric are)—their main subsidiary holding companies are in Delaware. ExxonMobil has more than sixty major subsidiaries in Delaware, including holding companies for operations in places as disparate and dissimilar as Belgium, Australia, Chad, and the Marshall Islands.

In Delaware, U.S.-based multinationals can have their offshore networks at home as well as in Cayman. In Cayman, of course, the exclusively offshore corporation can steer itself away and completely avoid the onshore world, giving it the luxury of absolute detachment from onshore state authority, if that's what it wants. But an onshore presence in Delaware gives the multinational something crucial that is not available on its own in Cayman: political advantage at home.

The onshore political advantage helps fend off the attacks on a company's patriotism that follow a wholesale move offshore. Another fundamental reason to keep a foot onshore is that it provides the kind of influence onshore that a giant corporation deserves. Corporations, those that have customers, production centers, workers, even a national reputation—in fact, any of the onshore ingredients that complete a company's entire universe—depend on the state for their right to operate, hold assets, and just get on with business day in and day out.

Unless you can steal yourself away entirely offshore by running a business in which an onshore presence has nothing to do with what you do (and how many legal companies fall into that category?), you have to have some influence, the more the better, over what is happening on the ground where you physically operate. By remaining at least in part onshore, the corporation does concede a measure of its freedom to the authority of the state, but it gains freedom of a different kind.

Enron's Onshore Interior

Like other U.S. multinationals, Enron was incorporated in one state, had its headquarters in another, and split its numerous subsidiaries between Delaware and its offshore network. Like other multinationals too, Enron made now notorious efforts to influence domestic political decision making through lobbying and political contributions. It succeeded. In many respects, Enron's rise as a corporate power was directly attributable to its success in influencing government deregulation policy and to its development of political support in Washington and Texas. Just consider the impact Enron had on Houston, its "hometown," and you get an idea of how completely the company worked its way into local society to leverage onshore political influence. Not only was Enron one of Houston's largest employers, it threw money into regenerating downtown Houston, built Enron Field, a new baseball stadium for the city, and showered donations on arts and social causes. All of this helped a great deal when it came to pressing the corporate advantage in political circles.

Take, for example, deregulation in the core area of Enron's growth in the 1990s: energy derivatives. In 1992 Enron petitioned the Commodity Futures Trading Commission to exempt energy-derivatives trading from government oversight, largely on the grounds that regulation was preventing business from developing a vital new source of revenue. In 1993 the proposed exemption was quickly pushed through the commission, chaired by Wendy Gramm, the wife of Texas senator Phil Gramm. Not long after, Wendy Gramm resigned from the commission and took up a position on Enron's board of directors. In 2000 Congress approved an act that further exempted from regulation trading of energy derivatives, of which Enron was the market leader.

Political donations were a main route to Enron's onshore success. Enron spent $10.2 million in support of national political candidates in the 1997–2000 election cycle. It also applied pressure in its home state, Texas, spending $1 million on political action committees and state candidates, and $4.8 million more on eighty-nine Texas lobby contracts. And Enron did not spread its generosity only among the Washington elite: justices of the Texas Supreme Court received $134,058 from Enron, making them the court's biggest corporate donor. Coincidentally, of course, the justices reversed a lower-court decision that went against Enron in 1996 to cut $15 million from inventory taxes Enron owed to a school district.

The prime mover in Enron's journey into the political interior was Kenneth Lay, a close friend of the Bush family's for many years. As Texas governor, George W. Bush assisted Enron by deregulating state electric markets, taking a softer line on corporate pollution, and supporting laws that gave businesses protection from lawsuits.

Lay's personal friendship with the man who was to become president—as well as generous political donations—prepared the way for a deepening relationship between offshore corporate capital and onshore government once Bush was in the White House. Lay is thought to be the only executive to have had a private meeting with Vice President Dick Cheney when the latter was formulating Bush's energy policy. Lay is also thought to have given the White House two personal recommendations for the post of head of the Federal Energy Regulatory Commission, one of whom was later appointed by Bush. Earlier, Lay is alleged to have called the former head of the commission and offered Enron's backing for his reappointment if the company's views on deregulation were taken up by the commission.

Lay and Enron's onshore advantage translated into an expanding domestic market and political support at every level. The resulting freedom (from oversight and regulation) was the perfect complement to the freedom the company enjoyed offshore. Without such domestic influence, it would be hard to imagine Enron having been able to expand its business worldwide and boost its stock price.

In Britain, Enron's aggressive lobbying persuaded government ministers to drop regulations on the construction of gas-fired power stations. Between 1997 and 2000 the company's European arm donated thousands of pounds sterling to the Labour government, which reassured the British public that it was guided only by what was best for the market. All the while, enthusiastic cabinet ministers rushed to and fro from meetings with Enron executives, opened Enron offices, and made sure that restrictions on Enron's activities in Britain were kept to a minimum.

In August 1998 Enron spent £15,000 on a reception at Labour's annual conference in Blackpool. Three weeks after the reception, Labour's trade secretary, Peter Mandelson, approved Enron's £1.36 billion takeover of Wessex Water without referring it to the Monopolies and Mergers Commission. With Mandelson's backing, Enron could confidently expect to avoid regulatory and political opposition to the first-ever takeover of a British water utility by a foreign company. Their confidence was ultimately rewarded.

A former aide to Chancellor Gordon Brown, employed as a lobby-ist by Enron, shed some light on how far the company had traveled onshore into Britain: "We [Enron] have many friends in Government. They like to run things past us some days in advance, to get our view." This of course was best for the market, which really meant that what was best for Enron was best for the British government. End of conversation.

This may have been a new game for Labour, but it was old hat for Enron, who had been sniffing around in Britain since the early 1990s, pushing the Conservative government to privatize the country's electricity industry. Enron duly got what it wanted, and it started building power stations. John Wakeham, the Conservative energy minister who had overseen the privatization and soon after granted Enron the right to build power stations in Britain, got a lucrative job on Enron's board in the United States.

Corporate Welfare

Political donations and aggressive lobbying help multinationals get on the front foot onshore, creating synergy with their globalized offshore activities. Enron's political financing, though large in itself, was only a fraction of the total $3 billion raised to fund the cost of the U.S. House, Senate, and presidential elections in 2000. This record figure was broken in the 2004 election, and as before, many of the donations came from U.S. corporations investing for their onshore advantage. Their aim: to secure the protection and backing of the state at every level and then fuse onshore control and influence with offshore freedom, to brew a potent concoction that can extract maximum political and economic leverage at home and abroad.

Corporate welfare is an apt description for the onshore advantage available to the otherwise offshore corporation. Ralph Nader defines corporate welfare as "the enormous and myriad subsidies, bailouts, giveaways, tax loopholes, debt revocations, loan guarantees, discounted insurance and other benefits conferred by government on business."

When American Airlines and United Airlines came close to bankruptcy after the downturn in air travel following 9/11 and during the war in Afghanistan, the U.S. airline industry got $2.5 billion worth of federal government aid. The aid package, passed by Congress, more than offset the $2 billion the airlines claimed in lost revenue and higher costs related to the war and the threat of international terrorism. Yet the fact is that the downturn was an inevitable correction to the boom of the 1990s, when airlines lost control of their costs, expanding wildly and creating massive overcapacity in the industry. Was the World Trade Center disaster merely a convenient pretext for the bailout?

Despite the billion-dollar aid package, the U.S. airline industry is still struggling. United Airlines, US Airways, and Delta are all bankrupt or on the verge of bankruptcy. Now, however, the airline companies are trying another bailout tactic to get out of bankruptcy—terminating their expensive, guaranteed benefit pension plans and transferring their liabilities to the Pension Benefit Guaranty Corporation (PBGC), an already overstretched federal insurer. The airlines want to replace their existing "final salary" schemes with "defined contribution" pensions that don't guarantee the same level of benefits at retirement as final schemes do.

United Airlines—the sponsor of one of the biggest pension plans in the United States—wants to transfer $6.4 billion in liabilities to the PBGC, which, if the transfer goes ahead, would be the largest-ever pension termination. US Airways, back in bankruptcy a second time, is next in line, with $2.1 billion in pension liabilities it wants to off-load on the PBGC. Meanwhile, the PBGC, which would take on the airlines' pension plans, already has a deficit of $11.2 billion. There's a distinct possibility that more cash-strapped airlines, not wanting to miss out on the chance to save money, will off-load their pension liabilities onto the PBGC. If they do, the public insurer could well go bankrupt itself—possibly leading to an even bigger bailout by the government.

Corporate bailouts have been a feature of American political-business life for many years: Lockheed in 1974 and Chrysler in 1979 both received millions of dollars in government handouts to prop them up following disastrous business decisions. Government steps in, says Nader, "because private financial markets are not willing to invest or make loans to the troubled corporate entity or entities."

The savings and loan bailout of the late 1980s and early 1990s, after the U.S.-wide house lender collapsed, was the largest corporate welfare expenditure program ever, costing taxpayers $500 billion. Prior to their bailout, S&Ls successfully lobbied Congress in the early 1980s for a deregulation bill that "freed the industry from historic constraints and paved the way for the speculative and corrupt failures that came soon after." Savings and loan quickly transformed itself through deregulation into something other than the local onshore business it had always been—something akin to an offshore enterprise, supposedly far more exciting and dynamic. "In the end," writes economic commentator William Greider, "the government's regulatory system was perversely diverted to a different purpose—'socializing' the losses accumulated by freewheeling bankers and developers by making every taxpayer pay for them."

The modus operandi for the corporation is to pass the cost of its losses onshore onto society and its taxpayers, while the corporation runs off with the profit and parks it offshore. Risk back home accrues onto ordinary people who end up paying higher taxes. This strategy is possible only if multinationals do their political work—lobbying for special favors, policy deregulation, financial and political protection— and if the institutions that can provide that protection are softened up by corporations to act as a cushion for their onshore-offshore farrago. Then, when the whole enterprise falls apart, there are a series of federal mechanisms, agencies, and insurers already in place to pick up the pieces.

So corporations hedge risk by passing the costs of their failure onto society. To a certain extent, this should not come as a surprise to the citizens of market democracies. A vote for the free market is by extension a vote for corporations to keep on supplying consumers with ever more goods and services. We should expect that when a corporation goes belly-up, society shares part of the burden. It may seem unfair, particularly if a corporation falls apart owing to some internal fraud or crime, but in a sense this is merely the price paid for capitalism. You pays your money and you takes your choice.

The key battleground for corporate welfare is tax. The strategy of keeping as much profit offshore and exporting financial losses onshore in order to claim large tax refunds from the state—out of public funds, and in exchange for rising public taxes—is, as we have seen, common business with U.S. multinationals. It is a strategy that generally works.

As Nader points out, there is a gamut of federal tax expenditure lavished on American companies. "Special exclusions, exemptions, credits, deferrals, or tax rates . . . totaled more than $76 billion in fiscal year 1999, according to conservative estimates by the Office of Management and Budget. For the five-year period 2000–2004, the government will spend more than $394 billion on corporate tax subsidies."

When cases do go to the tax courts (in 1992, $32 billion in disputed revenue was tied up in proceedings), they drag on for years, becoming a further drain on public funds. Mobil Oil, now ExxonMobil, submitted 1.3 million pages of unlabeled documents as part of its evidence in one case that opened in 1989, delaying the matter for years. It was not until late 2003 that ExxonMobil finally reached an agreement to end another dispute that went back to the early 1970s. In this case, the resolute attempt to minimize taxes—while nominally remaining an

American company—paid off, on the grounds that the oil giant was entitled to tax deductions on the sale of natural gas in Texas. Exxon Mobil got tax refunds of $2.2 billion from the government, resulting in an additional $2.2 billion to its bottom line. For the offshore corporation, the inconvenience of a tax-court case, even one that lasts for many years, is well worth the onshore corporate welfare advantage in the long term, particularly when it involves such valuable tax concessions.

The American corporation—with one foot off- and one foot onshore, with the freedom to roam the world and maximize profits on the one hand and the freedom to soak up all possible corporate state protection and benefits on the other—degrades politics and weakens democracy. Losses are socialized onshore at a cost to social and public goods such as community and neighborhood cohesion, employment, education, health, and pensions—with a rising tax burden on citizens—all to the benefit of corporations whose tax rates decrease year on year. In the end, offshore freedom degrades to control and coercion at home.

The Offshore Solution?

The onshore interior of corporate welfare, its political machinations and wheeler-dealing, is as fixed and closed for the corporation as its offshore interior of transfer pricing, tax deferral, and corporate shell games. These closed, secret worlds, onshore and off-, are constructed in response to the real, existing challenges of market competition at home and abroad, challenges that include competitor corporations who ceaselessly develop their own internal spheres of preservation. Not to wrap yourself inward within the corporate body—as much at home as not—is to weaken your strength against an opposition that will profit at your disadvantage.

As one would expect, there are winners and losers in the onshore-offshore game. The winners will be those who can best maximize their business success through political lobbying, tax rebates, and various other means—by restructuring success to look like failure, for example. The winners will also be those who have achieved the corporate scale and size to take advantage of the onshore premiums their size makes available to them. The losers will be those who cannot extract sufficient onshore premiums and who, rather than see their businesses fail, reincorporate offshore, forgoing a measure of onshore advantage, most visibly in the political shame and embarrassment that the move offshore entails.

The biggest and largest of America's corporations—the Wal-Marts, the Fords, the General Electrics—are the best at the onshore-offshore game. They dominate and control corporate welfare largesse and political access, while with their Delaware incorporations and offshore networks of subsidiaries they expand and grow worldwide with as little restraint as possible. They also pay far less tax on their profits, in relative terms, than smaller companies do, and the difference is what enables them to pay for the onshore premium. In 1999 the largest U.S. companies paid the smallest percentage of their profits in federal income taxes. Of the 10,000 plus companies with assets of $250 million or more—with a total net income of $757.9 billion—there was a real tax rate of 20.3 percent. By comparison, for the 13,500 companies with assets between $25 to $50 million (and net income of $10.4 billion) there was a real tax rate of 36.7 percent.

To stay in business, to offset the onshore advantage the largest corporations enjoy, many American companies drift offshore almost inevitably. Large but relatively unknown companies, at least to the general public, such as the Texas oil drillers, reregister their parent companies offshore in droves. No one notices (the move offshore is a virtual, paper affair and involves no physical relocation of personnel or resources), so there is no great fuss.

Not so when the company is a household name. Consider the plight of Stanley Works, makers of the distinctive yellow-and-black tools known the world over. When Stanley of New Britain, Connecticut, proposed in May 2002 to reincorporate in the Caribbean island of Bermuda, there was much thumping and banging of congressional fists on the table: such a thing should not be allowed, the representatives thundered; it was unpatriotic, against the national interest, and just downright unfair to American companies that stayed at home and paid their fair share of taxes.

What irked the most was that Stanley was an American institution, founded by Frederick T. Stanley in 1843 as "a hardware company with unsurpassed customer service, product innovation and integrity," according to the company's Web site. And now this great institution was moving offshore to liberate itself from U.S. corporate taxation. Looked at from Stanley's point of view, however, the problem was that being part of America's industrial heritage did not necessarily make it a winner in the fiercely competitive global marketplace. A large proportion of its revenues and earnings were already derived from outside the United States, and the materials it used to make its tools came increasingly from global sources. Stanley wanted to free itself up and become a big boy, as it were, a proper multinational company doing things that proper multinationals did. Like having an offshore base in a tax haven.

In Bermuda, according to Stanley's CEO John M. Trani, the toolmaker would get the leg up it needed to compete as a global company—and hopefully make the type of returns its demanding shareholders expected. In Bermuda the tool kit for the global offshore corporation could be opened up: greater operational flexibility; better management of international cash flows; and better access to international capital markets. Sticking it out incorporated in Connecticut was not going to deliver the kind of competitive edge that Stanley aspired to.

The truth was that Stanley, for one reason or another, had not managed to acquire the homebound advantage that would allow it to survive onshore and buck the market to continue its drive for global growth. Perhaps it didn't even want to depend on onshore corporate welfare. As far as Stanley was concerned, it had little choice other than to exploit the advantage offshore, where, its representatives insisted, it would be able to reduce its tax rate to about 24 percent from 32 percent, saving $30 million a year in taxes.

Inversion

Stanley was following the Bermudan path taken earlier by a number of other American corporations, such as Ingersoll-Rand, Foster Wheeler, and Cooper Industries. Each had used a good trick known as corporate inversion, whereby a U.S. parent company sets up a Bermudan subsidiary, then smartly turns the subsidiary into the parent. For tax purposes, the corporate address is switched to the tax haven, but all the corporate hardware—offices, production, factories, as well as labor and management—stay onshore, in Stanley's case, in New Britain.

Stanley's proposal had U.S. lawmakers practically crying treachery and rushing to pass a bill to force corporate inverters in offshore jurisdictions to pay U.S. taxes. In late June 2002, New York congressman Michael McNulty, recalling the American soldier and turncoat who had once fled Connecticut for Bermuda, exclaimed, "I have no sympathy for the argument that these Benedict Arnold companies are justified in their actions, literally turning their back on this country because of problems they claim with our tax laws. No one should justify tax avoidance at a time of war by complaining about the laws." Meanwhile, banners held aloft by protestors handing out Stars and Stripes flags in New Britain read BLESS THE USA.

The ensuing controversy was more than a protest against Stanley. It was also the citizenry's terrified reaction to the glimpse it had gotten of the offshore interior, the disfigured world of capital into which American corporations had long since migrated. With the prospect of "turncoat" U.S. corporations, ordinary people felt social detachment, loss of economic control, and guilt. Stanley quickly became the scapegoat for all that was wrong and immoral about U.S. capitalism in the immediate post-Enron era.

Not long after Enron's collapse, but before Stanley made its announcement, Tyco inverted its corporate base to Bermuda. Its chief executive Dennis Kozlowski claimed at the time that Tyco was "a very healthy and viable company." Two months later, in April 2002, the criminal interior of capital raised its head again when Kozlowski was indicted with others at Tyco on charges of looting $600 million in the form of company loans, bonuses, and stock sales. And it raised its head again when Global Crossing, another Bermudan inverter and one-time stock market winner, collapsed in a financial scandal. At Stanley, no crime had been committed, but by the time it made its Bermudan intentions clear, the practice of offshore inversion had gained such a horrific reputation that the company appeared to be acting criminally just by default.

The specter of inversion came into the supposedly ordered and upstanding world of homespun, moral, law-bound U.S. capitalism like a wretched many-headed monster that had brooded in secret, then taken revenge on its innocent forebears onshore. If Stanley could be forced back into its box back home, thought the opponents of offshore incorporation, then the evil of capital could be contained.

In the end, Stanley never did leave New Britain for Bermuda. It backed down in July 2002 after an onslaught of opposition from labor unions and anti-inversion firebrands in Congress. Most damaging to Stanley's cause, though, was the prospect of a battle in court with the attorney general of Connecticut, Richard Blumenthal. Blumenthal alleged that Stanley had misled its shareholders by telling them that its Bermudan reincorporation would have no effect on shareholder rights. Blumenthal believed otherwise and threatened Stanley with a lawsuit, saying he would also ask the SEC to investigate the matter. Within a few days Stanley sent a revised statement to the SEC, which made the position quite plain to its shareholders: "Your rights as a shareholder may be adversely changed as a result of the reorganization because of the differences between Bermuda law and Connecticut law and differences in Stanley Bermuda's and Stanley Connecticut's organizational documents."

Suddenly, for those who had suspected a cover-up all along, it seemed there actually was something devious going on at Stanley. The company's straightforward commercial proposal to become a full-fledged multinational was perceived as just a pretext for Enron-style self-dealing, insider transactions, and criminal disregard for the laws of the outside, onshore world. Within weeks of Blumenthal's threatened lawsuit and the prospect of a SEC investigation, Stanley withdrew its plans for reincorporation in Bermuda. John Trani, Stanley's CEO, was left meekly asking his peers at Cooper Industries and Ingersoll-Rand, who were safely ensconced in their Bermudan refuge, whether they wouldn't mind returning home so they could all play on a level playing field. Needless to say, they stayed put offshore.

And there's the nub of the contradiction for a company pondering whether to become a real multinational player. It can either stay onshore, close to its shareholders, but forgo its global competitive prospects; or it can go offshore, where it can become more competitive and win profitable returns for its shareholders, but forgo shareholder rights and corporate accountability in the process. Quite a tough decision for a CEO to make, but one that ultimately depends on the type of capitalism that is deemed politically acceptable at the time. When Stanley made its bid for inversion, offshore was definitely persona non grata. A few months earlier, and the company would probably have got away with it.

Tyco—which made it to Bermuda and then turned inversion into such a political hot potato after its top executives' greed was exposed —is up and running again, under new management, and still in Bermuda. "Had the corporation been a U.S. corporation during fiscal year 2003," runs Tyco's annual report, "we estimate that the effective tax rate on income . . . would have increased from 28.1% to between 35% and 37% . . . The resulting impact could have caused a reduction in the Company's market capitalization amounting to $4bn to $5bn." In 2004, though, in the face of union opposition, Tyco held its shareholder meeting in North Haven, Connecticut, checking in onshore, as it were, just to reassure everyone it still had some attachment to the real world, however slim. Stanley, on the other hand, didn't fare as well as Tyco once its offshore plans were dropped. In May 2003, a thousand employees were laid off and nine factories were closed. "Sorry, Stanley," ran an editorial in *The Wall Street Journal*, apologizing on behalf of Connecticut's attorney general, whom the *Journal* blamed for Stanley's predicament.

If a company can't extract the onshore premium secured by the giant corporations, there is little to weigh up, financially, between the desire to remain at home, onshore, and the need to reincorporate offshore with all its benefits. When it comes to securing profits in a world of ever more fierce and aggressive markets, the question of national allegiance, of whether or not to locate a company at home, is irrelevant to the cutthroat demands of business survival. Under the economic logic of global capitalism, onshore has to be sacrificed for offshore. "Is it the right time to be migrating a corporation's headquarters to an offshore location?" asked an Ernst & Young tax expert who helps U.S. companies relocate to Bermuda. "We are working through a lot of companies who feel it is, that just the improvement in earnings is powerful enough that maybe the patriotism issue needs to take a back seat to that."

There is some hypocrisy in the attacks on Stanley and the other offshore inverters. The huge corporations who play the onshore-offshore game to their best advantage park most of their assets offshore and use corporate welfare to support such onshore presences as they maintain. It is hardly patriotic to threaten to leave—as the corporate welfare recipients do—unless the government essentially pays you to stay. In this sense, legislation meant to keep corporations from moving offshore altogether will only give the biggest corporations further cover to pursue their onshore-offshore games.

There is one other benefit to an onshore presence. Over time, cross-border mergers and acquisitions set up and networked offshore will inevitably reduce a global company's onshore tax obligations nearly to zero. At this point, the return on the offshore advantage will start to deteriorate, as there is nothing more to evade. The multinational will then intensify its search for onshore advantage, seeking more government subsidies and the like as incentives to remain "at home."

In the meantime, Stanley can continue flying the Stars and Stripes in New Britain without any further sense of betrayal. The new, improved Tyco, on the other hand, whose address for tax purposes is the second floor of a bright yellow office block in Hamilton, Bermuda, can proudly fly that country's flag. It may be bright red with Britain's Union Jack in one quarter, but for Tyco, it is the emblem of its offshore freedom.

Onshore Everywhere, Offshore Nowhere

The modern corporation is often described as having no home, no identity, no allegiance to any nation-state, only an "exquisite rootlessness" that makes it glide across the world, free from social restraint. This description is more correctly applied to capital itself than it is to the corporation. (To the extent that the global corporation is a financial machine operating through its internal offshore network, it has achieved liberty in the sense that capital is free. But it needs more than enough capital, and more than enough access to capital, for this to be the case.) Though developed market states take a liberal approach to the economy, it is still very much within their command to regulate and control, which means that even the most detached offshore corporation must pay some mind to the state, even if it appears, to its own advantage, not to do so.

In practice, the offshore corporate body remains bound to the authority of the state, for it needs to root itself onshore to do its business. How and where the corporation roots itself onshore is what counts. It is not that the modern state is being taken over by the corporation; rather, the interests of corporation and state are converging into single state-corporate identities based less on traditional historical, social allegiances than to pragmatic, global considerations of mutual preservation and opportunity. For each, harnessing capital is paramount, which is why on the economic front there will be no great reversals of economic liberalization. In other words, capital will continue to flow relatively unhindered. On the political side, the state can broaden its worldwide influence if it smoothly assists the offshore corporation in doing global business. That means giving the corporation some assistance to burrow itself onshore in a foreign state that is of political and economic interest.

These state-corporate identities will become further interdependent as states bolster their individual sovereignty through unilateral action in defense and security—or just plain military aggression— particularly in response to the new geopolitics of terror. The most recent, and blatant, example of foreign policy merging with the interests of big corporations was the move onshore of U.S. companies in Iraq soon after the end of the ground war in April 2003. A handful of large U.S. corporations won—and in the case of Halliburton were largely given—billion-dollar contracts from the Pentagon for the reconstruction of post-invasion Iraq. Bechtel Group got a $1 billion contract to build airports and schools. Fluor Corporation got the same amount to build water pipelines. And Kellogg Brown & Root, a subsidiary of Vice President Dick Cheney's old firm Halliburton, got contracts worth over $1.7 billion to provide U.S. troops in Iraq with food, accommodation, and other support services. Now, it wasn't just American corporations that could bid for the big contracts in Iraq, though that was obviously an advantage. If your country was on a list of 62 countries, such as Italy or the United Kingdom, deemed to be members of the "coalition of the willing" by the Bush administration, you were eligible to compete for U.S.-funded contracts in Iraq too. However, if you were Russia, China, France, Germany, Canada, or one of the other 130 countries excluded from the list, you were not.

The "with us or against us" thinking demonstrated by hard-liners in the Bush administration over Iraqi contracts will inevitably contribute to a hardening of states against one another in a range of foreign policy issues, of which trade is one. In the coming trade conflicts that arise between developed states, gaps will be prized open between states as they face one another down, and in these gaps multinational companies, tacitly supported by their sponsoring states, will find the competitive corporate advantage.

Exploiting the gaps between states in politics, law, and financial regulations; spreading out, here and there, in different geographic markets; making political connections where they matter most; touching down onshore where there is the least resistance and the most protection—there is nothing the corporation doing business across the world likes better. It will be the job of the state to harness this to their advantage and preserve the gaps between nations. Otherwise the advantage will be compromised.

The story of LNM Holdings, one of the world's largest steelmakers, in one particular incident as it unfolded in 2002 is instructive in the matter of the developed state's relationship to multinational corporations. The story illustrates well the contradictions of the corporations that "touch down" onshore to increase their global advantage, and of states that ride on the back of the financial power of corporations to enhance their trade and foreign policy interests. What becomes clear is that the global market is far from free. It is bent and distorted by state-protected markets, industries, and corporations, in which states and corporations seek each other out and, through the vehicle of capital, collaborate for mutual advantage when and where opportunities arise.

In July 2001 the British prime minister Tony Blair wrote to his Romanian counterpart Adrian Nastase, giving British support to a deal to sell Sidex, Romania's biggest—formerly state-owned—steelmaker, to LNM Holdings, the private holding company of the world's then third-largest steel firm. In the letter to Nastase, Blair said he was "particularly pleased that it is a British company which is your partner." But LNM Holdings, registered in the Caribbean tax haven of the Netherlands Antilles, was privately owned by Lakshmi Mittal, an Indian citizen. How then was LNM in any way a British company? Such contradictions and ambiguities are rife in the new world of offshore capitalism.

To be fair, Mittal did have a British presence. He had an office in central London, and he lived in the city too, though intermittently. His Mayfair, London–registered company, Ispat International Ltd., was indeed an onshore base for LNM's vast collection of steel factories across America, Europe, and Asia. Ispat employed some 100 people and in 2000 made a net profit of £2.3 million, properly paying its taxes to the Inland Revenue. The British "bit" of LNM was nevertheless quite a small part of Mittal's global empire, which had more than 125,000 employees in ten countries and profits of $99 million. And as British as it was, LNM's onshore base in London was wholly owned and controlled by Ispat International NV in Holland, the steel group's main operating subsidiary. In turn, Ispat in Holland was wholly owned and controlled by LNM Holdings NV in the Netherlands Antilles, the

Caribbean tax haven. And at the end of the day, this was the company that wanted to get its hands on Sidex in Romania, and the company that the British government said it was in partnership with.

In February 2002 the Sidex letter was uncovered and its contents made public by Adam Price, a member of Parliament for the Welsh nationalist party, Plaid Cymru. The party accused Mr. Blair of lobbying on behalf of "a foreign-owned" company in "direct competition" with steel plants in Wales. Why, Mr. Price wanted to know, was the British government lobbying on behalf of an offshore company in a tax haven, when British Steel, the former state-owned steelmaker and a direct competitor of LNM, was laying off thousands of its employees in Wales?

Perhaps in the mixed-up world of sometimes onshore/sometimes offshore corporations, that's how it was, and there was nothing the British government could do about those lost jobs in Wales. After all, British Steel was now part of Corus, an Anglo-Dutch multinational, so what place did the British have telling Corus what to do? None, said Corus, and government policy concurred. But in the case of Mr. Blair and his letter penned on behalf of LNM, the government's hands-off approach to multinationals didn't appear to be that consistent. And then there was the matter of Mr. Mittal's donation of £125,000 to the Labour Party just one month before the Sidex letter was written.

The fact of Mr. Mittal's £125,000 donation was no secret waiting to be uncovered by some hardworking M.P. or undercover reporter. It was down to Labour itself. When the party came to power in 1997, Mr. Blair said his government would be "whiter than white" in contrast to the Tory Party and their descent into sleaze in the 1990s. Labour turned rhetoric into action and made it compulsory for political parties to disclose the identities of all donors of more than £5,000, and the amounts given. With Blair's letter of support for LNM's Romanian deal out in the open, however, Mittal's donation and the crucial issue of its timing had only one possible implication for many political observers: Mittal had bought direct political influence from the government in order to purchase Sidex. The attempt to make political donations more transparent had badly backfired on the government, damaging their whiter-than-white reputation.

The government went on the defensive against a barrage of fevered headlines in both the tabloid and broadsheet press that screamed LIES, DAMNED LIES, BIG BUSINESS: POLICIES FOR SALE, and MITTAL: IT GETS WORSE. But it was the question of LNM's "Britishness" that was the hardest for the government to defend. It had to turn, in some way, a patently offshore tax haven–registered company into an onshore British company. Once that feat of transformation was accomplished, the home run—of justifying their support for the company solely on the grounds of the greater British interest—would be easy.

Initially Blair tried to make the justification without even dealing with the question of LNM's offshore status. He told Parliament that "the government will back companies to gain contracts the whole time. If we are not careful, we would be in the absurd position where the government doesn't have anything to do with promoting British business." Something more specific was needed, and it was left to officials to try to pull off the trick of turning LNM Holdings into a British company. Ispat International Ltd. in London, one step removed from direct control and ownership by a company incorporated in a tax haven, had now to carry the weight of the government's justification for supporting LNM. A government spokeswoman declared, "There should be nothing surprising in Mr. Blair supporting a British company—a U.K. registered company—winning a contract in Romania. What is important is that the Prime Minister uses whatever influence he has to encourage markets for British business." This rang as hollow as Blair's original statement, and a few days later the prime minister came back to the House of Commons to say that the government was in partnership with a "British-based company," a more accurate reading of a less-than-precise situation.

It was the essential ambiguity of the whole affair that spoke the truth about what was going on. And from that could be decoded the realpolitik of the British government's relationship with the offshore world. There was no doubt that the government was supporting a global offshore corporation in a third-party commercial deal. That it had the opportunity to do so, through Mittal's British presence, was what counted. The government calculated that the Sidex deal, even as it proved helpful to Mr. Mittal, would enhance British influence in Romania. And being helpful to Mr. Mittal could, in the long run, be even better for Britain, as it would put itself in a position to ride on the back of Mr. Mittal's future foreign deals, perhaps with very big fish like China. By giving Mr. Mittal their support and assisting his global ambitions, Downing Street decided they were backing a good horse for the country. Britain's own political and economic influence across the world would be broadened as a result of hitching a lift off the back of an offshore giant. What appeared to be missing from the government's argument, or was just plain irrelevant, was that LNM Holdings NV in its Romanian deal would bring little direct financial benefit to Britain. Income and profits accruing from the Sidex acquisition would disappear offshore to Curaçao in the Netherlands Antilles.

The explanation for the Sidex deal, in the context of offshore state-capitalism, appears rational enough. But when we enter into the relationships that form the new corporate-state compact, we find a hidden world of private and corporate wealth, national influence, and state power, ingredients that together degrade and negate democratic politics. We move into the secret realm, where the interests of capital and state conflict yet reconcile themselves in forms increasingly alien to our comprehension; where the political process is contorted, turned inward; where complex reality is not disclosed or comprehended; and where defiance and ignorance are papered over by doublespeak and spin and then reduced to newspaper clichés about corruption and the national interest, with the public left in the dark, uninformed, and disempowered.

Lakshmi Mittal has perfected the blend of offshore freedom and onshore control. His personal fortune is estimated at anywhere between £1 billion and £2.2 billion, putting him into the top five of the British rich list. LNM Holdings has surpassed South Korea's POSCO and Nippon Steel of Japan in steel production, and in 2004 it even surpassed Luxembourg's Arcelor, which now makes LNM the largest steelmaker in the world. LNM today has steel plants in the United States, Canada, Mexico, Trinidad, Germany, Indonesia, South Africa, France, Ireland, the Czech Republic, Poland, Algeria, Kazakhstan, and of course Romania, producing sixty-five million tons of steel a year, with annual sales in the region of $15 billion. Mittal's private holding company has further interests in shipping, railways, energy, banking, and consumer goods.

At age twenty-four, after working for his father's steel firm near Calcutta in India, Mittal junior set up his own steel business, Ispat Indo, in Indonesia in 1973. Combining new technology with smaller, more flexible factories that used scrap steel as the raw product, Mittal transformed Ispat Indo, made a fortune, then carried a business strategy—buying up failing steel firms and cornering the market in scrap metal—to other parts of the world, turning the firm into what Credit Suisse First Boston called "arguably the best steel company on the planet."

Mittal's fortunes accelerated in the 1990s, and in 1995 he opened his Mayfair-based subsidiary. A year later he bought a house in one of London's most expensive neighborhoods, Bishop's Avenue, in the leafy suburb of Hampstead, christening his £6.5 million purchase Summer Palace. His neighbors in Billionaires Row include properties belonging to the sultan of Brunei and King Fahd of Saudi Arabia. Bishop's Avenue might be more appropriately called Offshore Row, for most of the large mansions on the street are owned not by private individuals, but by offshore entities with names like Boston Offshore Federal Corporation; Mirage Holdings Ltd.; Quisai NV; Asturion Foundation; Sambar Deer (Bahamas) Ltd.; Green Canyon Foundation; Kirans Holding Limited; and Habib Bank Zurich.

Now settled in his offshore enclave in Hampstead, in a property held through the offshore bank and trust company Ansbacher & Co., Mittal set about working his way into the onshore interior. He began with the Conservatives, and in 1996 he received government backing for a £50 million soft loan from the World Bank to purchase a steel complex in Trinidad. A year later, with New Labour threatening to topple John Major's government in a British general election, Mittal wasted little time and donated £5,000 to Labour's election campaign, passing the donation through Keith Vaz, an M.P. who would become the new government's Europe minister before later falling from grace for failing to declare certain financial interests. Shortly after Labour was elected, Mittal's U.K. company, Ispat International, gave £8,000 to Labour, a donation it illegally failed to declare.

Mittal's financial investment in British politics brought swift returns. Mittal found the British government very willing to help him in building up his global steel empire. The government supported Mittal's bids for a series of World Bank and European Bank loans, all on favorable terms, to purchase formerly state-owned steelworks that developing countries were selling off as part of their IMF-imposed "structural adjustment programs," meant to bring their ailing economies into the world capitalist economy. The British government supported a loan of £315 million in 1997 to help Mittal buy steel plants in Kazakhstan, and one for £2.3 million in May 2001, the month before he made his £125,000 donation to the Labour Party and weeks before another general election.

For a steel company with aggressive global interests, getting in on the soft loans doled out by world bodies to buy up plants belonging to improverished states that had little choice but to sell off their assets was a great deal. Just as good was to have British government ministers, like Vaz, popping off on your behalf to the same states and telling them they should pass laws favoring foreign investors and be open to offers from U.K. industry. It was only a matter of time, and of more donations to the party, before Mittal gained access to Tony Blair and secured the prime minister's personal support for his foreign deals. One foot offshore in the Netherlands Antilles, one foot onshore in Britain was the way to success for Mittal.

With commercial support from the British state, Mittal established a good foothold on the mountain of information and intelligence held by other states that was critical to his business. It was claimed that the U.K. Home Office attempted to help Mittal obtain details from the Belgian prosecutor's office of a fraud investigation involving companies in Kazakhstan allegedly suspected of money laundering and corruption in relation to a £39 million pipeline project run by the Belgian company Tractebel. Apparently, one of the companies charged with fraud was a mining concern that had supplied Mittal's Kazakhstan steelworks. There was no suggestion that Mittal was involved in any wrongdoing, but the very fact that he could now leverage one government to supply him with highly sensitive intelligence obtained by another showed how close the British trade/foreign policy compact with Mittal had become.

At the June 7, 2001, British general election, Labour was returned to power in a landslide victory. To thank the party's most generous financial backers, Lord Levy, the party's fund-raiser in chief, held a private reception at his London villa. The prime minister was there to thank his party's elite benefactors in person. Among the 150 or so guests who mingled with Levy and Blair as they met and thanked the donors was Lakshmi Mittal, the Labour Party's second-largest donor that year with his £125,000 contribution, some £75,000 behind Labour's top donor, entrepreneur Sir Alan Sugar. Who knows what Blair and Mittal spoke about when they met at the party, but it was unlikely that Blair was unaware that Mittal was a donor, and a high-value one at that, a fact the government later claimed to know nothing about at the time. Whether Blair knew it or not, within seven weeks he would be signing a letter of support for Mittal's LNM in its purchase of a Romanian steel factory.

Mittal's prospective deal to acquire Sidex was already moving along nicely when he met Blair at Levy's reception in the wake of Labour's recent election triumph. For this, Mittal had the government to thank. He had British government support, in principle, for an application for a £70 million loan from the European Bank for Reconstruction and Development, capital that would help LNM absorb the cost of purchasing Sidex. That was the easy part. Now Mittal had to actually win the right to buy Sidex, against tough competition from other states sponsoring "their" corporations. This was where British support was crucial for Mittal, and he had the assistance of the prime minister himself when he needed it most.

"I am delighted by the news that you are to sign the contract for the privatisation of your biggest steel plant Sidex with the LNM Group," ran Tony Blair's letter of July 23, 2001, to the Romanian prime minister. Blair's letter suggested that the Sidex sale to Mittal was a done deal. But that was not the case. The letter reached the Romanians before draft contracts had even been exchanged, and just as French prime minister Lionel Jospin was en route to Bucharest to lobby on behalf of the rival French bidder, Usinor. It was the prospect of a sale to the French that had sent Mittal back to London empty-handed and in need of Blair's support. Working overtime, Britain's Foreign Office drafted a letter to the Romanian prime minister, Adrian Nastase, for Tony Blair to sign. It was to go to Nastase via the British ambassador in Bucharest and to include the claim that Blair was "a friend" of Mittal, but this claim was struck out by Downing Street.

Within a few days, Mittal, thanks to Britain, where he was not even a citizen, had won a £300 million steel plant, and the British government had gained, on the back of one of the world's richest men, some political and economic influence in Romania. It would claim that this deal was in the national interest, and for a while perhaps it was—but not for long. Having come onshore to gain advantage, Mittal returned offshore. Although he had a great deal to gain from his "partnership" with Britain, he was also making deals in other countries that would clash with the so-called British interest.

The key commercial relationship in question was with steel in the United States. Mittal had gained entry into the huge U.S. steel market in 1998 with the purchase of Inland Steel of Chicago, then the sixth-largest producer in a national steel market depressed by an influx of cheap imports. Mittal snapped the company up and did what he did the world over with his new acquisitions: downsized and introduced new, "smarter" technology for steel production. And as if this was not enough, the offshore corporation now turned the old onshore trick to embed its global expansion even further.

Mittal pressed home his onshore political advantage with donations of around $100,000 to Democrats and Republicans in the run-up to the 2000 election. After Bush became president, U.S. steel producers and steelworkers lobbied for trade protection, and in June 2001 they persuaded Bush (they had earlier failed to move Clinton on the issue) to authorize a U.S. International Trade Commission investigation into the country's steel industry. The so-called Section 201 investigation would, according to Bush, investigate steel imports coming into the United States to make sure that U.S. steel was "not being affected by unfair trade practices."

Inland Steel of Chicago, now called Ispat Inland and ultimately owned and controlled by Mittal's private offshore company LNM Holdings NV, had much to gain from the prospect of trade protection. Inland contributed $600,000 to the Stand Up for Steel campaign to push through tariffs on imported steel, particularly steel from British and European producers. In late 2001, as the U.S. trade panel ruled in favor of the protectionists that foreign interests posed a "serious threat to the U.S. steel industry," Peter Southwick, the president of Ispat Inland, said, "Today's action recognises that the U.S. industry has suffered for years because of unfair imports—the consequences are all around us." Offshore LNM, which had a few months previously benefited as a "British" company in the Romanian deal, was now claiming, under its American guise, to be a victim, in effect, of itself, in order to extract more government support from across the Atlantic.

Mittal, out of nowhere, popped up here, there, and everywhere—in the United States, where he was pushing policy and support his way, and at the same time in the United Kingdom, where he worked on the government to develop a base for his expanding eastern European empire. Now that American markets were to be closed to steel produced in Britain, an export market worth £250 million put jobs, livelihoods, and communities there at risk. "It now seems that Tony Blair was not only supporting someone who only had very minor interests in Britain, but a company which is actively supporting interests which go against British industry." So declared Plaid Cymru, the Welsh nationalist party, recognizing that with Britain about to have steel dumped on it by foreign companies excluded from the U.S. market, what was left of the once great steel industry in Wales could well be heading for complete decimation.

In March 2002 the U.S. government unilaterally announced tariffs of up to 30 percent on imported steel from abroad. This was bad for British steel producers, good for Mittal in the United States, with his Delaware-incorporated Ispat Inland, and even better for Mittal's offshore entity that owned and controlled the Delaware company. And it was excellent for Mittal's steel plants outside the United States—such as those in Romania and Trinidad, which Britain had helped him acquire—because these and other countries were excluded from tariffs on steel sold to America by virtue of their developing-country status.

As a global strategy, Mittal's onshore ducking and diving—his exploitation of the differences between states and their fears of competitive disadvantage—worked wonders. At a time when the developed world was engaged in a fight over barriers to protect national steel industries, it was not free trade and open markets that (as corporate rhetoric would have it) allowed him to dominate global steel production, but trade protection and tariffs, which granted him access to markets from which his competitors were excluded. In the world of offshore capitalism to which he contributed so much, Mittal was free to choose a nationality as (and if) it suited him.

Today, guess who is looking to push his way into steel production in Britain? Surely, should LNM Holdings control what remains of the British steel industry, the U.K. government can put its hand on its heart and say that it truly acted in the national interest when it enabled Mittal to dominate global steel production. At that moment, offshore freedom and onshore control will have completely merged.

The Competitive State

Faced with multinationals operating like LNM, states have little choice but to try to ride off the back of such offshore freedom and somehow turn it to national advantage. If the state does not, some other state will take that freedom away. If the power of offshore freedom is not sufficiently tapped, the state faces grave economic dangers: direct foreign investment from global corporations will dry up; unemployment will soar; the country's export industry will collapse; the currency will devalue; the cost of imports will rise; inflation will rise; interest rates will run all over the place. Very soon, as the last drop of capital flees the country looking for a safe haven, the economy will stagnate and production will come to a standstill. This is the prospect that states face if economic stability is taken for granted. It is the horrors of political instability and long-term economic depression revisited on them that keeps the developed West disciplined and attuned to the demands of offshore capital. If the offshore pact is not sealed, they fear, stability will be exchanged for crisis overnight.

Sadly, the admittance of offshore corporations and offshore capital to its shores will not save the state from economic peril—just look at what happened to Latin America, Asia, and Russia in the 1990s as off-shore capital inflated their economies, then exploded them—but without offshore freedom, the state, in a globalized economy, can never hope to make it in the world. Without offshore freedom, the state would have no geopolitical influence, no foreign policy beyond obstruction and rejection, no global pulling power to alter or change anything that could bring it sovereign advantage. It would be left either as a relic of an old Soviet state, like Cuba, or a failed, ruined state, like Sudan: the state of development of its domestic institutions—or worse, lack of institutions—the only measure of the country's status in the world. Rather sacrifice themselves to the offshore world than find themselves in the predicament of a Sudan, is the judgment the West makes, raising themselves, they imagine, to the moral high ground of the geopolitical universe, distancing themselves ever further from the world's losers as the latter are admonished and wept for in turn.

To keep on winning, the competitive state has no choice but to court offshore capital and corporations, to welcome them through the front door, give them direct and immediate access to political leadership, and accept on their behalf payoffs to politicians before, during, and after elections. This is why corporate welfare must be doled out, tax benefits arranged, and new laws brought in to deregulate markets and business to make the offshore corporation, in whatever guise, feel completely at home. Meanwhile, the global corporation will arrange its onshore presence to be as detached, virtual, flexible, and pragmatic as it needs be to tally up similarly advantageous arrangements with states elsewhere in the world. And for this the global corporation will employ its network of offshore paraphernalia, essential to store profits and assets, raise finance, speculate in foreign exchange markets, and capture and retain the earnings it has made tax free in the countries it operates in so they can be reinvested where in the onshore world it is deemed profitable. The state will not, and increasingly cannot, intervene in these convenient arrangements for corporations.

States go on endlessly about playing a leading role on the world's stage. To play that role, they have got to go out and catch offshore capital, bring it home, and keep as much of it there as possible—on the grounds that something is better than nothing. Hence, in the United Kingdom, the government now encourages multinationals to locate in Britain by cutting taxes on their capital gains and intellectual property assets and by taking a permissive line on their use of offshore tax havens to avoid British tax. It was this liberal, offshore-welcoming environment that made Britain such an attractive base for Lakshmi Mittal in the first place.

But what happens when these policies are followed? The consequences hardly enhance Britain or its people. The cost of the new freedom granted to corporations is offset onto higher taxes on labor, which, unlike the mobile corporation, is comparatively static and cannot move about to play off the gaps between states. As tax competition between states intensifies to lure in offshore corporate capital, the trade-off between tax incentives and the return in tax on captured corporate income deteriorates. Each time the government bends the rules, it gets a little less in return. No amount of privatization, asset sell-offs, and tax giveaways can then stem the decline in public sector investment. In Britain, this has led to a situation where health, education, housing, and transport investment has declined every year since 1975, even as the earnings of "British" corporations have skyrocketed.

Yet the relationship is not all one way. When competition is on a global scale, corporations cannot survive, let alone begin to profit, without the support and protection of the state. The onshore advantage kicks in increasingly as the offshore advantage levels off for corporations competing to lower their global tax exposure. True, unfettered economic globalization would be a frightening prospect for corporations used to feeding from the onshore trough of corporate welfare, protection, and strategic state support. With no national governments to lobby for market protection, anti-import measures, and

export incentives, corporations would be truly stranded offshore, com-
pelled by their freedom to be utterly detached in their search for
profit—to actually earn their money, that is.

Enduring Advantage

With so much largesse to gain from the state, why then do corporations bother to go offshore at all? Because, at the outer limits of competitive advantage, some things really do need to remain hidden.

There is a murky stream of offshore capitalism that spends its life
incubated, hidden offshore, such as the many private investment vehicles behind which stand secret beneficiaries operating as corporate
raiders, silently creeping up on companies in order to steal away control. But it would be a mistake to imagine that the instigators of this
type of business have no great onshore foothold as well, for often they
do. The point is that their onshore activities and the advantages that
accrue from them in politics or public life, for example, are secretly
manipulated for financial returns that are hidden offshore. The accumulated returns can then be reinvested onshore to buy even more political influence. This is not far from the game that Mittal was playing.

However, even the respectable public company, to all intents and
purposes embedded onshore, will set up secretive offshore entities to
facilitate lucrative joint ventures, monopolies, trusts, contracts, loans,
or sales it wishes to shield from public scrutiny. These entities constel-
late around the margins of the greater corporation, acting as cutouts
and fronts for business that is less than respectable.

With monopolies, offshore corporate vehicles are means for corporations to covertly secure—through the hiding of beneficial
interests—concentration of ownership that would otherwise be illegal.
In the generally monopoly-weakening environment of economic globalization, such underhanded methods can have their uses. Offshore

vehicles facilitate a way for multinationals to evade regulatory or antitrust controls and are directly used as secret financial intermediaries for corporate bribery and corruption in state privatizations, particularly those in developing countries and emerging markets. One example of such corruption was in the Swiss bank accounts opened in the name of offshore corporations when the French oil company Elf Aquitaine allegedly bribed the Gabon president El Hadj Omar Bongo for concessions. A recent estimate of the bribes paid by Western companies to gain influence and contracts puts the figure at US$80 billion a year, with secret offshore entities used most frequently as the funnels for illicit payments.

Offshore entities used in a deliberately corrupt and criminal manner are marginal to the corporation to the extent that they are structured to escape detection by the public eye. However, their criminality and corrupting influence reaches right into the corporate center and out again into the onshore state in which the corporation operates and invariably secures protection. Slowly but surely the public realm is hollowed out. Slowly but surely the prospect of freedom for a society that is not controlled by corporate-state interests is expunged.

The Interior Becomes the Exterior

The Founding Fathers and the framers of the U.S. Constitution were men who had closely studied Jean-Jacques Rousseau, Adam Smith, and, later, Immanuel Kant, whose philosophy of freedom and enlightenment expressed the zeitgeist of the late 1700s. With the ideal of the classical liberal state that Jefferson, Hamilton, and Madison inherited from these old, wise Europeans, there lay for these young Americans the hope of a conciliatory, pastoral harmony among many competing interests, a universal goal of progress and moral advance. Harmony would extend naturally to the relationships between states, and old conflicts based on irrational prejudices would be resolved through the unimpeded development of free trade. In harmonious America, state would link up with state to form a constitutional federation of United States.

Thereafter, from a principle that would unfold naturally, overseas states would link up with other states until the world's continents touched each other in brotherhood. Commerce, trade, and capital would provide the energy to liberate the human race to achieve this great end. Government would be morally synonymous with the market, together a kind of portable machine, fired up by the interactive presence of buyers and sellers, and exported around the world wholesale as an instrument of freedom maintained by the merchant class for the benefit of civilized society. Through a coalition of willing states, a perpetual peace for humankind would be secured.

How tragically removed our world today is from such noble visions of political and economic grace. Capital has indeed realized a kind of freedom and mobility, but humanity is far from reconciled with the violent and unjust external world that capital's offshore interior has reproduced for the lives of those who live onshore. None of the providential naïveté that motivated the Founding Fathers' undoubted charms survives. No matter how "free" trade is said to be, the secret realm perpetually secures the interests of the wealthy at the expense of the less so, and thus gives rise to war, hatred, and violence. The noble vision expires, starved of the clean, rooted air it needs to resuscitate itself, "sacred to patriotism" no more.

In theory, on some level, the liberal onshore state exists external to the fortunes or ruins of offshore capital and corporations that "tie national and local economies more closely into the global economy." But the dream of market freedom as the handmaiden of political freedom turned out to be a nightmare of control for the state, which depends on offshore capital without reaping any obvious social benefit from it. Now the petrified state, isolated in its autonomy, rings out with the cries of citizens desperately longing for identity with society, but finding that the state can deliver only the promise of greater wealth.

This means that in a global capitalist society, the state is in many ways redundant except as a servant of stateless capital. The point is conceded by states themselves. Robert Cooper, an adviser to the British government, writes, "The primary concern of governments is to satisfy electorates, not to reach compromises in international institutions. Thus we live in a world in which co-operation is increasingly necessary but is made extremely difficult. Everything else may become global—markets, currencies, corporations—but the state remains stubbornly territorial."

Why not do away with states, then? Because the robustly sovereign state is what capital and its associate agents depend on for profit; it is their fertile ground. This is why they desire a world of competing sovereign states, where international rules on tax, trade, and labor can be dismissed or avoided by states and, even better for capital, where the state (while professing the virtues of free trade) bends trade rules in practice to suit its corporate cronies.

Thus, in a world of state against state and corporation against corporation, states can only build strategic alliances with capital, however distorted and ambiguous. "It is perhaps most useful . . . to view the relationship between [trans]nationals and governments as both cooperative and competing, both supportive and conflictual. They operate in a fully dialectical relationship, locked into unified but contradictory roles and positions, neither the one nor the other partner clearly or completely able to dominate."

It is no wonder, then, that international trade talks, so full of rhetoric about the need for "free" trade, not protectionism, are exercises in rich state protectionism, as the rich states jealously guard "their" corporations against other states with "theirs," all to the detriment of developing states who have no corporate allies, merely their own land and labor, resources destined either to destitution in a sovereign isolation of their own making, or in sacrifice and alienation to the rich states and corporations wearing the masks of freedom and economic progress.

Global trade is determined in the last instance by the balance between offshore freedom and control, the point at which the respective competitive advantage of both capital and state can be seen to be best traded off by individual business interests and government. Such positions are not taken in isolation, but in the context of competing states, where corporations and governments will see how much they can get away with together over time. We owe to this situation the constant state of flux and insecurity that we experience in our everyday onshore lives.

In the era of offshore capitalism, the modern nation-state, with its immense capacity for international business and war, fashions the world on the back of its mutually willing corporate allies. This is no mere mercantilist fantasy, but a question of global empire, where the world is structured inside out by and for the United States and its self-same market and military allies. Behind their ideology of freedom has long been crafted a careful repression.

5. Interlude: The Secret Realm

Look into your heart, and it will tell you that the good man is in society, and that only the bad man is alone.

—DIDEROT, *LE FILS NATUREL*

Origins

We take leave, momentarily, from the profane world of multinational corporations, offshore capital, and governments to embark on a philosophical prehistory of the secret realm, a story that begins with myth, monsters, and man's primal search for individual and collective identity. Nascent capitalism and scientific rationalism in the West soon join the narrative as the principal forces underpinning what would one day become our detached offshore world.

Before we arrive at that conclusion, however, the scene is set for a groundbreaking philosophical reaction against the proto-offshore world of capital and controlling reason as it got established in the eighteenth century. Jean-Jacques Rousseau and Immanuel Kant, thinkers to whom we owe much in Europe and America's embrace of Enlightenment and liberalism, took on the dogmatic inhumanity of the times in which they lived, and they developed a counter-theory to the offshore world they sensed enveloping them. Their common objective was to set apart from this spiritless, natureless world a space for the individual where one could be true to oneself and not be corrupted by outside powers irrational or unjust.

For a moment, with these thinkers, there was a flicker of hope for a free realm that man could inhabit to allow society's natural instincts for liberty and goodness to blossom unopposed. Tragically, though, this genuine attempt to bring man back home in the world, to ground him onshore, as it were, dovetailed with those very forces of capitalism and instrumental reason from which they had set out to protect him. In the process, man, to retain his freedom in the modern world, would increasingly turn to deception as the means by which to assert his own individuality. This in turn would lead to the inauguration of the secret realm—the negative, dark spirit that today pervades the offshore world and its network of secret paraphernalia and hidden practices that are so closely bound into the global economy.

The Myth of Proteus

Our offshore but utterly controlled world is pretold in myth. The story of Proteus, the old man of the sea—and his capture—forecasts man's dominion over nature, and feeds finally into a history of capital and state in the modern era, their great five hundred years of covering the world in exchange and financial systems and the institutions and agencies of nation-states and governments. There is no real separation

between state and capital—they form a totality—but there is great an-
tagonism and contradiction between them.

The space of that contradiction is the secret realm, where freedom
has fallen, capital is preserved, and power is protected. It is the inner
sanctum of a world withdrawn from nature and spirit, a world where
tricks are played on the hapless, where gains at their expense are
made, accumulated, and preserved. "Authority has no strength in this
secret realm, this happy realm, this band of brothers, who spread the
light of pure confusion into the hearts and lower intestines of the
common man."

It is in the *Odyssey* that we find the sea god Proteus, in the story of
Odysseus' epic return back home onshore after many years away, detached from family and his people. The journey home requires him to
practice cunning and deception in a chaotic world in which equally
deceptive gods and demigods assume wild forms of nature. The
homecoming of Odysseus is the triumph of the human spirit of self-
preservation, survival, and knowledge: freedom secured through the
control of nature.

We meet Proteus in a story told by Menelaus, the husband of
Helen, for whose freedom Odysseus, Menelaus, and the Greeks fight
at Troy, successfully recovering Helen by using the Trojan Horse in a
master act of deception. But after the Greek heroes have returned
home, Odysseus remains lost, wandering his way across strange lands.
Telemachus, the son of Odysseus, visits Menelaus to see if he knows
anything of Odysseus' whereabouts. Menelaus recalls that he himself
had been stranded on the island of Pharos while trying to get home.
"It was here that the gods kept me," Menelaus tells Telemachus, "and
all that time there was never a sign of the offshore breezes that speed
ships out and into the open sea." As the tale continues, Menelaus, eager to get home, finds out that the island belongs to Proteus, the son of
Poseidon, and that if he catches Proteus and ties him down, he will
be released from Pharos and will reach home at last.

Proteus is no easy prey. To evade being captured and having to tell the truth, he possesses the power to transform himself and change "into every sort of beast on earth, and into water and blazing fire." Unperturbed, Menelaus prepares an assault on Proteus, and disguising himself in a sealskin so that he looks like one of Proteus' seal flock, he creeps up on the sea god. Proteus is "entirely unsuspicious of the fraud," and Menelaus pounces on him, holding him down. "But the old man's skill and cunning had not deserted him. He began by turning into a bearded lion and then into a snake, and after that a panther and a giant bear. He changed into running water too and a great tree in leaf."

In the end, Proteus gives up, and Menelaus takes control. He learns the truth from Proteus: what he has to do to get home, and also about Odysseus, whom he learns is held hostage by Calypso on another, far-off island. And from Proteus too Menelaus learns of his destiny—to spend the rest of his days in the Elysian Fields—"where living is made easy for mankind," a state of ideal happiness granted him for taming Proteus. Menelaus' great return home, or onshore, which he brings about through techniques of deception, cunning, and mastery of wild nature, is a mini-narrative within the Odyssey's epic portrayal of the human spirit released from external control.

The basic opposition between metamorphosis and its arrest and containment, the power of transformative nature and its control by man, is clear from the myth of Proteus, and it echoes a primary concern of ancient Greek thought about the cosmos—the enigma of cosmic flux and everlasting stability. It is not hard to fast-forward from this story to the dialectic of capital and state: capital's intrinsic transformative qualities, its mobility and flexibility over space and time; the state's inherently fixed and stable nature, and the state's relation to the wild transformations of capital—to its containment, control, and stabilization.

The myth also suggests the essential qualities that drive the state:

harmony, social and political order, and the pursuit of a particular moral end, the very ideal of the Elysian Fields that Menelaus is guaranteed once Proteus is mastered. Elysian is the well-run state in which the regulative elements—law and authority—give to the state its identity as a self-determining historical nation or community. In order to maintain itself, the state must employ deceptions and tricks against its more flexible, mobile opponent—nature—as a means to securing higher authority and rule.

The conflict between shape-shifting capital and the stable state can be abstracted further to a conflict between nonidentity and identity, and various economic and scientific concepts can be fitted into these categories. Nature and capital as nonidentity: changing and flowing, liquid and chaotic, volatile and spontaneous. The state as identity: order and control, constant and rooted, permanent and singular.

Marx, for one, was obsessed by the nonidentity of capital as it took different forms in the process of production and consumption, changing from money capital to productive capital to commodity capital and back again to money capital. The forms that capital takes today far outnumber those of Marx's time, as seen in the elaborate and complex range of financial instruments that exist in today's markets.

Capitalists have always been seduced by capital's ability to transform itself endlessly, and one of the key tasks of modern financial technology is to turn capital's nonidentity into an asset: to give shape, substance, and identity to capital in order to manipulate it for profit. Financial technology acts on capital the way Menelaus acted on Proteus, pressing it into service for its own ends.

But the task of ordering is no straightforward matter. The external world of nature, referring back to the Proteus myth as our guide, is full of powerful, dynamic transformations, a terrible chaos that resists control, wrestles with it, and evades it. The hard resistance of this wild nature to control—the tricky nonidentity that eludes capture—comes to define and condition the state that attempts to contain it. In other words, the state inherits some of nature's elusive qualities, even as it tries to overcome them.

The same can be said of individual identity. Individual identity, in the form of a person, is not some preformed totality, ready and waiting to take on the world right at the start of history. Rather, identity emerges bit by bit in the long historical struggle with external nature: as much through the sheer presence of nature in the inhabited environment—the weather, the form of the land, and so on—as through the material that the natural world is made of and the use made of it by man for such primitive needs as food, clothing, and shelter. In this respect, what Marx had to say about the formation of individual identity in precapitalist societies is instructive: "He himself is not only the organic body, but also the inorganic nature as a subject. This condition is not something he has produced, but something he finds to hand; something existing in nature and which he presupposes."

Marx contends that our identities as individuals are inextricably bound to the external world. We have a piece of nature within us, internalized as it is by our attempts to master and control external nature. We cannot separate ourselves from this part of our nature or try to distance ourselves from it. It is who we are. However, given that we connect to nature in this way, a space now opens up for a relationship to nature that is not bound by its control and is instead closer to the nonidentity of nature, closer to a spontaneity that could be called spirit or freedom, and therefore to that freedom within us *as* nature. It is from the revolutionary possibility of such a freedom within us that the secret realm will emerge.

This freedom could be equivalent to life in the Elysian Fields, a life of happiness, harmony, and the good, a final release from the internal command to control nature, a journey back onshore, in the way of Odysseus and his associates, from the detachment demanded by survival and self-preservation. This myth (to take a cue from Marx) perhaps underpins the drive toward collective identities that form tribal, community, and then primitive state allegiances structured around shared labor, communal ownership of land, family reproduction, and, inevitably, war against foreign identities perceived as threatening. The lesson, of course, is that the ideal is never realized. We are never reconciled with that free piece of nature within us. The internal detachment of self-preservation can never be put to rest; therefore, control of nature progresses with indifferent technological forms that drive identity forward, in the state and in the individual, still in the hope that freedom can be found.

The Sea

It is not just through ownership of the land, however, but also through possession of the sea that one can trace the emergence of the modern state and its search for freedom. And it is in the sea that we can also grasp something of the origin of capital. "The natural element for industry, animating its outward movement, is the sea." The sea is surely one of nature's most nonidentical forms—liquid and flowing, with a terrifying, mysterious disorder of its own—and historically for man one of the most difficult of natural phenomena to control. Yet, of course, the sea is the source of commerce cultural and economic, trade and exchange, and the basis of civilizations and empires, ancient and modern. It is the radical, free nonidentity of the sea that Proteus represents—and which early societies struggled to order and control to make economic progress.

There is a medieval manuscript from Baghdad, produced at the height of the Muslim enlightenment in the last quarter of the first millennium, that depicts Sinbad, the Arab world's own Odysseus, carrying on his back a creature half fish, half old man, whose arms are around the legendary sailor's neck. This is the Old Man of the Sea in another incarnation, yet still tamed for the service of man. A bountiful tree frames the two characters, its fruit dropping into a basket held by Sinbad, a symbol of economic advance through the control of nature.

Arab mythology took from Ptolemy's *Geographica* the idea of a world center, halfway between east and west, a summit that was the best place to see the heavens, the place closest to God. To the west, for the Arabs, was the "sea of darkness"—the Atlantic—a life force so alien, unknown, and strange that its dread existence, which could not be denied, defined in contradistinction the city of God. Yet the seas to the east, which the Arabs knew and traveled themselves, were a realm of freedom, a source of prosperity through trade, and the channel through which ideas from elsewhere in the world—from India, China, from Christians, Jews, and pagans—could flow, producing a rich culture of diverse interests, of science and reason.

The path to statehood in Europe was a more abrasive and dominating affair than this, but the sea was no less significant in its development. European states began to take their present shape at the turn of the fifteenth century, when nations expanded their "maritime networks across the Atlantic, Indian and Pacific Oceans into regions where their political and economic power had previously been of little or no significance." Though the Europeans were by no means the first to use the sea to trade and extend their influence, no state until this period had actually claimed exclusive ownership of the sea for itself. The civilizations of antiquity made no jurisdictional claims over the sea. The Romans had accepted the sea as common to all by natural law, as a *res commune*, a thing incapable of ownership. Other states in the Near East and Asia had regulated sea trade to protect their commercial interests, but again, the sea was not something that could be owned.

This changed in 1493, when, following Columbus's first voyage to the New World, Pope Alexander IV declared a formal partition of the Atlantic, dividing sea as well as land between Spain and Portugal. The papal bulls granted a monopoly of commerce within these regions to their respective crowns so that other states could not trade in them. From now on, the state would enclose sea and land within itself to form a protective, sovereign identity, ruthlessly impervious to outside forces.

For the next three centuries European states would expand such sovereignty through war, conquest, slavery, and trade, linking the lands of their dominion to their nations at home, turning them into resources for their disposal. Europe's sovereign powers had tamed Proteus the sea and brought the outside world under their command. Here the first breath of offshore freedom and onshore control was drawn.

The old economic order of feudalism began to dissolve, and a new order started to grow up alongside it, slowly choking out ancient and medieval practices like withering weeds. This was the independent realm of capital, fed by growing world trade and a rising class of merchants. Newly acquired monetary wealth was put to use producing exports, using new methods of production that completely altered the way men had previously worked, tied as they had been to their localities. Now that relationship had begun to fragment, and man was increasingly separated from nature, "the laboratory of his forces." Feudalism decayed, throwing man into a baleful freedom from the ties that had bound him; capital sought him out in terms of the value that he could now command for the exchange of his labor. It appeared to be a fair bargain, an exchange of equivalents, but man's labor was now given up to ownership by another, on terms that were less than favorable for the work he was required to do.

In the bold, new thrusting world of global trade, of new commodities in circulation, of new desires and needs, of vibrant European cities connected to distant territories across land and sea, producing for and shipping to export markets far and wide, mere money was transformed into accumulating capital. Now Proteus—the earth's natural resource base—was tamed by the all-consuming identity principle of exchange, where things of utterly different identity could be equated to each other through the medium of exchange. This was the method by which the diversity of nature could be reduced to instruments of transaction in the market.

Now all nature and its produce could be brought via trade within the confines of the market, on the principle of "indifference," suppression of difference—freed, like labor, from what had held them stubbornly in place through traditional beliefs, uses, and practices. The identity principle shook it all up: in short, it made the world tradable. Lemons for guns. Ships for coal. Unlike for unlike could become like for like through the exchange medium of capital. Here at last, with exchange and the division of labor—itself a function of the identity principle—did the modern state bring its order and authority over the world and proclaim its freedom in it.

Of course, the state did not dissolve as the shoots of capital appeared. On the contrary, the state was behind the economic conquest that delivered new markets to traders, who were organized into monopolies that were founded—like the various East India companies—on national lines and tightly controlled by the state as instruments of economic expansion. The monopolies then became the source of much needed revenue for advancing state conquests and wars.

The state acted as a container of capital—regulating capital to its advantage, or, if there was no advantage to be had from it, hindering its growth. Royal currencies and taxation were introduced, allowing the expanding state to have "access to wealth in circulation." From the mid-seventeenth century in England, state finances were rationalized and centralized, reforming and nationalizing customs and excise, and introducing treasury departments of government to control the national finances. *"Tout est ici en regie"*—everything is under government control—was what one visiting Frenchman said about England in the early 1700s.

Nowhere did capital and the state oblige each other more in Europe than in the overt state economic policy of mercantilism, where trade was taken to be war by other means. Aggressive mercantile states conjoined world trade and colonial conquest from the fourteenth century to the eighteenth century. The policy was one of total competition among the European nations for economic and military control of the Americas and Asia. To this end, capital and state sided completely, to the benefit of capital in terms of a growing merchant and bourgeois class whose trade interests were protected by government tariffs, duties, and monopolies, and from which states could then gain revenue and keep a hold on economic activity to purchase foreign conquest.

The eighteenth century was the triumphant century of sea trade. "For some time now people have been talking only about commerce, navigation, and the navy," reported a contemporary source. But soon, as the industrial revolution got under way, manufacturing would be the main joint concern of capital and state; and capitalism itself, now fully emerged from its long gestation, would be the order of the day.

Reason and the Control of Nature

What was it that contained capital and put it under the rubric of identity? It was reason. That which turned nature into commodities to be bought and sold on the market brought nature under the control of science to produce knowledge. The intoxicating lens of man's modernity had two sides to it: on the one side it telescoped the passage to distant lands and far-off places over the seas, bringing the world under its control and profit; and on the other, with a microscope, it inspected matter close up, reducing it to certain definable laws, which nature, as observed in an orderly fashion, would prove in situ. From the sixteenth century, with Galileo, through the ultra-rationalist formulations of Descartes, who declared that reason made men "masters and possessors" of the world, did such activities prosper. With the experimental method was modern science born, a revolution in reason that would take man out of the chaotic soup of nature in which he had so long flailed about aimlessly.

Francis Bacon, the father of empirical science, invoked none other than Proteus, the sea-god son of Poseidon, as the image of anarchic nature that could at last be contained through the mechanical arts or technologies of science: "The vexations of art are certainly as the bonds and handcuffs of Proteus, which betray the ultimate struggles and efforts of matter. For like as a man's disposition is never well known or proved till he be crossed, nor Proteus ever changed shapes till he was straitened and held fast, so nature exhibits herself more clearly under the trials and vexations of art than when left to herself."

The force of reason brought the world into focus for modern, enlightened man situated in the acquisitive, proto-capitalist West. Reason had given him the world's dimensions, its feel, speed, and shape—such sensations were unique, particular, but at the same time were underpinned by strange yet very present laws, everywhere applicable. There was an amazement to reason, a divine astonishment at its power over nature. Was there no end to reason? man asked. Was not everything explainable by it? Was it not possible to move beyond the great advances in natural science to banish everything that was irrational, vague, old and unverifiable, mysterious? Were there not indeed timeless and universal truths that could at last be known to man, that *should* be known to man as the ultimate goal of faith?

The answer to these questions would, it was hoped, deliver to Enlightenment Europe that Elysian realm of perfection. However, the way to happiness was not guided, as it had been, by Providence on the one side and respect for the Cosmic Order on the other. This was an old method, to be banished alongside all superstition. In its place was the belief that what man needed could—and inevitably would—be discovered through knowledge alone. This concord with knowledge, by which human happiness and progress was guaranteed, was the ultimate moral goal. As Holbach, one of the most ferocious defenders of reason, put it, "Let us hope for everything from the progress of enlightenment."

What was this brave new world to be like? What could be hoped for? In the end, it was total control of the individual. Whereas earlier, in the discoveries of the new science, reason had liberated man from blind nature, it now returned like a new force to track man down and dominate him, to reduce him merely to an object of another's reason, malleable and plastic, without a mind of his own. This was surely the counterpart to the world of conquest, genocide, and capital accumulation that the West, with its telescoping of foreign lands, imposed on its victims across Asia, America, and Africa. Chillingly, Holbach invited man to "submit in silence to laws from whose binding force nothing can remove him."

Now that the ultimate goals of mankind's happiness had been determined and reduced to rational laws of nature (which, among many other things, gave absolute grounds for the decimation of foreign peoples and the plundering of their resources), man himself was just an indifferent variant of nature, to be controlled, like nature, for mere profit and exploitation. As a result, all man could rest on was his sensual, feeling self, searching for pleasure and avoiding pain. With reason absolutely in command, there was nothing else to aim for. How perfectly well this new, "progressive" man fitted into the emerging market states of Europe. Here was the engine for the scope of capital's enlargement into society, for there was much pleasure to be gained in capital's accumulation, and privation from its taking away. What a useful tool this man was, for in working toward his own gratification, he was working toward his nation's own glory. Was this not the best pleasure one could seek in society? And there were rewards too for such a state of mind—in commerce, in the administration of the state and the conquest of others—in service to reason, the highest good, colonial conquest and order.

Freedom and the Secret Law

Rousseau was the first to condemn the oppressive determinism of the Enlightenment, the impasse beyond which thought could not continue. For Rousseau, the Enlightenment's absolute identity of reason and morality produced a corrupt, hypocritical, spiritless world that alienated man from nature—indeed, man from his own nature—a sphere of life that had been suppressed by the utilitarian attitudes of the bourgeois state that preached above all the greatest good of the greatest number, which in the end, for Rousseau, came down to the selfish pursuit of wealth, status, and private happiness of the few. This for Rousseau was a kind of detached, offshore world in which man's nature, and his relationship to nature, was being subverted. Where was the good to be found in this detached world? asked Rousseau. What was the source of real value, not those deemed to be valuable by the grasping mores and desires of the bourgeois? It was that piece of nature inside us, Rousseau replied, that realm that was spontaneous and free from control. This was our own built-in onshore refuge from the depressing, disconnected world that Rousseau perceived around him. The point was to tap into it and then find salvation.

Unlike his intellectual opponents, Rousseau sought the good not in commanding reason or knowledge, but inside himself. Conscience, he said, "speaks to us in the language of nature" and so was to be our inner guide to the good. Man needed to transform himself, come back onshore as it were and cleanse himself from bogus modern society, its pretensions, airs, and graces, and reconnect with his own internal "true" nature. Once there, man would know what he ought to do for right moral action. It would be up to the individual himself to choose the good—in other words, man was free to choose between good and evil—and this freedom to choose was part of his own rational nature. But without getting back in touch with his onshore self, there was no free basis for making the moral choice.

What Rousseau promised, and what was so radical in his thought, was that man could break out of the prison house of reason as a grand, detached, and ultimately oppressive machine and seek instead refuge with nature on an attached, internal level, and from that move toward the good.

Immanuel Kant, the solitary but not unsociable philosopher who lived alone in Prussia, had only one picture on his wall. In his *Observations on the Feeling of the Beautiful and the Sublime*, Kant wrote, "Newton first saw order and lawfulness going hand in hand with great simplicity, where prior to him disorder and its troublesome partner, multiplicity, were encountered, and ever since the comets run in geometrical paths."

In this remark, Kant is much the conventional rationalist paying tribute to the detached heights of Newtonian empirical science. But the picture on the wall was not of Newton, but of Rousseau, whose almost sensual presence led Kant to his next observation: "Rousseau first discovered amid the manifold human forms the deeply hidden nature of man, and the secret law by which Providence is justified through his observations."

It is through Kant's devotion to and study of the laws of man's secret nature, something upon which his entire system of philosophy is based, that we begin to deduce the origins of the secret realm that inhabits our world today and is so extremely present in the conditions of global capitalism. For this is where freedom—individual, social, political, and economic—first finds its moral refuge in the West. It begins, in the late eighteenth century, as a realm of immense possibilities, amid ideals of individual and political liberation from the tyrannies of various forms of absolutism, and it ends in our times embedded in absolute capitalism as a tragedy of freedom, its original ideals so debased that this secret realm knows freedom no longer, just its ruin.

The critical component of morality for Kant, and hence for freedom—and this is where he drew inspiration from Rousseau—is the absolute autonomy of the individual. Without this self-autonomy, in which the individual inhabits a sphere of moral existence that is contained absolutely within him, with no exposure to outside interference or control, there is no morality and no freedom. This is precisely what Kant diagnosed as the sickness of his age—rigid, dogmatic, illusory thinking, driven by utility—which had debased science and was above all "indifferent to humanity." Science had been used to alienate the individual from this natural, free condition. In the process, a space for "the moral use" of reason had been closed and shut off to the individual, who had become in effect merely an instrument of reason, just another cog in its hungry, amoral machine.

Like Rousseau, Kant felt that the relationship between detached reason and morality had to be rearranged and fitted back together again to form a new identity, one that gave the individual a space to determine himself in his own way, according to his own natural rules. This did not mean that Kant rejected reason, far from it. Reason had to be upheld where it was applicable to external nature, such as in the formation of scientific understanding and knowledge. However, the moral sphere was not open to scientific understanding in the same way as nature was, so a new relationship with reason had to be found that did not efface man's own inner, "deeply hidden" nature as a moral being, yet gave him a basis for rational action. The idea of an onshore refuge had been critical for Rousseau. It was to be so too for Kant, and central to his philosophical scheme to protect the individual from what he saw as the irrationality and meaninglessness of so much eighteenth-century thought.

Kant's achievements in mining away a moral autonomy for man utterly changed the course of Western thought by giving the concept of freedom a power that was both individual and deeply resonant with the wider political struggles of the time. But in the end, the consequences were far from what Kant intended, for rather than breaking away from the machine of instrumental reason that the modern capitalist world was constructing, man in his secret realm was left ever more exposed to, and implicit in, reason's control for the purposes of capital accumulation and human repression.

Kant's first task, in *Critique of Pure Reason*, first published in 1781, was to determine how far theoretical reasoning could actually go in explaining the world. No further than our experience of the world, he concluded, against the babble of existing theories that took supposedly rational explanations to impossibly irrational depths. He reminded us that theoretical reason can tell us nothing about morality, the purpose of the individual, freedom, art, or beauty—it is strictly empirical, scientific knowledge based on the a priori principles of time and space that make experience possible in the first place. And more radically still, the knowledge we have about objects in this way is only of the appearance of what actually exists, not of those actual things in themselves. Science could now, with the *Critique of Pure Reason*, have a complete and isolated realm of reason for itself, where natural phenomena were determined in a closed system according to universal laws.

In constructing his new identity of reason and morality, Kant radically separated human experience into two parts—one of the inner self of morality, and one of the outward world of matter. The former was an onshore refuge for the individual, the one and only place where moral questions had any validity. In the latter, nature was regarded as an assemblage of fragmented phenomena, just nonidentical bits and pieces that had no substantial onshore connection with the individual, which nonetheless the individual, with the use of reason, transformed into a rigid, controlled identity.

From the ironfisted criteria of what regulates knowledge, Kant turned, in his *Critique of Practical Reason*, to the moral realm of man's hidden nature of freedom. This was where man's secret, onshore interior would be opened up and revealed as man's rule-bound gift from God.

In *The Social Contract*, Rousseau had written of freedom as "obedience to the law that one has prescribed for oneself," where man was his own self-legislating master who lived in concert with his true self, practically forced to be free by the law.

Kant's moral theory began—and ended—with an extension of Rousseau's core idea: man must submit to no other rule than that which he himself has set up as a *universal* norm and proposed to himself. From this duty emanates Kant's famous categorical imperative: "Act only according to that maxim by which you can at the same time will that it should become a universal law." Here then was the sharp rule of reason butting up against man's secret, moral nature, giving it the universal, rational law it should obey. The choice was there for man: he could act as he ought to, live up to his true nature as a rational agent, or he could act against himself, against reason, and be subject to external control, to the base world of desire, pleasure, and pain. It was up to man himself. Did he want to be controlled by the law of freedom to remain fixed and grounded onshore, or by the law of nature with all its randomness and prerational incoherence? For Kant, the law of freedom was consistent with man's secret nature, so it was rational to submit to it. If he acted against reason, he would be at the mercy of blind necessity and the indifferent, mechanical laws of matter, no longer a free being, merely another piece of nature, floating by, offshore.

But man's onshore preservation against the detached, random world of nature required no less a detachment itself. The realm of freedom was possible only if the individual was completely separated and protected from the effect of any law other than the categorical imperative. The individual was to be sealed up against the outside world and preserved as an autonomous rational unit. No noise from outside that conflicted with the moral law was to be tolerated on the path to freedom, no infection from the common world of experience could be permitted to enter the fortifications of the moral individual lest they set him off course on the sorry road of passion and pleasure. Only through the authority of the moral law could one break through the surface world of phenomena and reach finally into oneself, as one really was in nature, onshore and absolutely free.

God, Freedom, and Immortality—the purpose of morality—would be waiting as one broke through to the hidden self, discovered not through experience and the mechanical laws of nature, but through absolute faith in reason. "I must therefore abolish knowledge, to make room for faith," Kant declared, instructing us that the goals of morality were to be something we chose to believe in as a matter of free will guided by our reason, not something determined from the outside and fixed onto us, like the laws of science were to nature. That we could never attain the ultimate goals of morality, and could only ever lead a life that tried to be directed toward them, was the best we could hope for, said Kant. With this, Kant erected the final brick in the barrier he constructed between freedom and nature, between an onshore interior of total self-control and an offshore exterior of fleeting, meaningless phenomena. Had not his objective been to rescue the moral dimension, freedom, from dogmatic reason, to find the source in man's hidden nature? It looked more like man was to be left abandoned, alone in his secret realm, bound into submission to the moral law and divorced from nature.

Man's aloneness was necessary to preserve freedom, argued Kant. Autonomy was essential, but just the start. There was much to aim for beyond—men acting as ends in themselves and coming together to form the "kingdom of ends," the ideal where harmony would be found and man would finally be reconciled with the world. Man was not then to be alone in his autonomy. He would move from that bottom line of individual freedom to join with other like-minded folk, acting in the best interests of their collective rational will to reach universal freedom. Even there, though, at the end point, autonomy would not be given up. "Only in a person is the idea of the end in itself and the ultimate end fulfilled."

This ideal of universal harmony transposed into the political realm expressed the great hope of the late eighteenth-century bourgeoisie in Europe and America—a reconciled social order, at once free from external political interference yet abiding by common interest in the moral law. This was truly the onshore kingdom to come. The hope is expressed in Beethoven's early piano concertos, the sudden crescendos of freedom breaking out of the classical straitjacket toward a new realm of possibility where "all might be well." As with Rousseau, the individual will would conform to the general will in the ideal state, in a greater freedom in which one would sacrifice one's particular interest "to the moral welfare of the community." There would be no contradiction between individual freedom and political authority in this state, because of the secret law of man's freedom, which was rational, preordained, and only had to be discovered to be seen that it was right.

Kant's bourgeois optimism reaches its height in the concept of a new world order comprising a federation of nations sharing the same values of freedom under universal law. Such an ideal and its language permeate all the way through to the supposed morality guiding contemporary U.S. foreign policy today: the oft-cited "coalition of the willing," the constant spinning of freedom as the justification for preemptive war in Iraq. "The world is more peaceful and more free under my leadership," declared President Bush a few months after the ground war, the old bourgeois rhetoric finding its place in the modern world, cover for the grossly instrumental realpolitik of political reelection while, in secret, Iraqi detainees were being tortured and humiliated. This was morality, all right, but one that had "degenerated into ideology, into a mask which concealed a dirty business."

The Tragedy of Freedom

Kant's dream of global harmony, with man reconciled with man, and reason with nature, in freedom, was a necessary bourgeois fantasy. The bourgeois struggle for autonomy, for emancipation of the individual against absolutist rule in seventeenth- and eighteenth-century Europe, was nonetheless bloody and real. The ideal was the reward for bourgeois victory. But for the sake of political freedom and the onshore kingdom to come, everything was suppressed: happiness, experience, affection, and sympathy. Only harshness would remain to withstand the battle.

This was the view of the philosopher Theodor Adorno, who had long labored to work out how the great liberal tradition in German thought and letters had ended in Auschwitz and the death camps. Today we cast our eyes over the photographs of brutality at Abu Ghraib prison in Baghdad and, amid the declarations of freedom by Bush, ask similar, though not comparable, questions about America.

Was autonomy really freedom if the individual had to endure such self-denial, such separation from sympathy that only harshness remained? For this is what freedom felt like in submission to the moral law. But where had this law come from? And how was it a basis for freedom? It was by merely thinking it so, said Kant. God, Immortality, Freedom—the principal interests of morality—were given to us as fact. We should therefore obey the law. That was all there was to it.

It is here that the contradiction in the secret realm becomes undone, for obedience to the moral law appears to be commanded from somewhere outside our onshore autonomy. The moral law in itself is not sufficient on its own to make us obey. Something else is acting on us, pushing us to conform to the moral law. What pushes us are the rules and controls of bourgeois capitalist society, in particular the work ethic, to keep us in order and disciplined. This is the real, practical choice we make—to stay on the right side of bourgeois law, in our own self-interest. There is no compelling universal reason otherwise to obey the moral law. In this light, freedom becomes an entirely pragmatic decision to comply with the norms and standards of bourgeois society. What was billed as freedom in fact turns out to be a pretext for coercion. In social terms, this is what really stands behind Kant's secret law of man's nature.

The notion of free nature that had guided Kant in his moral philosophy—to carve out a space for morality and freedom in relation to reason—was abandoned, in effect, to what the philosopher was originally trying to get away from: reason as control and domination over nature. However hard Kant tried to get away from controlling reason in his search for a moral space, he could not resist his Newtonian inheritance, the ice-cold rump of reason left over from his first *Critique*. Now that touchstone of control was targeted at the moral sphere, as if to pin it down, the much-vaunted autonomy put under the command of bourgeois law and order, and, with that, its progressive incorporation into the market economy. That free piece of nature within us, that vital element spirited onshore, would be slowly buried by the controlled detachments of modernity, and morality would be snuffed out. In return, we would become hardened against each other and lose that vital spirit of spontaneity, so essential for real freedom.

With the categorical imperative and its "ought principle," the conscious, self-reflective, rooted, and experienced spirit of free, moral nature was forsaken by the secret realm. Desire, passion, happiness, and attachment—genuine inner freedom—were banished, not in the end for reason or the moral law, but for the sake of bourgeois control and the dictates of the market. Freedom had to be proclaimed, as a matter of political and moral pragmatism, but on the strictest, most limited and exclusive terms. All were to be bound to the necessary division of labor, the work ethic, and the banishment of indolence and laziness. From this our onshore, rooted autonomy—the means to protect and express our inner freedom as moral, social beings—would be subverted, through the misapplication of reason, by the detached offshore world that onshore autonomy had sought to define itself against in the first place.

"Laws in reality reflect power relations," said Adorno, seeing an authoritarian element creeping into autonomy in order to keep freedom and morality in their places within capitalist society. Even though there were formal laws to protect and guarantee freedom in bourgeois society, there was a tendency to abolish freedom, to dispense with it entirely, while all along proclaiming it as the ideal. Freedom was eliminated and reduced to an instrument of control.

At the dawn of the nineteenth century, the technological promise of modernity gave birth to industrial society. Capitalism began to develop and expand globally. The disengagement and detachment between man and nature increased in proportion to the complexity of modernity's bold new structures. This was not the capture, but the slow destruction of Proteus, the free nonidentity of nature taken over by rational control. The hope of a providential order of harmony, something that had consoled Kant and Rousseau and given them faith, was now a distant, antiquated memory that had no bearing in the technological age of progress. The ancient conflict between duty and desire had been resolved in favor of bourgeois discipline. Meanwhile, the desire to seek one's own interest, as long as it conformed to that discipline, was encouraged and promoted by the state as the common good.

All that was left was the form of freedom, emptied of any real social content. The husk of individual autonomy became the fossil of freedom, the secret realm where the individual, in his "obsessive isolation," was concerned primarily with his individual right. This was a detached, private ethic of denial, a refuge of the will from the external, social world. The ideal of freedom would be held aloft, but always accompanied by a sense of loss at the gap between the "ought" of the moral interior and the reality of the outside world. Yet the gap would provide the pragmatic solution by which the individual could at once shield himself from the outside world and profit at its expense. All hope of a genuine, shared onshore freedom was lost to the jostling of position between competing interests.

The secret realm would be no protection from the guilt of one shut inside his private domain, never measuring up to the ideal. As recompense for this trial, the suffering of others would be demanded. Only by the force of violence, retribution, and punishment could the world outside be made to measure up to the ideal. This was the merciless road to absolute freedom, total control, annihilation, and evil.

Modernity

The tune was to change from the expressive optimism of the ideal to its tragic loss—from Beethoven to Schubert's A-major Sonata, described memorably by Isaiah Berlin as a "deeply tragic, deeply beautiful, deeply melancholy work of painful innervision." This was the mood of Romanticism, the lost inner voice with nothing to connect to, stranded offshore, its despair at the chasm between the isolated individual and society. Science, technology, and national economy moved together in the modernizing state, instrumental reason at its service. A homogenous materialism crept over the world.

Individual autonomy in the secret realm became ever more the refuge from the dreadful realities outside. Yet the secret realm knew this reality well, for in a sense it was wholly responsible for its existence. Romanticism as an art form was the counterpart to this sheltering, bombarded consciousness of the disembodied. It sought to overcome the detachment of the modern world either in substantiality on the ground, in the nation, or in the completed logic of its supreme inwardness. These were the poles on which the Romantic aesthetic turned: Wagner's ideal of *Ganzheit*, or "wholeness"—in which art would realize the total identity of national German culture, the very Valhalla of onshore mythology—or the absolute subjectivism of Kierkegaard, in which the outside world would also be entirely blocked out, but as an individual act of self-defining choice. Both were responses to the secret realm in which enlightened society now found itself.

By the end of the nineteenth century the suffering soul of autonomy was declaimed as the spirit of a decadent modern age. Wagner's dream of wholeness, of freedom and social identity regained, gave way to a nightmare of wholeness's impossibility—the language of morality, truth, and art completely debased and corrupted in modern technological society. All that was left were the shattered remnants of identity. On this barren, silent landscape artistic modernism was born.

The angst-ridden, romanticized secret realm was most sharply expressed in fin de siècle Vienna, in artists and musicians such as Gustav Klimt, Oskar Kokoschka, and Arnold Schoenberg. It is in Peter Altenberg's poems, written on postcards to friends and set to discordant, atonal scores by Alban Berg, that we attest to the extremities of self-obsessive withdrawal:

> *Here is peace. Here I shed endless tears over everything!*
> *Here I give vent to the unimaginable,*
> *Immeasurable grief that consumes my soul . . .*
> *See, here are no people, no settlements . . .*
> *Here is peace! Here the snow drips quietly into pools of water . . .*
>
> —ALTENBERG, *LIEDER, V*

One can think too of Freud in the same period, with his pioneering work into the unconscious world of dreams, the recognition and mining of the hidden landscape of the bourgeois psyche in order to better understand the darkness that disturbed the normalcy of otherwise respectable people. Indeed, politics and society in late nineteenth-century Vienna has been characterized as a crisis of liberalism, where liberal politics lost its way, unable to deal with its own contradictions or public responsibilities, stuck as it was in the brooding private sphere of the secret realm.

It was against this almost irreversible sense of decline and stagnation that political ideas whose sole purpose was to lift man out of his social isolation came to prominence. Earlier in the nineteenth century, Hegel had teased man out of the secret realm and connected him to the flow of history—substituting Kant's weak Providential teleology with something much more forceful and up-front, no less the idea of history as freedom itself. Later Marx politicized man's alienation in the secret realm with an economic teleology. History became freedom, but only through class struggle and the radical alteration of the economic conditions of society. Rather than transforming individual will to create a better world, as Kant had urged, man would do better to transform society first to find his liberation.

Marx's philosophy appealed to an era that had become disillusioned with liberalism and its pallid ideal of freedom. Socialism, and nationalism, were both germinated in the late nineteenth century by a belief in making man whole again and vigorously connecting him to his "true" nature by some great social revolution. It was the search for a new Providence, a way to resurrect freedom and raise it up again out of the secret realm, that would lead to the ideologies of absolute transformation in the twentieth century. We well know freedom's double tragedy in totalitarianism, the millions who would perish in the wake of the command to transcend the individual secret realm in the interests of the state. That, of course, was not possible, for the secret realm was etched into the core of modernity too deeply for its traces to be obliterated. How could modern identity elect to get rid of itself except through mass annihilation and genocide?

There was no way out of the condition that itself had built the detached world. All that could be hoped for was to sink further into oneself to seek refuge. Individual autonomy was paralyzed in its collusion with modernity; it complemented modernity's detachment yet recoiled in fear from its overbearing power. The will wanted to rush out and do its own thing; then it had to take cover from the shit that came back at it from outside. There was a constant shuttling back and forth between freedom and control, one moment part of nature, another removed from it, though lost to know which was which. On the whole, homogenous modernity pushed toward control. In our secret domain we drew a protective veil around us to preserve the very last drop of our authentic, onshore freedom. Only from under that cover could we try to take advantage of the world, to trick it and regain control. This deceit was our only power.

Arcades

In his work on the arcades of nineteenth-century Paris, Walter Benjamin detected the way capital and state gained identity in opposition to each other to create structures that dominated our experience of the modern world. The first Parisian arcades were built in a heated wave of financial speculation that covered the city early in the nineteenth century and represented everything that was dynamic and energetic about modernity. The arcades became spaces in which capital came alive in the form of luxury goods, countless commodities, fashion, and technological invention. They were spectacles of modern life, immensely popular destinations where city dwellers reveled in a newfound sense of mobility and heightened stimulation. Capital in the arcades had a kind of phantasmagoric presence, an illusory quality that pervaded not just the items on sale but the whole ambience of the experience. The arcade was a threshold through which capitalism passed into modernity.

Soon after the arcades gained such popularity, Benjamin discovered, the state also emerged as a resolutely modern force. In antithesis to the wildness of capital, the state strove for control and regulation in a "quest for order" to structure the strange, chaotic world that had sprung to life. State prisons, hospitals, and schools appeared. Naming and classifying became the way by which the state took control, identifying and keeping track of the populace by the introduction of formal names, numbers, and addresses. In the arcades, the crucible of modernity, policemen and detectives arrived on the scene to keep order under newly fitted electric lighting.

By the end of the nineteenth century the arcades had become shabby, forgotten relics of the past, in which the dynamic interplay between capital and state had been frozen over. Benjamin used the metaphor of an archaeological dig as he set about uncovering the encrustations of modernity sealed up in the streets of Paris. In his excavations, he revealed a whole cast of characters whose experiences exemplified and were shaped by modernity. Flaneurs, prostitutes, ragpickers, conspirators, gamblers, and salesclerks were all figures that crisscrossed and intersected in the arcades and streets. The most significant, though, were the criminals and the bourgeois.

Balzac contemporaneously related the rise of the criminal in the nineteenth century to the rise of capitalism and the poverty, displacement, and unemployment that accompanied it. "Each morning," he wrote in his *Codes des Gens Honnêtes*, "more than twenty thousand people [in Paris] awake with no idea of how they will eat at noon." Benjamin sifted through the Parisian data and pieced together how the criminal learned to cover his tracks against the police and their new administrative technologies of mug-shot photography and fingerprinting. The criminal would hide his traces undercover in the proletarian crowd that swelled in the rapidly modernizing city. There he would remain undetected in the mass, his presence erased from sight. No name, no address, no identity could be pinned on him. Unknown to the police, without identity, he could evade capture and remain free.

Yet no one was more adept at preserving himself in modernity than the bourgeois. Like the criminal, he would go undercover, but his cover was the interior of his home. He would escape into his private dwelling, where secrecy would become a fetish against the outside world. The bourgeois would cover up his traces in the interior as he would no doubt cover up the traces of his expropriation scams during the Haussmannization of Paris, with the proceeds and evidence of his criminality kept out of sight of the authorities. "To live in these interiors was to have woven a dense fabric about oneself," wrote Benjamin: as the crowd was a veil for the criminal, so the interior became a veil for the bourgeois.

The criminal and the bourgeois both hid undercover from modernity, obliterating their traces and protecting their freedom. The criminal hid his traces from the police—undercover, underground. In the bourgeois interior, objects and ornaments were covered in plush and velvet, sealing away what was under them. The bourgeois preserved his freedom with covers and boxes; his home became a shell, his possessions and wealth "removed from the profane eyes of non-owners." The bourgeois would seek refuge in his library, his art, in his assets, which were the sacred objects of his ideal, free identity.

That the bourgeois continues to preserve his traces in a shell is evident to this day in the private banking and asset management schemes that run through the global offshore financial system, where wealth is protected against its uncovering through mechanisms that completely remove the identity or trace of ownership. The offshore system, built for the bourgeois by a network of other bourgeois—lawyers and accountants—also provides cover for the proceeds of organized crime and white-collar financial crime, money launderers, and corrupt presidents who have stripped their countries bare of assets, proving Benjamin's point that "a criminal career is a career like any other." The offshore system today is to corporate, private, and criminal wealth what the nineteenth-century interior was to the bourgeois and what the crowd was to the criminal: a cover behind which to hide their traces from modernity, where the criminal is masked as a bourgeois and the bourgeois unmasked as a criminal.

Freedom and Deception

There is a famous aphorism of Malraux: "A man is not what he hides but what he does." We might say "A bourgeois is what he hides *and* what he does." In the gap between what is private and what is public, we can isolate the secret realm.

The bourgeois sought refuge in the interior to remain true. Outside, in the public realm, he got on with his business. He sought refuge to free himself from the self-control that his class demanded of him under its laws. In the interior, he could be his own master and fulfill his responsibilities without interference. There he could dream of the truthful world that the private ethic promised. But he knew full well that this ethic contradicted and conflicted with the real world outside, where there was no prohibition against lying.

The modern world was driven by means, instrumentality, not truth. It had no qualms about employing deceit for its ends. If one was not prepared to bend to outside norms, not prepared to lie, one would not make it in the world, for that was where material reward was found. Self-preserving, instrumental reason regulated private action in the outside world to keep one in line and on board. The alternative was personal failure or punishment.

This was the social—and moral—contradiction that was lived in the secret realm, the inner world of conscience that strove for the good and the outside world that did not measure up to the ideal. The moral law decreed that one could not use oneself as an instrument to further one's aims. One had to be true to one's nature, and not deceive. One had to be a moral being, free in one's own autonomy, not subject to the rule of impulse, desire, and passion. This would be a violation of duty and a betrayal of freedom. The moral law, in other words, demanded human perfection. We are no less familiar with this contradiction today. We know well how the ideal becomes too demanding, too unreal in the outside world for us to close the gap between what ought to be and what is. Nevertheless, the ideal remains, and we contemplate it in our isolation. The question we find ourselves asking is: How can one obey the strict terms of the moral law and not be a hypocrite without pushing away the outside world?

This was the question the historical bourgeois found himself asking when he saw that his duty conflicted utterly with reality. But at least the political and economic structures of the liberal era served his interests. Hypocrisy was then just a fact of life, in the way that decadence was an art form. But there came a point where even pragmatic self-preservation, in keeping with the tune of the day, was not in the bourgeois interests. This was felt when the private interior was threatened by the enlarging, modernizing state—and, worse, a state whose interests were robustly antibourgeois or socialist. Everything would then be at stake.

Fear gripped the bourgeois of Europe as the nineteenth century progressed. The threat of socialism was real; nationalist forces were gaining strength, threatening liberalism and the sanctity of the private individual. The unarguable insight these populist forces brought was that liberal values were decidedly two-faced. Freedom was preached, as was liberty for all, but only the wealthy elite prospered. The liberal state was corrupt and did not express the interests of the People, the Nation, or whatever group was stirred up to oppose the political and economic status quo. In liberalism it appeared that action could never link up with morality without resort to hypocrisy. The newly politicized masses smelled the rat of the secret realm in the liberal state, and they vowed to banish it. In time, that reaction would bring its own catastrophe.

Of course, the bourgeois was a hypocrite, but this was his right. He did one thing in public and thought or said another in private. It was the means of detachment by which he protected himself from the outside world. He tricked the public realm to distance it and keep his sovereignty intact. Conscience could remain free in private, yet the game outside could be played as roughly and in as unruly a manner as it needed to be played. In any case, these were the hidden but accepted rules of bourgeois society. Everyone was doing it.

Deception was the means by which the outside world could be controlled and adapted to private interest. It extended individual power in the public realm and provided a means by which the conflict between private interest and public authority could be overcome.

A veneer of authority would survive, of course, enough at least for the protection of private property under the rule of law. Through the artifice of deception—through lying and covering up, changes of appearance, and hidden intentions—private interest could be presented to the world as something other than it was. This was the trick that could be contemplated in the secret realm and pulled off to gain competitive advantage. With deception well practiced and evidence concealed, one could remain respectable and violation free in the eyes of public authority and still true to oneself, still good.

From the inner security of the secret realm, the bourgeois negotiated the chasm between individual freedom and external authority. To evade the inconveniences of the latter, he could deceive it and appear to be acting according to the law, while in secret he was not. This technique—in substance no different from one used by any criminal, though more elaborate in its reasoning—would stand the bourgeois in good stead as the modern state centralized and enlarged its scope of activity, particularly in the economic sphere.

Bourgeois autonomy needed to be strengthened in these unfavorable times. Techniques of financial protection would emerge that involved deceit and the removing of the traces of ownership from the public scene. The offshore networks that exist today owe their social existence to the strategies of deception and freedom first practiced by the bourgeois as modernity closed in on them. Through these networks, the secret realm would be mediated into a revived capitalism that would, in the late twentieth century, take revenge on the authority of the states that had driven bourgeois freedom and capital undercover. Modern capital would seek a new settlement with the state, on terms favorable to its newfound freedom. No more would freedom have to hide, it was hoped; the ideal would become reality at last. Yet in the era of offshore freedom and onshore control, the world would become ever more untrue.

6. Offshore Heaven, Offshore Hell

Today the boundary line between respectable and illegal rackets has become objectively blurred and in psychological terms the different forms merge.

—THEODORE ADORNO AND MAX HORKHEIMER,
"DIALETIC OF ENLIGHTENMENT"

A Caribbean Revolution

The modern world did not properly arrive in Cayman until the 1950s. It landed with the first airplane to touch down in 1952, no doubt bringing tourists to Benson Greenall's Galleon Hotel, the first hotel to be constructed on Seven Mile Beach. Greenall cleaned up—he bought acres of beachfront real estate for $1 a square yard, selling it in the 1960s for $750 a square yard. With the scent of money in the air, Barclays Bank opened a branch in George Town that serviced the now regular flights to and from the island operated by Caribbean International Airways. The new bank also made it easier for native Caymans working at sea on the North America–South America oil tanker runs to send money back home to their families, income upon which much of Cayman's domestic economy then depended.

Cayman's emergence as an offshore finance center was a deliberate affair. A bunch of young lawyers put their heads together and decided that Cayman was ripe to turn into a tax haven like the Bahamas, another British colony, where a free port and tax benefits for incorporating businesses had built up a good legal and financial infrastructure to attract foreign capital.

There was much that could be learned from the Bahamas about building a tax haven. In the early 1930s, Bahamas-based Canadian banks on Bay Street, Nassau, became a popular destination for capital fleeing economic meltdown in the United States. Then, as personal and corporate tax rates in the United States jumped during the Depression (in 1936 the maximum individual rate was 79 percent), wealthy U.S. citizens took to setting up foreign personal holding companies in the Bahamas to avoid taxes at home. Despite legislation passed by the U.S. Congress to tighten up tax avoidance and restrict the use of foreign holding companies, U.S. capital did not stop flowing offshore. A joint congressional committee on tax evasion and avoidance set up at the request of Roosevelt in 1936 showed the continuing growth of holding companies in Panama and Newfoundland, but most significantly in the Bahamas, where in 1935–36 alone, sixty-four companies were created to evade tax.

U.S. tax evaders were lured to the Bahamas because the islands' company laws, which were based entirely on the British 1866 Companies Act, offered total financial and personal secrecy to shareholders, with no requirement to publish financial accounts. Apart from the appeal of the Bahamas-incorporated company, U.S. citizens also discovered in the tax haven the benefits of the English common-law trust. Typically, a trust was structured to stand behind a Bahamas company as its shareholder, with its beneficiaries in turn remaining absolutely secret. Bahamas trust and company formation firms, dominated from the mid-1930s by Canadian newspaper magnate Lord Beaverbrook's General Trust Company, ensured wealthy Americans maximum protection from onshore tax authorities. In return, the Bahamas, throughout the 1930s and during World War II, made a good living from hiding the wealth of the rich, their corporations, and even, it is said, currency stolen by the Nazis.

In 1960 Canadian lawyer Jim McDonald, who had some experience in the Bahamas, came to Cayman with the intention of drafting new company laws for tax-exempt business. McDonald took the Bahamas as his tax haven model, and the authorities in Cayman, looking to their future, embraced his ideas with open arms. McDonald was joined by Bill Walker, who settled permanently on the island and busied himself trying to turn it into a tax haven. "I began by spending a lot of time traveling, visiting bankers, law firms, and accountants, trying to convince them to come to Cayman," Walker later recalled. "At that time, we had no trust law, no sale of goods law, no banks and trust companies law. However, the government said they would pass any laws that were necessary."

The Cayman government bent over backward to help, but politics elsewhere speeded up the islands' development as a tax haven. The election of Harold Wilson's Labour government in the United Kingdom in 1964, ousting the Tories, prompted the wealthy to seek protection against the introduction of higher taxes on income and inheritance. Milton Grundy, a tax expert who had drafted tax law in the Bahamas, was sought out by Bill Walker and his colleagues in Cayman to help capture private money fleeing Britain. What Grundy and Walker came up with was the tax-exempt trust, a radical innovation modeled on traditional English trust law—and just what the wealthy were after to keep their assets out of the hands of the state.

The Cayman Islands were reborn in 1966. In that year, permissive bank and trust laws were enacted, a new airport opened to cater to large jets, and an international telephone link was established. Cayman was now connected to the rest of the modern world of capital— and ready for its business.

External events, closer to home, were to advance the islands' fledgling financial services sector even further. In the Bahamas, Lynden Pindling and his socialist-leaning Progressive Liberal Party came to power in 1968, promising the colony full independence from Britain. The Bahamian financial elite—the so-called Bay Street Boys—were extremely concerned that their running of the Bahamas as a tax haven fiefdom would be checked by Pindling's redistributive economic policies and plans for political independence, so they took their capital and ran with it to Cayman, clearing out well before Bahamian independence in 1973. "The timing was terrific," recalled Bill Walker. "Telephones first, then the airport, then business. The other way around wouldn't have worked. Bahamians used to say that we should build a statue in Cayman to Pindling, since his government wrecked the Bahamas offshore financial industry and gave us a kick-start."

By the end of the 1960s Cayman's new existence was being gleefully and proudly recorded in British Colonial Reports. "These islands are now known to be a tax haven because of the absence of any form of direct taxation" was the news sent back to London. With the backing of its sovereign protector, Cayman set up a tax haven committee in 1970 to "expand and promote tax haven facilities on the island." Company and trust registrations took off, and other foreign banks settled down beside Barclays in George Town. It seemed that Cayman had never had it so good.

"Geometric shapes are altering the skyline as large office blocks push upwards acquiring concrete flesh to their steel-girder bones," the local glossy magazine, *The Nor'wester*, rhapsodized in 1972. All this activity and purpose meant there was much to be proud of. And it was justified in more intellectual terms, but with no less passion, by

Charles Adams, Cayman's own antitax ideologue, in theory and practice, who taught at the islands' International College and was manager of the Euro-Dutch Trust Company Ltd., set up "for legitimate alternatives to the secret bank account"—the trusts that had made Cayman so popular with the tax evaders.

Adams personified the radical neoliberal zeal of the tax haven revolutionaries. "The moral foundation of the tax haven is well justified because of the violent injustice of the progressive tax as well as the inquisitorial methods of an income tax system," he thundered. "Few people in the world are fortunate to have such liberty today" as they did in Cayman, he argued, as opposed to states where mail was opened, telephones were tapped, tax inspectors fished for bank information, and all generally interfered in one's private business. Adams's denunciations, however paranoid, did not belie the fact that the state in the industrialized West, let alone the Soviet bloc, had never been so large, bureaucratic, and controlling, with top rates of tax at over 90 percent in most countries. It was in reaction to this that the politics of the secret realm, which would soon return triumphantly onshore with the New Right revolution, first gestated, then raged in the tax havens, where it had been able to construct, with all the assistance of the state, its own economic experiment with freed-up capital.

To resist the monolithic power of the state was tantamount to a religious requirement for Adams, and there is more than a hint of messianic fervor when he quotes from the Book of Joshua to support his idea of the tax haven as "a kind of economic sanctuary, a modern city of refuge, for those oppressed with taxes." With Cayman's infrastructure placing it at the avant-garde of tax havens, the "economically oppressed" now scrambled to Cayman for its sovereign protection. "We have a solemn duty to protect their property and their privacy from attempts to snoop into our financial community," Adams solemnly reminds his fellow islanders. "It would be a betrayal of the worst magnitude to aid fiscal and tax investigators of foreign countries, who will often come under some pretence to collect information, as wolves in sheep's clothing." In the righteous conviction of Adams, the paralyzed private ethic is expressed as a war cry: the enemies of freedom are to be denounced and hounded until they expire. Yet these freedom fighters would poison even the last drop of spirit in a world trapped inside their secret realm.

The Fall of Doucet

"It was like Switzerland had come to town," recalled Lem Hurlston, former Cayman Islands chief secretary, about the roller-coaster era of Jean Doucet and his Cayman-based financial empire. That was back in the early 1970s, when anything and everything was possible in the shiny, forward-thrusting tax haven with a world reputation to build. Doucet, with his own distinctive style and ambition, was going to be the man who put Cayman on the map of international capital, who would break the mold of the old staid world of finance and banking and give it a bit of tax haven panache, flair, and cosmopolitan glamour.

Doucet started out as a banker in Canada, then set up his own company, Sofico, in 1965 to bring U.S. capital into Canada, where he directed it into large real estate projects. Before long, Doucet was moving in the nascent tax haven circles of the Caribbean, where tax lawyers had realized how useful the havens could be in freeing up investment capital from U.S. tax and monetary controls. Doucet was dealing with men like Marshall Langer, a U.S. tax attorney who had written the rule book for the Bahamas as a postwar tax haven. For a period, Doucet and Langer were involved in financing hotels in Freeport, Grand Bahama. Then Langer suggested that Doucet might turn his attention to Cayman, an up-and-coming tax haven, with perhaps more opportunities for Doucet to get a leg up in than the Bahamas. In 1966 Doucet set up Sterling Bank in George Town, one of the first private banks to be licensed under Cayman's new tax haven laws.

But Doucet wanted to do more than just use his Cayman bank interests from a distance. He wanted to get involved in Cayman, make a name for himself on the island, and be somebody in international finance. All this was possible in Cayman: it was small enough to make an impact on, and, by God was it willing and looking for the attention of the outside world, waiting for someone to push it into the modern financial age.

Doucet trod carefully at first, not wanting to offend the more conservative elements in Cayman society. He took up residence in a modest bungalow way up West Bay Road from George Town, refurbished its garage, and opened up a branch of Sterling Bank for domestic banking business. On the private banking side, he promoted a booklet by Langer and Bill Walker extolling the very considerable tax advantages of Cayman for foreign companies and trusts, mailing it out to twenty thousand potential investors. Quietly, business grew.

Not much more than a year later, Doucet opened the doors of Cayman's very own homegrown financial empire. The timing was perfect: the corporate banks were flocking downtown, erecting their shiny new offices on the back of roaring trade in Eurodollars, with Cayman's name on every Wall Street banker's lips. But Doucet's Interbank Group, as his company was now known, was something else: a couple of whitewashed bungalows up the West Bay Road, the sands of Seven Mile Beach just a minute's dusty walk across the road, and then the sea. And from here a financial and banking group with offices in Miami, Montreal, London, and Geneva was headquartered, offering everything from bank loans to local folk up in West Bay to international mergers and acquisitions, trade and real estate investment, and tax and investment planning for corporations and the rich. The specialty of the house was two-ounce gold bars stamped with the distinctive IB logo and on sale at Interbank House, a luxury available only to

Doucet's offshore clientele as they passed through the new financial paradise of Cayman.

Doucet impressed the islands' great and good with all of Interbank's pizzazz. "They were very futuristic in their outlook," remembered Lem Hurlston, then the rising star of Cayman's civil service. "It was a real fascination to be linked to a group of companies that was engaged in doing so many exciting things, all headquartered in Cayman." Doucet's appeal was that he invented, self-consciously, a kind of tax haven style to go with the financial adventurism of capital that had slipped the leash and the old ways of the nation-state. In short, he made the world of offshore capital look sexy. He introduced a style that gave a seductive identity to the secret realm dream of freedom, a lifestyle of offshore cosmopolitanism, easing of restraint, glamour, mobility, "Cartier" luxury, all set cozily around traditional bourgeois family values and a taste for light classical music. Doucet's offshore style was the epitome of 1970s kitsch, the essence of every glossily aspirational ad that promoted a life free from the moral constraints of conventional society. Here in Cayman was the life of freedom as it was really lived.

COME IN AS YOU ARE read the sign on Interbank's entrance on West Bay Road. In his office, Doucet would greet you in his open-necked short-sleeved shirt and floral cravat, his chubby face with slicked-back hair exuding an oily charm, offset by serious black-rimmed spectacles. Soon you would be discussing philosophy and French wines and sharing Doucet's enthusiasm for escargots and gourmet cooking. Then the charming Mr. Doucet would show you around Interbank House, where "a charming array of girls bustle about the warren of offices," all to the sound of piped music, perhaps Stanley Black and his Latin Rhythm Orchestra in playful renditions of "Fly Me to the Moon" or "The Breeze and I." Finally, you would be introduced to the stunningly beautiful Mrs. Doucet, dressed up in all her finery, posed over the latest hulk of an IBM computer with state-of-the-art international bank transfer technology busily pumping away.

Doucet was the offshore world's very own Renaissance man—banker, financier, playwright, filmmaker, poet. A man of action, not just dreams. The man who produced films like *The Cayman Islands*, a feature-length documentary that had premiered to the sight of the "Sterling Girls" posing in an array of catsuits and miniskirts designed by none other than Mrs. Doucet. So cool, different, modern. So unlike the dull tedium of life onshore, with soaring inflation, rising taxes, and unemployment.

By 1974 Doucet had captured Cayman society and sold them the offshore life. But he still needed to make a good impression as a banker and show that he had not gotten too carried away. Doucet's way of doing this was to prove that he was at heart a man of the people, that he understood the common man, his dreams and aspirations. So his next bright idea was to open a new subsidiary—the Cayman Mortgage Bank—which would deal only with personal mortgages for local Caymanians, offering them large advances at preferable rates. The venture would show, once and for all, that Doucet was committed to Cayman, not just using the island for his own convenience.

Nevertheless, Doucet celebrated the opening of his new mortgage company in his usual over-the-top kitsch way: a gala evening for a thousand guests at the Holiday Inn, with champagne, caviar, Scotch and meatballs, beer and bangers, opera from Quebec, and the governor of Cayman as the guest of honor. Lem Hurlston went to the Holiday Inn party with his sister Delrose, who worked at Interbank. Apart from the opening of the Cayman Mortgage Bank, they had another reason to celebrate, as Delrose had just been promoted to vice president of the new company. Furthermore, Delrose was going on holiday the very next day. This was news to Hurlston, and he asked his sister, "That's rather odd, isn't it? You have just been promoted, you've got all these new responsibilities, and you are going on holiday?" And in the thick of the gala, his sister replied, half in jest, "Yes, I'm going on holiday because we haven't got that much money to lend anyway!"

It was true. Sterling Bank's depositors were cashing out amid rumors that Doucet was involved with the Mafia. Questions were being asked about who was behind the purchase of the Governor's Harbour development, a huge marina and real estate project that stretched across the width of western Grand Cayman. Were the Mafia behind this? Was this why Jimmy Hoffa, the infamous chief of the Teamsters Union, had allegedly met up with Doucet after Hoffa's release from jail? Was Sterling Bank the Teamsters' private bank? Although many of them proved not to be true, the rumors did not die down, and they sparked a crippling liquidity crisis at Sterling.

Just two months after the gala celebrations, Interbank shut its doors for the last time. CLOSED BECAUSE OF LIQUIDITY PROBLEM read the notice that replaced the jolly request to "come in as you are." In the investigation that followed, no evidence of Mafia involvement or anything else was uncovered at Interbank. However, it emerged that Doucet, to cover his liabilities as the cash crunch set in, had mishandled one hundred ounces of gold entrusted to his bank by Cayman's International Monetary Bank for Interbank's famous gold bars. There was also a poignant note found among Doucet's belongings, written just six days before Interbank closed: "Must pay US$2.8 million." The day before the bank closed, Doucet chartered a Learjet and hopskipped it to Monaco. Soon he was charged with a US$1.25 million fraud, extradited from Monaco, flown back to Cayman, and locked up.

The Cayman government deliberated over whether Doucet should be tried before a judge and jury or merely sent to a magistrate for summary trial. It opted for the latter, fearing that a lengthy trial might expose too many uncomfortable truths about Cayman's young tax haven and destroy its reputation. By this, Cayman's elite tacitly accepted that their survival as a financial center exposed them to risks that could be overcome and dealt with only through institutional cover-up and denial. Cayman's celebrated openness toward capital and finance was accompanied by a strictly imposed veil of secrecy over its activities.

This, it was believed, was the key to self-preservation, financial free-dom, and control over its own destiny. They were not about to throw all that away for some pretentious Canadian who had got himself in a fix desperately trying to save his bank. Doucet was sentenced to nine months in prison, served his time at Her Majesty's Prison at North-ward, left Cayman, and was never heard of again. Cayman breathed a huge sigh of relief, demolished Doucet's bungalows, and built a busi-ness center over them.

A Postcard from Hell

Up in West Bay, off a side street, is Hell. Over an area of about an acre, jagged spikes of rock sprout up from the ground like flames that have burned themselves out in a hellfire. The rock is ironshore, com-mon in Cayman and more than a million years old. But in Hell, acid-secreting algae have turned the once pure white stone black, eroding it into the shape of flames. In the old days, everyone knew where Hell was, but no one actually went there except for local lads who would come down and walk barefooted on the rocks to show each other how tough they were.

In the boom years of Cayman's financial revolution, Hell became a tourist attraction, with no one who visited the island for a cruise stop or a week's vacation missing out on the special trip up to West Bay. In a smart bit of marketing, a sub–post office was set up on-site, where tourists could buy and send postcards back home stamped with the postmark HELL. "I've been to Hell" was the alarming greeting on a million cards that arrived from Cayman and dropped into mailboxes around the world.

As the tourists flocked to Hell, the hot money rolled in downtown. Cayman was booking Eurodollar loans by the hundreds: short-term bank loans for multinational corporations and trade deals; long-term loans sold by banks to developing countries eager to jump-start their passage into the modern world, the fevered atmosphere of apparently cheap and abundant money belying the fact that these loans would later come back to ruin these countries in the form of catastrophic debts to Western creditors. And offshore funds multiplied as private banks and trusts raked in capital, fleeing currency controls at home, breaking national laws, and damaging financial stability in the process.

Suitcases arrived, full of cash. You'd walk through customs at the airport, they'd open the Samsonite and just nod you through. Into a taxi, and off you'd go to any bank in town to make a deposit. All the banks had special cash counters. Some charged a 10 percent counting fee.

From the beginning, Cayman got a reputation for laundering drug money. But the government was not too bothered about all the cash coming in. "In fact, they used to boast about it," remembered Benson Ebanks, a former member of Cayman's executive council. Learjets would arrive at the airport, and executive types with loud, kipper-shaped ties would walk off with briefcases carrying a million dollars in cash. Jet pilots would lie on the beach or possibly take a trip to Hell, waiting while the cash was paid in before the return flight later in the day.

These days, tourists don't go to Hell much. If they do, they are not that impressed. Expectations had led them to believe they were going to see something quite terrifying. Instead they find a man dressed up in a devil costume, greeting them at the gates of Hell around the corner from an Esso service station. The bare rocks of Hell have themselves been dressed up with cardboard cutout figures of little devils and suffering sinners. Hell has turned into a rather banal theme park. In the gift shop you can buy a degree from Cayman's University of Hell for $7.50. Many subjects still available: Money Grubbing; Lying, Cheating and Stealing; and Tax Dodging.

Pressure

Whether they knew it or not, Maples and Calder, Cayman's largest law firm, with its swanky offices on the George Town seafront, had registered all the critical entities in Parmalat's Cayman portfolio. Bonlat Financing Corporation joined the electronic roster of Maples and Calder's offshore registrations in early 2002 and now sat alongside various other subsidiaries of the Italian multinational dairy products group: Parmalat Capital Finance Ltd., Bonlat's parent company; Epicurum, a mutual fund that Bonlat had invested in; Dairy Holdings Ltd. and Food Holdings Ltd., two special purpose off–balance sheet vehicles; and about half a dozen other funds and subsidiaries. Parmalat was exactly the high-end corporate business that firms like Maples and Calder prided themselves on capturing, and exactly what Cayman as a financial services provider needed in order to show the world that it was a respectable and mainstream operator.

From its small-scale origins in the 1960s as a local milk producer in Parma, south of Milan, Calisto Tanzi's company had grown to be Italy's eighth-largest corporation, with more than 35,000 employees across thirty countries, nothing less than an Italian-based multinational giant. In the early 1990s, fresh from a public listing on the Milan Stock Exchange, the company embarked on a period of rapid expansion and acquisitions, making expensive inroads into Latin America, particularly Brazil, where it became the dominant milk producer.

At first Tanzi kept a lower public profile than other Italian business tycoons—such as Luciano Benetton and Silvio Berlusconi, the future Italian prime minister—but in time he made a name for himself, flying off with his family in his private jet to inspect prospective deals, and offering the Parmalat helicopter to Catholic prelates as they toured Italy. Before long, football, always the populist dominion of the business oligarch, became a family concern, with Tanzi's son Stefano becoming chairman of the 1993 European Cup winners AC Parma.

Behind the public face of Parmalat's growth into a multinational player were two factors, both hidden from the outside world: an expanding offshore network of Parmalat entities, and a growing debt problem. Parmalat's offshore network—which covered Singapore, the Netherland Antilles, Malta, Mauritius, and the Cayman Islands, as well as onshore havens such as Luxembourg and Delaware—was used in a way no different from any other multinational to operate an internal corporate market through which profits and losses could be exchanged and transformed within the company and "landed" in whatever jurisdiction provided the best tax advantages.

However, for a company with a growing debt problem—one that had come about through greed, stupidity, and corporate adventurism and would eventually lead Parmalat into bankruptcy with debts of $18 billion—the offshore network provided the secret mechanism to defy the reality of the problem by hiding debt and craftily turning it into equity and other assets, all of which would keep Parmalat turning over and looking good where it mattered most, on the world's stock and bond markets.

In this respect, as with Enron, the entities that helped Parmalat engineer its growth and global expansion were reengineered by Parmalat to disguise the costs of capitalist greed. The point at which this reengineering becomes fraud is moot for the defenders of capital, who try to draw a line between legitimate and illegitimate behavior. The reality is that the line is relative to the overall cost that such behavior has for capital in general. Thus, if there are no major scandals and everything is successfully hidden away, people are generally willing to turn a blind eye to fraud and deception. It is much easier and more lucrative for all those involved in the deception—capitalists, corporate accountants and lawyers, banks—not to rock the boat, to just get on with business.

However, there is a limit to how much fraud can be contained before self-combustion takes place when the fraud is on the scale seen with Enron, Parmalat, and the other well-known cases. For the defenders of capitalism, these excesses cause them considerable embarrassment, and the defenders hasten to add that there are always a few rotten eggs in boom times. They shrug their shoulders: these debacles are unavoidable, natural, to be expected. What helps considerably is that the well-known frauds are accompanied by the specter of individual greed at the top—Andrew Fastow and Calisto Tanzi shamelessly stealing from their companies.

Yet these characters are the fig leaves of capitalism, the fall guys, against whom the calculated moral indignation of those more concerned about being found out—no less than those genuinely concerned about the health of capitalism—can be aimed as a distraction. They are useful too as memento mori for those who would let their crimes come to light, barbaric decapitations that instill a dreadful lesson in the aspiring capitalist and in the markets and corporations in general. The lesson is simple: deception is the royal road to freedom, but moderation and ruthless discipline in its execution—to the point where the exacting administration of business merges unknowingly with deception—are nonetheless vital for the self-preservation of capitalism. It is only for failure in the correct practice of these dark arts that the capitalist will find himself denounced by a bourgeois society eager for punishment and revenge. That is why they are an object lesson in those "corporate responsibility" symposia where poor, humbled souls, formerly "driven" executives, are solemnly discouraged from stealing.

The first outward but generally unrecognized signs that Parmalat was in trouble came in February 2003, when a planned Parmalat bond issue worth $360 million was met by the markets with a 9 percent fall in the company's share price. The bond issue was hastily withdrawn amid market murmurings questioning why a supposedly cash-rich company like Parmalat needed to raise money on the capital markets. But markets move on quickly, and Parmalat's withdrawn bond issue was just a quick distraction. No one at the Milan stock exchange gave it a second thought.

Parmalat was briefly the subject of attention again when the group's chief financial officer, Fausto Tonna, resigned in April. It was not until September 2003 that Parmalat began to receive sustained interest from the markets and regulators. This came only after the company's much coveted investment-grade rating was put under review by Standard & Poor's, bringing with it the dire prospect of a ratings fall. Further pressure was added a month later when the governing body of Milan's stock exchange asked Parmalat for extra guarantees for debts coming due before the end of the year.

In response to the growing demands as to how it would meet its debt obligations, Parmalat revealed to investors, for the first time, the existence of a Cayman-based mutual fund, Epicurum, in which it said it had an investment of US$600 million. In a press release the company said, "The [Epicurum] investment was made in order to assign the management of a portion of the group's liquidity to professional fund managers, partly based on an unexpected return in excess of the average returns provided by the securities currently in portfolio." Stefano Tanzi, son of the founder and a Parmalat director, told analysts that the Epicurum investment had earned the company US$50 million thus far in 2003, but curiously, he was unable to tell them the current size of the fund or how its assets were used.

A few weeks later Parmalat announced that it was not going to be able to recover its multimillion-dollar investment in Epicurum. Immediately Standard & Poor's cut Parmalat's investment rating to junk bond status. By now the company was staggering, its shares losing over half their value in one day before trading was suspended. Its chief executive and founder, Calisto Tanzi, resigned, and then came a final revelation that brought Parmalat to its knees: the truth about Bonlat.

According to Parmalat's 2002 accounts, its Bonlat subsidiary in Cayman had an account with the Bank of America consisting of (it said) cash and securities worth $5 billion. Not so, Bank of America now declared. A few days later, files were seized in a police raid on a Parmalat office outside Parma, and documents were uncovered that confirmed that the Bonlat account and assets had been completely made up by Parmalat. The signature on one Bank of America statement letter for Bonlat had been copied from other bank correspondence that Parmalat had in its possession. The Bank of America logo had been simply replicated on a PC.

There was Cayman again at the center of a monstrous fraud, the largest ever in Europe, an instrument of ruin in the collapse of one of Italy's largest industrial groups, the prospect of thousands of lost jobs ahead and billions of dollars of foreign investment scared off by a country unable to lose its reputation for corruption and lawlessness. In his New Year message President Ciampi, onetime governor of the Bank of Italy and a former finance minister, told Italians that the Parmalat affair was a blow to "the prestige and credibility of the entire financial system"; most of all, though, it was a disaster for Italy.

The Italian government moved in to deal with what swiftly became a national crisis, fearing that the country's ambition to become a serious global economic player might be permanently derailed. Parmalat must be saved at all costs, the government declared, while critics said the scandal was a direct result of Prime Minister Berlusconi's relaxation of corporate regulations in Italy, undertaken largely to suit his own commercial interests. In any case, whatever the reason, the protective hand of the state was swift: Parmalat was brought under creditor protection in an emergency government decree. At the same time, Tanzi and two dozen others were arrested, including executives from Parmalat's audit firm in Italy and two former finance directors. Even before charges were laid, Tanzi and his closest associates started to confess to their crimes. The scale of Parmalat's "black hole"—to translate from Italian the name of one of its subsidiaries, Buconero, set up allegedly to disguise debt as equity—was $17.8 billion, equal to the combined foreign debt of Angola and Tanzania, or the total sovereign debt of Bangladesh.

"I was in agreement with the objectives, that is, the need to make the company appear in good shape from the point of view of the balance sheet," Tanzi told his interrogators at Milan's San Vittore prison, where he was held for questioning following his arrest. But, he added, "the instruments used to achieve these ends were dreamed up by my colleagues." Predictably, Tanzi's former finance chiefs said that they were just obeying his orders. The likely truth is that the men at the top of Parmalat acted deliberately with their auditors to exploit their offshore network to hide losses and invent assets in order not only to make the balance sheet look good and prop up the company's stock, but also to finance group activities through various credit and loan transactions that looked like real, arm's-length transactions with outside parties, though they were in fact shams manipulated from inside the company. In one of these so-called back-to-back transactions, Parmalat received loans from banks that were guaranteed by receivables owed to the company. The receivables turned out to be intracompany credits shunted through various offshore companies to disguise their origin and to make it look like real money was coming into Parmalat when it was not. That is, Parmalat claimed to be receiving money from other companies when the money had simply been shifted from the offshore to the onshore column of its balance sheet. Often, banks themselves structured such illegal transactions, entwining themselves in the deception.

One of the largest and most spectacularly concealed back-to-back loans concerned Food Holdings and Dairy Holdings, two Cayman-registered special purpose vehicles. Until their direct link to Parmalat was revealed in investigations following Parmalat's collapse, the two Cayman companies were assumed to be independent vehicles set up in late 1999 to raise $300 million for third-party investors supposedly interested in buying 18 percent of Parmalat's Brazilian operation. But it turned out that they were not independent companies, and there were no third-party investors poised to purchase a large chunk of equity in Parmalat Brazil. Food Holdings and Dairy Holdings had in fact been set up by Parmalat to acquire, through the private sale of debt, a $300 million loan from the Bank of America that was to be guaranteed by an 18 percent stake in the Brazilian unit. This was quite different from the open-market equity transaction that Parmalat publicly informed the markets it was engaged in.

Indeed, making the Bank of America loan look like it was a case of investors keen to buy a large stake in Parmalat Brazil signaled to the markets that Parmalat as a whole was an undervalued company. Consequently, when Parmalat announced in a press release that Parmalat Brazil had "increased its share capital in favor of a group of North American investors," shares in Parmalat jumped by 17 percent, their largest one-day gain ever. Of course, if the transaction had been seen for what it was, that is, another loan on Parmalat's books, Parmalat's stock price might well have gone down in value instead of up. This was exactly the calculation made by Parmalat, and it was something they wanted to avoid. So they chose the route of deception.

For its services in arranging the transaction, Bank of America earned a $4.5 million commission, and the Italian bankers who arranged the deal out of the bank's Milan office received a separate commission of $3.75 million, deposited, the bankers later confessed, into a Swiss bank account. Parmalat's $300 million loan was merely sunk into the company's growing debt bubble.

Besides back-to-back offshore loan schemes, Tanzi made personal use of offshore companies to siphon money out of Parmalat and into personal accounts—he initially admitted taking $445 million—and those of his family's private interests, such as Parmatours, a travel company run by his daughter, who claimed no knowledge of these events, which stole (there is no other word for it) at least $1 billion from Parmalat. In Cayman, besides the forged Bonlat statement, the Epicurum mutual fund in which Bonlat had supposedly invested $642 million was another fiction set up by Parmalat, as was the investment itself, turning out to be another forgery of Bank of America documents. As a Cayman-registered mutual fund, Epicurum was subject to minimal supervision by the islands' monetary authorities. The only real Parmalat assets to have passed through Epicurum were believed to have been directed by Tanzi to a private bank account in Luxembourg.

In the wake of Parmalat's downfall, allegations about it and Tanzi's offshore foray multiplied: a "missing" $250 million held on account for Parmalat at the Cayman subsidiary of Santander Central Hispano, Spain's largest bank; and several Cayman companies set up as trusts with Tanzi as sole beneficiary. Elsewhere in the Parmalat offshore network, details emerged of a set of companies in the Netherlands Antilles that legitimate Parmalat customers had settled bills with, but which (the authorities alleged) were actually offshore bypasses to private bank accounts held by Tanzi in Europe. The investigation into the offshore network led to Delaware, where two more Parmalat companies were discovered, their incorporation documents indicating as the managing director a man who turned out to be Parmalat's switchboard operator in Italy. The lowly employee had no idea that Parmalat had used his name in this way. He was even more surprised when told he was the managing director of thirty other Parmalat affiliates as well.

As the civilized onshore world surveyed the ruins of Europe's largest-ever corporate fraud, the eyes of blame shifted away from the wreckage to that offshore devil with which the world of respectable capital and responsible global governance was so disgracefully entwined. Once again, following Parmalat's collapse, a surge of moral disgust rose against Cayman and all the sordidness it supposedly stood for. There was talk of new brooms needed to sweep away the dark mysteries of the offshore system, and there were pledges to rid the world of this unspeakable evil. Signor Giulio Tremonti, Italy's economy minister, went off to a G7 summit meeting to try to persuade his fellow finance ministers to force multinationals' offshore networks to conform to strict regulations.

Strange, this, for a minister of what is Europe's most flagrantly offshore capitalist state, its Prime Minister Berlusconi embroiled in financial scandals and trials, its governance the epitome of secret realm misrule in which economic and political control are brought together and totalized through the instrument of television. "The unification of these three forces in one man and in one group has a name well known to political theory," wrote the philosopher Norberto Bobbio. "It is called, as Montesquieu called it, despotism."

Just look at Milan. Take a stroll around the haute couture district of Monte Napoleone. Be dazzled by the storefronts parading the likes of Prada and Dolce & Gabbana. Here, in the smartest district of all Italy, is a splendid fashion industry. But how much of this business is based in the republic? Travel, instead, to the Swiss tax haven of Lugano, just an hour away, sheltering at the foot of the Alps. There, behind the cafés and restaurants that overlook misty Lake Lugano, in streets smarter even than Milan's finest, are the little offices of law firms and trust companies where Italian fashion multinationals register corporate entities. They come to Switzerland for the private banks, financial secrecy, and tax evasion opportunities. So does even the smallest pizzeria in Italy. And now, as further evidence of this state-sponsored offshore sport of national destruction, here was Parmalat embroiled in a Cayman scandal and bailed out only through an $18 billion tax on the people.

Yes, soon, Signor Tremonti, we must tighten the rules, it will not be long now, his colleagues back at the G7 replied. Next was a European Union summit, where Tremonti complained that Europe had diverted attention from its crackdown on tax havens. Yes, soon, Tremonti; soon, this will be dealt with. And in Cayman, they really believe it will be this time.

7. The Politics of Offshore

Consider the darkness and the great cold
In this vale which resounds with mystery.

—BRECHT, *THE THREEPENNY OPERA*

Heroes and Victims

It may seem a rather outrageous proposition, but the political and financial elite of Cayman genuinely believe that they are unwitting victims of globalization. But hang on a second: Cayman, victims? GDP per head far higher than the rest of the Caribbean, higher even than the United States. Unemployment virtually zero. Political stability. This is not exactly a strife-torn economy accelerating into chaos, let alone a failing state. Yet Cayman is an oddity in the global system. Its development has been so caught up in the vanguard of forces that drive globalization through the world that in the end, its own survival is put at risk by its very strange success.

That success was built on the cultivation of Cayman's difference, its competitive advantage over other states in the post-1945 period, when the door of the nation-state was only marginally ajar to utterly free trade and capital mobility. Taxes were at astronomical levels, and state regulation and control bounded national economies. Offshore tax havens like Cayman introduced into this slow-moving world a certain spark of economic electricity in the form of tax competition. Go off to Cayman, do a deal there, and there'll be a discount on the costs that accrue to regulation and tax. Go off to Cayman and do a deal you cannot do back home. And get a tax refund at home into the bargain.

Thus Cayman and its like were a new force in the old world economies of borders and barriers. It put pressure on political leaders to take down the barriers a bit, open up their economies to external capital and foreign corporations, and (most significantly for the electorates that voted in Margaret Thatcher and Ronald Reagan) cut taxes at home. Competitive tax cuts to corporations in the 1980s turned the United States into the global growth machine it became in the 1990s. The chain reaction of tax cuts followed through into other Western economies, principally that of the United Kingdom. Economic growth—in theory—created a broader tax base and therefore brought in more state revenue. The competition to get tax down looked to be a win-win situation. And, as many countries became in effect onshore tax havens for footloose capital and certain major corporations, Cayman and other offshore tax havens became integral parts of the international financial system, now normal and central rather than marginal, enabling the corporation and private capital to gain that little bit of extra advantage on tax and regulation and, by doing so, gnawing away at national financial controls.

Alas, not so long after the developed nations jump-started capital's release into the world through fiscal relaxation and competition—a trick learned from the tax havens—they began to realize the damage being done to the national tax base. The calculation between economic growth and its associated tax revenue did not add up. Economic growth did not mean growth in government revenue. And how could it? That economic growth had been brought about by letting the corporations out of their obligation to pay taxes on their earnings. That growth *was*, in effect, their taxes, simply retained as profits and parked offshore. What had caused the problem was the very thing that had been promoted as the solution: capital and ownership freed up to roam the world. Mortified, the finance ministries looked for a villain, and they found one. The chief offenders, they claimed, were the offshore tax havens. Remove competition and introduce tax harmonization, was the message put out by the rich men's club of Europe at the end of the 1990s. The world has moved on economically, been taken to another level, they said, and there is a point where the pressures of tax competition have to be controlled and a new, "fair" level playing field implemented.

Suddenly Cayman and the rest of the offshore network were out in the cold. Globalization was now leveling out; the epic era of capital's revenge and freedom in the 1990s was finally over. There was a new sobriety in the air even as the financial bubble of the so-called new economy showed signs of bursting. It was now a time for global standards, for multilateral platforms that would iron out the differences in the global economy. Real, cutthroat competition had a kind of animal power: it had put a spell on the world, and it was time (to switch metaphors) to put the offshore talisman back in its box before too much damage was done. This was especially the case after 9/11, when Al-Qaeda was judged by the United States to be a multinational terror business hiding in the offshore network. For a while, the offshore system became a prime target in the war on terrorism.

Cayman's elite saw themselves as victims of a world that had used them when it was politically convenient to do so, then cast them off. In the process, Cayman had made its way in the world, gained a purpose and an identity. It was no less than the fifth-largest financial center on the planet. Who would have thought that a few decades ago, when cows, not capital, roamed the backstreets of George Town? Now all of a sudden it seemed all over. This was the hard truth of the offshore dialectic: Cayman had served as a loyal instrument of global capital; its service had been exemplary, even heroic, but the political world had got enough of what it wanted for now, thank you very much.

So, the Organisation for Economic Co-operation and Development, the European Union, and a whole band of multilateral bodies wanted Cayman to do their bidding. Cut this. Cut that. Stop this. Cut off the advantage. Close up the gaps. Implicit in Cayman's response to these agencies and their new agenda was this thought: "We found our own way in the world and thought we were free at last, but the industrialized West wants to control us in return for that freedom we bequeathed them." Such is the tragic lament of Cayman, a slave to global capitalism.

Controlling Freedom

Cayman had always suffered the duplicity of its masters. In the early 1980s the U.S. Justice Department started to aggressively attack Cayman's bank secrecy laws in a run of cases involving tax evasion and drug trafficking, where the U.S. authorities demanded confidential bank account data from Cayman. This was based on the suspicion that Cayman laundered a large amount of the $25 billion made annually by the drug trade. For three years the United States caused havoc with Cayman's secrecy laws—which make it a crime to reveal bank account details to any external authorities—by putting pressure on the islands' banks. The banks relented and gave up documentation to the United States.

There was something other than the urge to combat organized

crime that motivated the United States to target Cayman: that was its own financial and corporate self-interest. In the early 1980s, following U.S. bank deregulation, New York was pushing hard for its banks to get a share of the huge Eurodollar market that traded U.S. dollars washing around the world free from government control. This lucrative business had long been denied U.S. banks onshore, and as a result, they had spent the decade of the 1970s in exile offshore playing the Euromarkets there. The time had come to bring the business back home and give the tax havens and the City of London, which dominated Eurodollar trading, a run for their money. Putting pressure on Cayman, and in effect giving it a bad name through its association with drug money, might frighten Eurodollar business in New York's direction. Though this suited its government policy, the United States had its own more explicit reason to attack Cayman and the other tax havens.

There was much hue and cry in the U.S. media about the ways wealthy individuals and multinational corporations "routinely indulged" in legal tax avoidance. What better than to divert attention from this by denouncing the tax havens for their role in illegal tax evasion? Although—in the early 1980s—offshore was a much less substantial fiscal issue than mainstream tax avoidance, there was good political mileage to be gained at home in appearing to be tough on tax havens, particularly Cayman, with its proximity to the United States.

However, behind all this political posturing, Cayman's traditional secrecy in its tax affairs was left untouched. The United States and Cayman reached a compromise agreement whereby the island would consider U.S. requests for bank information related to suspected drug traffickers. Cayman saw the deal as a historic and exceptional compromise, beyond which they would move no further in opening up their banking regime to fishing trips from outside authorities. Sir Vassel Johnson, Cayman's financial secretary, proudly asserted that any matters "relating directly or indirectly to the regulation, imposition, calculation or collection of taxes, unless this involved the unlawful proceeds of crime," were excluded from the agreement with the United States.

Throughout the rest of the 1980s Cayman was pretty much left to get on with business as it saw fit. The Americans were satisfied that they had at least some control over Cayman's offshore advantage, and in any case Wall Street was soon enjoying a boom with the recovery of its status as a player in the international Eurodollar market. Yet this did not spell a decline in the fortunes of the tax havens, as had been predicted. Rather, they prospered in their servicing of capital's global ambition and saw a marked increase in the presence of U.S. multinationals incorporating on their shores. Deposits by U.S. citizens in Cayman's banks more than doubled between 1980 and 1988. Thus the Cayman boat had rocked a bit on choppy waters but was now to be left alone.

A "Dark Side" Discovered

In the high tide of capital's revenge on the world, a period that lasted at least throughout the last decades of the twentieth century, there were few global standards and rules that transnational capital actually obeyed. The international financial system developed over and outside existing national and regional financial apparatuses, sometimes absorbing them, sometimes radically altering them. Capital, by its votaries' accounts, was outpacing outmoded structures, breaking the binds that had tied it, and taking the path of least resistance as it spread across the globe, digging in and taking root wherever it could.

Here emerged a web of unconnected, fragmented entities going off and into the world in their separate ways as corporations, investors, market makers, currency dealers, financial middlemen, consumers, and, of course, criminals. Each group sought to serve its own interest, yet they were all in it together as brothers in the joint enterprise of a world market. Indeed, they had a greater sense of collective self-interest than Marx's envisioned proletariat ever did. Here the differences in the world—between national systems of regulation, supervision, law, and taxation—could be arbitraged and played off against one another for profit as the skein of the market covered the earth. Here the world's economic diversity could be the basis for increased returns as transactions were structured to take place where there was the least expense, the least regulation, and the most room to maneuver.

The offshore network was the outrider and agent for this ambition, the venue through which business, trade, capital, and crime could be lifted from the restrictive jurisdiction of its origin into a free, virtually detached world of no borders, no controls, and wonderful possibilities. In this new offshore world, an enterprise at last could operate transnationally, on its own terms, in its own way, subject only—in optimal circumstances—to its own will. This was an entirely new phenomenon: as if the lead of capital as a base metal had been transformed through alchemy into gold.

It was not until the collapse of the Bank of Credit and Commerce International (BCCI) in 1991 that any government raised serious concerns about the new offshore world. Here was a banking enterprise that epitomized the offshore freedoms to escape government control and regulation so as to achieve a breathtaking internationalization of operations and expansion of services: with holding companies in Cayman and Luxembourg and a head office in London, BCCI grew faster than any other bank in the world in the 1970s, opening 146 branches in 43 countries. By the mid-1980s BCCI had expanded into Africa, the Americas, and Asia, as well as the Middle East and Europe. It had offices in 73 countries and balance sheet assets of $22 billion, compared with assets of only $200 million a decade earlier.

When BCCI was closed down by the Bank of England with losses of $10 billion—amid allegations that the bank had defrauded individuals and corporations, falsified its accounts, and laundered money for drug dealers and organized crime groups—it became clear how far the whole enterprise had escaped the attention of regulators. Because BCCI had a head office in one country and holding companies elsewhere, no one national authority could take an accurate global snapshot of it. Here was a monster that had grown up in the gaps between national financial systems and authorities, and analysts began to see that these gaps—and what was contained within them—were what constituted not only the dynamism of the international financial system but the risk to its sustainability.

In response to the BCCI collapse, the United States and the European Union put in place measures to strengthen cross-border bank supervision, and they produced various anti–money laundering directives for international banks. For the first time, there was some multilateral pressure on the Cayman authorities to take at least some notice of the outside world. For Cayman's bank supervisors could not claim that they were unaware of BCCI. The bank had a prominent, visible presence on the island in the form of its garish offices, and it openly publicized its unusually high interest rates on deposits through marketing material and word of mouth. But the hundreds of shell companies through which many of BCCI's most suspect loans were transferred, and by which fake assets were invented for other parts of the group, all operated behind the scenes under the near-perfect protection of Cayman's secrecy laws. Following BCCI's shutdown by the Bank of England, the Cayman authorities moved in swiftly to bring the bank's operations on the island to a close. A receiver was appointed for BCCI's operations in Cayman, and the assets of several Cayman companies believed to be linked to BCCI were frozen. Such immediate and direct action against criminal enterprise on the island was, however, the exception rather than the rule as the 1990s progressed, despite the new multilateralism on bank regulation and supervision.

But the "downside" of the system that BCCI represented to capitalist states was nothing compared with the upside it represented in the international financial system. BCCI made clear that the global spread of capital was taking place far more quickly than any attempt to counteract it. Just when BCCI was coming apart, the former Soviet Union and its satellite states were reintroduced to the free world, ripe for transformation by capital. Suddenly there were "emerging" mar-kets everywhere—from Russia and former Eastern bloc states like Czechoslovakia to the much-heralded Asian "Tigers" of South Korea, Malaysia, and Indonesia. With these distracting—and (from capital's point of view) highly lucrative—developments, there was no urge to take up, nor was there even much interest in, post-BCCI multilateral initiatives on financial regulation. In fact there was no compulsion to do so, as U.S. and EU legislation aimed at increasing bank supervision and countering money laundering were not applicable to the golden lands of fortune that had appeared on the horizon as the sun was setting on BCCI.

. So Cayman was left alone once again, free to be played as an in-strument of global capital. In the 1990s, as the world economy ex-panded and Cayman became secret capitalism's preeminent service station, you just had to look around George Town: it had all but a few of the world's biggest banks; a booming captive insurance industry; a huge increase in company registrations; a rank as the leading mutual fund provider; and its own stock exchange. Cayman's offshore spell helped set the world alight in the era of capital's global triumph.

By the end of the 1990s the high tide was ebbing away. Capital's speculative free-for-all had turned into crisis and disaster for econ-omies across the world—Russia, Malaysia, and Argentina—and Cay-man, along with the offshore network as a whole, would find itself the scapegoat once more, urged to excise its "dark side" for the sake of global capital's survival. But for that to happen, U.S. capitalism would first have to discover, to its own horror, that the dark side had well and truly pitched up on the shores of the United States.

The Lessons of Near Ruin

Long-Term Capital Management was a hedge fund that operated out of offices in Greenwich, Connecticut. It was, like other hedge funds, a private and exclusive club that allowed extremely wealthy investors to pool their money and have it gambled on precise (and it was believed predictable) price fluctuations of virtually any security or asset that was traded in the world's markets—from stocks, bonds, and currencies to the complex financial instruments derived from them. Speculation of this type was increasing in quantity in the 1990s to the extent that capital was pounding its way across the world and through the old iron curtain.

The U.S. Congress had seen that hedge funds were not overburdened with regulation and oversight, as it judged that the wealthy were wise enough individuals to self-assess the risks of their gambling habit and in any case were rich enough to cover their own losses if things turned nasty. In the United States, hedge funds were not required to reveal the names of their investors, their investment strategies, the strengths and weaknesses of their investment positions, or even their financial leverage gained through bank borrowing.

It was logical, then, that hedge funds, fully sanctioned by U.S. lawmakers and able to operate unimpeded onshore, should incorporate offshore, where they could maximize the freedom already granted them. The hedge fund in conception and in practice was therefore an entirely private affair, regulated only by private morality—sealed off, separate, and indeed secret from the outside world, so much so that the outside public realm had no legitimate bearing on it, and all that mattered was the free rein of an autonomous realm immune from any external interference. In short, it represented nothing less than the highest stage of the secret realm's technical materialization in the modern financial age.

Founded in 1994, Long-Term Capital Management duly incorporated in the Cayman Islands, then set up offices in Greenwich to manage the fund. The firm's partners were a top-ranking bunch: two Nobel laureates in economics; a former vice chairman of the Federal Reserve Board; and several ex–Wall Street bond traders. The firm quickly raised $1.25 billion for the fund from those who agreed to hand over a minimum $10 million investment, including Hollywood agent Michael Ovitz, Nike chief executive Phil Knight, and several Wall Street executives, as well as foreign banks and university endowment funds. The firm's partners and staff contributed to the fund too.

LTCM's specialty was bond arbitrage, where it would aim to make a profit in the price differential between the relative value of bonds traded against each other on the markets. These could be mortgage bonds, government bonds, or bonds issued by emerging market countries. Typically, LTCM's sophisticated computer programs would predict a sudden and temporary divergence in value between two sets of bonds, say government bonds issued by the United States and by Russia. These two sets of bonds, call them Bond A and Bond B, would be tracked in the market, then hedged against each other.

If, for example, Bond A (issued by the U.S. government) was predicted to gain extra value relative to Bond B (issued by the Russian government) at one moment in the future, then there would be an opportunity to buy Bond A and sell it later for a profit just before its value dropped back down to where it normally was in relation to Bond B. At the same time, Bond B's relative decline in value to Bond A could be sold short—that is, Bond B could be borrowed and sold at a higher price before it was actually bought at a lower price relative to Bond A. To make a profit, the hedge transaction had to be made at precisely the moment Bond A was temporarily a better value than Bond B. The art of arbitrage was in being able to spot the minuscule fluctuations in relative prices between different sets of bonds, and then, it was hoped, to cash in on the price differential before the blip in the market returned to historic norms.

In economic terms, the practice of bond arbitrage at the microlevel was broadly similar to the arbitrage that corporations and banks engaged in through offshore centers at the macro level—that is, exploiting the differences in regulation, tax, and other costs and benefits between national financial systems. LTCM and all the other offshore hedge funds were doing both things at the same time. They had arbitrage as the core of their business as hedge funds, and also as corporate entities registered offshore, where they traded (or arbitraged) tax differentials and other costs to their advantage as a corporation. Thus, LTCM was supremely detached and free-floating from anything external to its insular private realm of capital.

LTCM's directors also incorporated in Cayman because the island was itself a "powerful magnet" for U.S. capital that could be invested in hedge funds like LTCM. According to Robert Morgenthau, the Manhattan district attorney, in testimony to the U.S. Senate Permanent Subcommittee on Investigations in July 2001, Cayman had some $800 billion U.S. on deposit: "More than twice the amount on deposit in all banks in New York City and the equivalent of nearly 20 percent of all the dollar deposits in the U.S. This amounts to almost $3,000 for every man, woman and child counted in the last U.S. census. It is about what the federal government now spends on Social Security, Medicare, and Medicaid combined in a year."

The advantage of LTCM's insular detachment, even among all this equally detached wealth, was made clear when the magnitude of its investment returns became apparent. This of course was the only justification that counted. LTCM earned investors 28 percent on its arbitrage trades in 1994; 59 percent in 1995; and 57 percent in 1996. In 1996, its profits of $2.1 billion exceeded those of McDonald's, Disney, Xerox, or Gillette. In the same year, its assets of $140 billion made it a rival to the world's largest banks. And at its height, the $7 billion LTCM had amassed in capital was greater than the holdings of all but a few of Wall Street's largest global financial institutions. These numbers were proof of the power of unregulated, free private capital. There was no need to worry about a downturn; everything was under control: just look at those great minds with their deep pockets and computer predictions! And just look at those returns!

Then, over a period of just a few weeks in the late summer of 1998, the great giant was brought to its knees as suddenly as it had risen to glory. Offshore, LTCM had imagined that they were free and unimpeded, and they acted as if they were so. That had brought success. But this success was bought at a price: that of dismissing the outside world as merely a force to be controlled, to be acted upon for profit. LTCM's supposed control centered on two factors that at the end of the day were revealed, in the circumstances, to be grave disadvantages.

The first was a view of markets as a machine that constantly sought equilibrium, in which the behavior of certain variables—in LTCM's case, bond prices—could be observed and predicted on computers. This would prove to be a disadvantage because, in a volatile market, prices behaved unpredictably and were impossible to track using LTCM's equilibrium-dependent computer models. The second disadvantage was the colossal size of the positions that the fund took in its trades. In many cases, the spreads between the prices of price-fluctuating bonds LTCM hedged on were relatively tiny, only a few dollars per bond. The bonds themselves had a face value, typically, of only about $1,000. To make the hedges pay off with huge returns, the fund had to spend millions, sometimes billions, on them; and to do so, LTCM had to borrow huge sums from its lending banks. Getting credit from the Wall Street and Swiss banks did not prove hard, given the elite reputation LTCM had quickly gained. After its first year in operation the fund was operating on borrowings of just under $100 billion, and thereafter its leverage rose to a sum of $1.25 trillion, or a thousand times the capital held by the firm.

There was a third factor that underpinned LTCM's supposed control over the world: secrecy. The fund's trading method was a closely guarded secret and subject to no external review. None of the firm's creditors—the banks who provided the billions of dollars in leverage—knew any of the details about its trades. And investors themselves were none the wiser. This secrecy, rather than putting LTCM in control, would prove to be another major disadvantage to the hedge fund.

Thus, in the summer of 1998, when the fallout from the collapse of the Russian economy began to upset U.S. markets, LTCM's computer programs were unable to adapt and predict accordingly. LTCM's assumptions about the bond market were literally turned upside down—with bonds bought long going down in price, and those sold short going up. The fund began losing hundreds of millions of dollars a day in the markets; its capital reserves were fast eaten away. The firm was left with huge liabilities toward its creditors—a perilous situation, for it meant that a LTCM collapse might have a domino effect on the banks, creating a crisis in U.S. markets. "Losses of this magnitude are a shock to us as they surely are to you," the firm's founder, John Meriwether, wrote to investors in early September, "especially in light of the historical volatility of the fund."

At the very brink of default, on the twenty-third of September, LTCM was saved from inevitable collapse by a U.S. Federal Reserve scheme that locked the fund's Wall Street creditors into a room and didn't let them out until a rescue package for LTCM was agreed to. Did the U.S. Federal Reserve step in to prevent the "systemic" collapse of the U.S. economy or merely to protect a perversely rich men's offshore club from going under? This question has never been answered to anyone's satisfaction. It probably did so for both reasons. What is known is that, just a day away from ruin, the Federal Reserve got LTCM's main creditors—Goldman Sachs, Merrill Lynch, and JP Morgan among them—to agree to together put in $3.65 billion to save the firm. "Why should the weight of the Federal Government be brought to bear to help out a private investor?" asked Paul Volcker, a former Federal Reserve chairman, amid widespread criticisms of the bailout and complaints that it showed, yet again, that "there was one rule for Main Street and another for Wall Street." Though no federal or taxpayers' money had gone in to rescue LTCM, there was no doubt the Federal Reserve had intervened to protect the fund from the mess it had got into by playing the markets recklessly.

A few days later, as U.S. markets continued to react uncertainly to the Russian economic debacle, Alan Greenspan told Congress that much more had been at stake than the survival of LTCM: "Had the failure of [Long-Term] triggered the seizing up of markets, substantial damage could have been inflicted on many market participants, including some not directly involved in the firm, and could have potentially impaired the economies of many nations, including our own."

For the capitalist elite, Greenspan's management and public response to the LTCM default was, for U.S. capitalism and its future preservation, particularly astute. He clearly saw what was at stake: Wall Street's elite institutions had to come together at this moment of danger in their own collective self-interest to preserve private capital's freedom and power in the world. Capital had to help out capital. In good times, capital was in flight from the state, indeed contemptuous of it. But in bad times it took the hand of the state to protect capital from its excesses lest it destroy whole societies.

Once the worst was over with LTCM, there was no rush to bring in regulations to open up secretive hedge funds to external control and oversight. Greenspan, sure that the LTCM episode was just a bad blip and one that in any case had been steered away from danger, was particularly sanguine about hedge funds. If there was a problem with hedge funds, he told Congress, it was one generally inherent in the new financial technologies that accompanied economic globalization. In common with other offshore phenomena, hedge funds were, Greenspan said, "only a short step from cyberspace." Try to regulate them, and they just take off and settle in a new jurisdiction. The best the U.S. authorities could do to control them was to regulate the domestic sources of their funds. To this day, Greenspan maintains that hedge funds and their wealthy investors are an essential fluid of capitalism, a secret realm that should not be regulated.

The Politics of Reform

In June 2000 Cayman suddenly found itself a pariah of the global financial system, having been "named and shamed" in a G7 blacklist of fifteen jurisdictions regarded as money laundering havens. The blacklist included the Bahamas, the Cook Islands, Dominica, Israel, Lebanon, Liechtenstein, the Marshall Islands, Nauru, Niue, Panama, the Philippines, Russia, St. Kitts and Nevis, and St. Vincent and the Grenadines.

At the same time, Cayman's offshore finance center was judged by another set of multilateral agencies, the International Monetary Fund among them, to have "serious deficiencies in supervision and cross-border co-operation." Along with twenty-five other, mostly Caribbean, havens, Cayman was placed in the lowest category of offshore centers, those said to constitute "weak links in an increasingly integrated financial system." It was also targeted by the Organisation for Economic Co-operation and Development as a tax haven that facilitated "harmful tax competition" and tax evasion, and was therefore guilty of hurting global trade and investment. It kept itself off the OECD's blacklist of thirty-five tax havens only by making an immediate "advance commitment" to deal with its supposedly disruptive practices—that is, to discuss them with regulators.

Suddenly it was open season on offshore financial centers, now likened to "gangster states" that licensed their laws to the highest bidder, whether global crime syndicate, tax evader, corporate fraudster, or third world dictator stealing his country's assets. Cayman was used to such accusations—the LTCM crisis had sparked the usual anti–tax haven backlash, despite the fact that the Cayman-incorporated hedge fund had not broken the law—but the orchestrated platform of aggression this time was unprecedented.

Why pick on us? asked the princes of Cayman and other Caribbean tax havens. What about the millions of dollars that get laundered through banks in New York and London? How can you turn on us after what we have done for you rich nations in pushing back barriers and opening the world to your trade interests? After all, that same opening up decimated our Caribbean economies, its fruits once protected by you and your once great empires; and we, backed all along by you, found other means—financial services—to survive and prosper in the global economy, means by which your own interests were served too.

"OECD members are finding difficulty adapting to the new global environment, of which they have been the chief architects," responded CARICOM, a regional grouping of Caribbean states whose finance centers had all been named and shamed in the blacklists. In order to protect their own interests, the rich world, now aghast at the competitive world they had urged on everyone, wanted to change the system that had effected that competition. It was "a dark day in the history of international relations," CARICOM's Secretariat declared; nothing less than rich-nation blackmail.

Why had this unprecedented multilateral program to tackle money laundering, tax evasion, and lax financial regulations come about now, and with such force? It was not as if these were in any way new issues. The G7 with its Financial Action Task Force had been working away on anti–money laundering policies since before the BCCI scandal. The OECD had been concerned about the negative side of tax evasion for national economies for several years. But the one great unknown area was the role that offshore financial centers played in the workings of the global economy. It had always been taken for granted that the offshore network was a boon to economic and financial globalization, a great instrument for putting pressure on states to open markets and take down trade barriers, but the nature of the offshore involvement had not been analyzed in any depth, owing in part to offshore's code of secrecy. And while the global economy was strong, who really cared what was going on offshore? Offshore was some paradise island experience, complete with yacht, seafront mansion, and domestic servants, all stoked up by Wall Street bonuses and executive options.

The global economic downturn made the role of offshore financial centers a technical issue in international economics by the late 1990s. At this time, in order to prevent crises that might put the whole enterprise of global capital at risk, the IMF was trying to understand just what had triggered the run of financial crises across Asia and Latin America. In early 1999 the IMF revealed—internally—what they thought was to blame: offshore banking, which, they argued, had played a "catalytic" role in the run of crises. In each case they looked at, economically faltering countries had parked their risk-laden liabilities and assets offshore, in the hope that by doing so, losses, loans, and debts could be kept off the country's public accounts and the domestic economy could be made to look much rosier than it in fact was.

The IMF's chief concern was that when the markets in the countries where the risks had been covered up offshore took a dive, bringing down exchange rates and other market values, the secret part of the economy—the vast accumulated debts and liabilities hidden offshore—would be suddenly exposed, putting the domestic economy in a far worse state than was already acknowledged. A rolling collapse of local banks would then lead very quickly to the breakdown of the whole economy.

With that zeal for emerging markets to exploit in their hedge funds, investment portfolios, and loan schemes, it was the offshore funds and banks that "pump primed" countries in Asia and Latin America with plentiful supplies of capital to get their economies hooked on market capitalism. Western—mostly U.S.—banks acted as super-conduits for the flow of foreign investment into Asian and Latin American economies, bringing about the growth of a domestic banking infrastructure that enabled local companies and investors to borrow money and take their own financial risks in the market. But the supply of offshore capital could be withdrawn just as easily when a downturn in any given emerging market made it a less promising investment for Western banks. And when that happened, the loans and investment that had fueled the economy dried up. For local banks that had lent well beyond their means, often in ventures that incurred huge losses that were hidden offshore (sometimes in the same offshore banks that channeled capital into the economy), the withdrawal of ready capital to the local market was a disaster. Once the market dried up and there was no more capital to borrow, the only thing left was the hidden losses. And when the magnitude of these losses came to light, Asian and Latin American economies collapsed.

The IMF noted the same pattern of offshore banks triggering economic meltdowns in Venezuela (1994), where billions in problem loans were hidden offshore; in Argentina (1995), where some $3 billion to $4 billion in losses were held offshore; and in Korea, Thailand, and Malaysia (1997), where, respectively, insider dealing offshore bypassed regulatory limits on bank lending, poor lending decisions were "rolled over" offshore, and $10 billion in losses were hidden offshore. The IMF also made clear that economic collapse in one country had a domino effect in neighboring countries that had joint investments or shared trade and banking operations. Thus the stage was set for "contagion," where meltdown passed from one country to another.

It was the collapse of the Russian economy in 1998, though, that catalyzed what came to be known as the reform of the "global financial architecture." The desire for reform was not motivated by altruism or even by a desire to restore the health of Russia's economy. No, the reform was meant to protect American investments, pure and simple.

The United States had not been immune to the Russian financial crisis. Indeed, it had struck U.S. markets very clearly with the default of LTCM, which analysts were now saying was in part because of the hedge fund's secretive and unregulated existence offshore in Cayman, particularly nondisclosure of the fund's huge financial leverage. But it was not LTCM's Cayman connection that led to the campaign to name and shame the tax havens. It was Russia's fast disintegrating state—in particular the pathologically destructive use of offshore banking and tax havens by Russia's elite—that posed the greatest immediate threat, not to the abstract global financial system, but to the United States itself, on its own shores. For the Russian elite, imitating their American brethren, had mastered the use of offshore tax havens and so siphoned off the billions of U.S. dollars meant to bring Russia into the family of capitalist nations.

The great hope of Western investors in the post-Soviet era was to turn the moribund mammoth that was Russia's economy into a glittering jewel of market capitalism. In a sense, the new Russia represented a chance to put offshore freedom in place onshore. Here was a blank canvas to work upon from scratch, a chance to start anew with hope, energy, and the naive enthusiasm of a creed that believed absolutely in its own rightness. It was thought that Russia could be induced to turn into a model capitalist economy through IMF-led "shock therapy": deregulation, privatization, and the setting up from scratch of new markets and exchanges.

So the IMF pumped billions of dollars into Russia, overseeing the hoped-for transition from command to liberal market economy. Working remotely from Washington, its officials dictated action on the ground, making reference to textbooks that told them how the transition should proceed from one stage to the next. No setback could stop the costly experiment, for in the IMF's view (and that of its investors) the project's success was critical to the just revenge of capital across the world.

Foreign banks and investors poured capital into Russia, assured that their risks would be offset by the IMF's commitment to bankroll the fundamentals of the Russian experiment, including its failings. For a while the transition looked to be going very well. By 1997 Russia had become the hottest of emerging markets: outside investment reached $45.6 billion, or about 10 percent of the country's $450 billion GDP; foreign cash poured into Russia-focused mutual funds; and the Russian stock market, only a few months old, became a hothouse of trading, with newly issued stocks immediately soaring in value. Western banks steamed into Moscow and set up shop in the frenzied casino of Russian market speculation, lending huge sums to ventures with dubious credentials. Russia's debt to the IMF and foreign banks grew larger and larger, but while there was money to be made, no one was too bothered.

The experiment came to a quick and sudden end in August 1998, when the fallout from the rolling collapse of Asian economies brought on a steep drop in demand for Russian oil, causing the ruble's value to drop sharply and the economy to melt down. The IMF was faced with the costly embarrassment of the first $4.8 billion of a $22.5 billion "crisis-saving" loan to Russia simply "disappearing" amid the crisis, and Western financial institutions, with losses of $40 billion in defaulted Russian bonds, scrambled over one another to exit the country as fast as possible.

What had happened was no secret: outside investors had been so focused on the money they were making that they'd turned a blind eye to how Russians themselves were doing business. In short, while Western capital and investment were pouring into Russia—at a time when the legal status of the country's assets and public institutions was in chaos—the new Russian capitalists were sending their profits out of the country and leaving their debts behind. They would borrow from the West, make a quick profit, and then send their bounty out of the country as fast as possible. And where to? Offshore, of course.

Because Russia's laws had no effective authority, the rules of the game were determined by sheer speed, ingenuity, and force. Any organization that could mobilize itself to grab hold of Russia's asset base did so: the immediate family circle around President Yeltsin, whose private companies received overinflated state contracts; the business oligarchs who supported Yeltsin politically and in return got their hands on Russia's most lucrative industrial and financial assets; and organized crime, who got their hands on anything left over. In practice, there was often little distinction between the various organizations involved in looting the country.

It took no IMF report to reveal the extent to which offshore networks were instrumental in the wild and raw brand of capitalism that emerged in Russia, and the role they had played in its fall. Behind the surface phenomenon of Russia's experiment in "overnight" capitalism was a hidden offshore economy based entirely on deception, private gain, and brute power. Yeltsin's oligarch cronies were believed to have run off with more than half of Russia's entire GDP and removed it to personal offshore holding companies. Cyprus was a favored haven, and these oligarchs had bought plots of beachfront property there and built monstrous villas along the southern coast of the island. Federal funds were transferred through the oligarchs' own commercial banks into offshore bank accounts and then reinvested in speculative market ventures in Russia and elsewhere. For every dollar of inward investment in Russia during the 1990s, between ten and twenty dollars were lost to offshore accounts.

Just a few weeks after Russia's economy collapsed, the offshore element of the national economy became a matter of public record. The Russian Central Bank admitted that $74 billion had been transferred from Russian banks to offshore accounts so far that year, with $70 billion going to accounts held by banks in the tiny Pacific island of Nauru.

The Central Bank was itself a prime mover in the establishment of Russia's offshore economy. It had its own subsidiary, FIMACO, in the Channel Islands, which it used to hide money (and later debts) away from the IMF and Russian creditors. A subsequent review by

PricewaterhouseCoopers commissioned by the IMF demonstrated that "Russia's Central Bank used FIMACO to bank government liabilities offshore, artificially boosting its balance sheets by some $1.2 billion, with the result of misleading the IMF into believing Russia's currency reserves were stabilizing." Such indicators of fiscal health would be used to extract further advances from the IMF, and so, when the ruble devalued, the debt situation was far worse than had been expected, triggering the economy into meltdown.

At first the elite's plundering of Russia's resources and wealth, and its self-destructive offshore addiction, appeared to be only a Russian problem. True, IMF credibility had taken a knock, and the Russian crisis had nearly struck U.S. markets. But swift and judicious action by the Federal Reserve had prevented the United States from succumbing to outside chaos.

Still, there was a sting in the tail of Russia's disintegration. Inevitably, the Russian offshore economy of deception became entangled with the American one, making a mockery of the U.S. banking community, which had boasted of its probity and diligence and considered itself safe from the effects of economic crises elsewhere in the world. In late summer 1999—a year after the crisis—a report in *The New York Times* revealed the Bank of New York, a pillar of Wall Street, as the passage through which at least $7.5 billion of hot Russian money had been laundered. The money had come into the States through the thousands of correspondent accounts that BNY had with banks in the offshore network. There was nothing unusual or illegal about such accounts. They were the way in which onshore and offshore banks had "talked" to each other for many years; they provided the routes by which money could move around the world on demand at great speed.

The money that found its way into the BNY accounts came from a variety of nonrespectable sources: Russian corporations evading taxes at home; the oligarchs; stolen IMF funds; Russian federal funds from state privatizations; and the proceeds of Russian organized crime groups, which had expanded out of Russia and linked up with crime groups in the Americas and Europe. Once laundered through on-shore banks, this money could have its origins washed away and made ready for use in the outside world. Cayman and Nauru appeared to be the principal offshore links to BNY, with one single offshore bank registered in Nauru acting as a turning point for $3 billion of illegal flight capital from Russia to the United States.

What was most disturbing about the BNY laundering scheme was that it was an inside job facilitated by a close-knit circle of senior bank executives of Russian origin. They not only had the freedom to bring in Russian clients and their money and to arrange for the correspondent banking transactions, but (it was alleged) they had direct links to oligarchs and organized crime figures whom international law enforcement agencies had been investigating for several years.

The BNY story was front-page news in *The New York Times* for several months. The paper's reporters broke the story, effectively derailed U.S. law enforcement's own covert investigations, and forced embarrassed BNY board members to admit in public how careless the company had been. Already the government knew that BNY was by no means the only conduit for Russia's dirty money coming onshore. There were other U.S. banks that had been hit. Capital had taken its revenge via Russia's secret realm and come to corrupt capital's great sponsor, the United States.

Russia was a big problem, but its secret realm was by no means the only one to have found a welcome footing in the States. In November 1999 a minority staff report for the Permanent Subcommittee on Investigations—"Private Banking and Money Laundering: A Case Study of Opportunities and Vulnerabilities"—estimated that half of the $500 billion to $1 trillion in criminal proceeds laundered through banks worldwide each year moved through U.S. banks. The report said that private banks in the United States were particularly vulnerable to money laundering: "the products, services and culture of the private banking industry present opportunities for money launderers, and . . . without sound controls and active enforcement, private banking services have been and will continue to be used by those intent on laundering money." The BNY scandal was now set against a wider picture emerging in public of a U.S. banking system that looked rotten to the core. It was at this point that the Clinton administration resolved to fight back and take aggressive action to protect the United States from the corruption and crime associated with money laundering and reckless banking.

But it would not do for the United States to admit how, in a sense, its own progeny had come back to infect it. The fault was not with the American system, the government insisted; it had just been taken for a ride by outsiders. Nor was the fault directly with Russia, for blaming Russia alone would threaten U.S. commercial interests there and draw further attention to the embarrassing domestic implications of the BNY scandal. Likewise, the $100 million that Raul Salinas—the brother of the former president of Mexico—laundered out of Mexico through the United States to accounts in Switzerland in the mid-1990s couldn't really be blamed on Mexico, when it was Citibank in New York that had set up the secret banking apparatus that permitted Salinas to expedite the transaction.

"There is a dark side to international capital mobility," proclaimed the U.S. Treasury secretary, Larry Summers, putting a name to the problem that had washed up on the shores of the United States. Fighting "the dark side" and "cleaning up" the international financial system would be the way to manage offshore capital, to control its excesses while preserving its more dynamic and creative attributes and the profits they created.

The problems associated with offshore capital run riot, where the secret realm made itself visible, could be transferred onto the "global financial architecture." From this position the fight back could start. The problem could be turned into an "issue" that the developed world could engage with and the United States could control. If the circuits of global capital needed to be adjusted in some way to protect the United States from the secret realm's becoming destructively manifest, then the United States needed to make sure that the adjustments were entirely in its own interest and did not squeeze out what advantages offshore capital brought the state. Clearly, international rules and directives would form part of the action to be taken, and these rules had to work for the United States.

By the end of 1999 the U.S. Treasury–led campaign to mobilize governments to take multilateral and concerted action to protect the world's financial system had succeeded in gaining the support of the G7, in particular the United Kingdom, which had felt the threat from Russian organized crime on its shores. "Coalitions of the willing can successfully influence and enforce international standards, especially if the coalition partners have a predominant interest in and influence over the subject at hand," said William Wechsler, the U.S. Treasury's special adviser, in language familiar in another context after 9/11. "The initiative showed that U.S. leadership was essential . . . no other country could apply anywhere near the same degree of diplomatic efforts and legal and regulatory resources to this project."

And so in mid-June 2000, a three-pronged program was launched: the Financial Action Task Force named and shamed fifteen countries as money laundering havens; the Financial Stability Forum drew up a list of three categories of offshore finance centers, ranked from good to very bad; and the OECD declared that thirty-five jurisdictions were guilty of distorting trade and investment through "harmful tax competition." The program had teeth, with the threat of sanctions against noncompliant countries, particularly those accused of assisting money laundering. It was no coincidence that the jurisdictions on the money laundering blacklist centered on Russia and on the most prominent on- and offshore territories implicated in BNY and other Russian illegal flight capital operations: Israel, Liechtenstein, Cayman, and Nauru.

In Cayman, the reaction of the financial and political elite was one of shock to their shaming in the money laundering blacklist. In an attempt to fend off outside attacks on its sovereignty, the island had introduced a series of new financial regulations and laws over the 1990s, but these new laws had not stemmed the continuing incidence of financial scandals in Cayman. Now Cayman had to be seen to act, and according to a swift timetable, or face sanctions. Already, multilateral teeth were biting hard and closing down unregulated and unruly private banking business. In late June 2000 Liechtenstein's police raided LTG Bank, owned by the principality's ruling family, as part of a wider investigation into money laundering that saw the country move quickly to show the world it had cleaned up its banking sector. In July, Switzerland stepped up investigations into allegations of money laundering by Russian oligarchs, and they froze bank accounts holding hundreds of millions of dollars said to have been stolen from Nigeria and Pakistan by corrupt regimes there in the 1990s. The net spread to the Caribbean too, with the closing down of banks in Grenada, Dominica, and St. Vincent. Cayman rushed to adapt (or to appear to adapt) so-called global standards; its very survival as a tax haven seemed under threat.

Reformers and Their Detractors

The campaign to clean up what it called the dark side of the international financial system was the moment when the identity between the secret realm and capitalism was first questioned by the powers who had ushered capital into the world. These powers had sat back and adapted themselves, always painfully, to the tough demands of life lived with such a forceful and dominating partner as capital. But there was a certain explosive dynamism there, and capital had been left to go about its business. At times it appeared that capital had no limits, this wild animal let out of a cage, so long held hostage by the state.

Capital had quickly adapted to its new circumstances; it had broken down barriers and outrun regulation and control. The onshore world of cities and people was slow, its governments no less so in catching the tail of this new phenomenon. National economies were intertwined through markets and exchanges. Crises in one locality could no longer be isolated or contained. They had a way of feeding back through the system, upsetting it, and throwing distant economies into instability or sparking explosive growth in another. The behavior of capital—all computer models notwithstanding—was random, mysterious, and inexplicable.

Now the main industrial players in the global economy—the United States, Japan, Germany, France, the United Kingdom, Canada, and Italy—decided that the system they had helped put together should be pared back, ordered, and controlled a touch. Capitalism had its limits; it had to, for safety's sake. The detachment from control, its forms of secrecy—both of which had enabled capital to burst through barriers—were liabilities likely to invoke crime and corruption. This, of course, involved some element of economic sacrifice, a clipping of the wings of capital at the point where capital's pure freedom could be more firmly balanced by the control of states acting in concert. Yes, believed the global powers, there was a collective trade-off required to control wild capital and make it politically acceptable and palatable to the public. G7 finance ministers announced, in July 2000, that if jurisdictions named in the blacklists did not take immediate steps to bring their "counter–money laundering regimes into compliance with international standards," then ministers would "begin to consider additional countermeasures, including the possibility to condition or restrict financial transactions with those jurisdictions and to condition or restrict support from international financial institutions to them." In other words, jurisdictions that didn't comply with the G7 directive would be banished from the global economy and left to fester as globalization's outcasts, all contact with the world of offshore finance and foreign investment removed. Any state that chose the path of resistance to the G7 took the shortcut to failure and ruin.

But this supposedly enlightened globalism did not go uncontested. Far from it, and from the first blacklists condemning tax havens and offshore centers a conflict got started within capitalism—a conflict between those who believed that the secret realm within capitalism was a necessary component to be preserved, promoted, and protected, and those who believed it should be root and branch reformed or outlawed altogether. The former (by and large economic neoliberals) argued that any effort to give up or trim capital's offshore instruments was an attempt to pander to voters in tax-hungry European democracies and was doomed to fail. The latter (economic reformers) believed some economic sacrifice in the form of more regulation and control of capital was a price worth paying to keep capital in check.

The neoliberal position was immediately that taken by Republicans following the blacklists of 2000. Congress voted against anti–money laundering bank regulations, in a move prompted by Texas bankers, with some, like Allen Stanford, holding significant business interests in Caribbean territories whose economies, it was argued, would be hurt by stricter controls on offshore banks and companies. Such moves were accompanied by the claim from some that anti–money laundering regulations were "part of the broader context of a surveillance society," a threat to individual liberty, and the harbinger of a global tax police. The Heritage Foundation argued that the "ultimate target of an organized and global anti-competition campaign is likely to be the world's largest tax haven—the U.S. itself." Senator Don Nickles, assistant majority leader in the Senate, argued for the reversal of multilateral agreements, which he said were an attack on U.S. sovereignty by high-tax European states.

In both the neoliberal and reformist positions there was a strong element of naive idealism: in the former that a world of unrestrained economic liberalism would not bring about such catastrophe that the state would need to step in to sort out the mess. Yet neoliberals in their neoconservative garb are also the most resolute supporters of U.S. sovereignty and unilateralism, and so have hedged their economic free-for-all with a good dose of state protection and U.S. exceptionalism.

With the reformists, there was a naive belief that through multilateral intervention the good, legitimate side of capital could be preserved from its rotten excesses. Enthusiasm for this was observed in the work that produced the blacklists in 2000. Toward the goal of a modified capitalism, young men and women, eager to make a name for themselves in the great cause of global financial transparency, bit their lips and got to work to make capitalism nicer. Global finance and capital should be transparent, open, freely competitive, and not distorted by secrecy. Technocrats and policy wonks got to work, trying to separate the bad from the good through a kind of impossible moral alchemy.

Yet there is little distinction between the good and bad use of capital in the global economy. The secret realm — for better or for worse — is there at every move and twist and turn it takes. The secret realm, much less its worst excesses, cannot be distilled away; it is the essence of the global economy. In this the economic neoliberals hit on a truth about the global economy that the reformists were unable or unwilling to grasp. A distinction cannot be made between the use and abuse of offshore tax havens any more than it can be made between the light and dark side of the international financial system. If you want a dynamic, expanding global capitalist economy, with giant corporations and offshore capital relatively free to roam the world, then, the neoliberals argue, you must accept the secret realm as it is, even the fact of its deceptive and potentially criminal instincts, for without those instincts there is no prospect of freedom for capital in the global economy. In short, the exploitation of the offshore system by the Mafia or any other criminal enterprise is a price worth paying for the huge advantages and benefits to liberty that the same system provides for the likes of IBM, Citibank, or Wal-Mart in the advance of capitalism.

If offshore tax havens are the instruments that rightly support corporations and capital to thrust the global economy forward, the neoliberals argue, then their exploitation by organized crime, money
launderers, and fraudsters by no means suggests that these instruments
are to be found wanting or should have their freedoms scrapped. Tam-
per with these instruments of freedom, say the neoliberals, and you
risk draining away the dynamism that is needed to keep the global
economy alive. Crime, corruption, and fraud flourish when the state
distorts capital by meddling with markets and the economy. The alleged "abuse" of offshore structures and financial systems is merely
the symptom of a wider, more fundamental abuse of economic freedom by governments. Cracking down on offshore instruments to clear
up crime will not have the consequence intended by the reformers,
say the neoliberals. Crime will merely find some other means to survive, while legitimate business will pay the price through the burden
of added regulation and supervision. This, the neoliberals claim, will
inevitably lead to the emasculation of the global economy, with no
less opportunity for crime to prosper. But for all its logical consistency
and idealism, the neoliberal argument is blind to the fact that criminality is embedded in offshore structures and practices, whether used
by "respectable" business or just plain criminal enterprise. What the
neoliberals see and value in offshore structures is an extension of what
they find so valuable in the secret realm: the restless, driving spirit of
economic and individual freedom. For them, there is no "dark side" to
the secret realm, only the guarantee of freedom in the economy,
which for them is a kind of enlightenment. No wonder that the neoliberals' adoration of the secret realm in the economy provokes the
accusation that capitalism is a system of organized crime.

The reformers' take on the dark side of the global financial system
falls foul to idealism, but of an even narrower, meaner kind than the
neoliberals'. Unlike that of the neoliberals, the idealism of the reformers is devoid of any moral argument about the type of economic sys-

tem that is right for human nature (as the free market is for neoliberals); it is merely a technical, legal idealism, driven only by questions of economic and political utility. The reformers cannot deny that the "positive" aspects of the secret realm are consistent with market capitalism, the system of course preferred by reformers for its supposed economic and political benefits. However, as reformers, they hardly make the values of economic and individual freedom the explicit center of their political universe. This is because, unlike the neoliberals, the reformers do not accept the darker, deceptive side to economic freedom, in particular the side that harbors criminal and destructive intentions. At the level of the global economy, the dark side, for the reformers, manifests itself most visibly in what they term the abuse of offshore structures. As far as the reformers see it, their clear task is to forensically analyze the offshore financial system for traces of abuse and distortion and then, once the rotten wires have been identified, to surgically and clinically remove them. In this way, the dark side of the financial system can be cleaned up, leaving only the legal, "respectable" side of the secret realm, which can then be turned over to capitalism in the interest of preserving economic dynamism. In the final analysis, this is capitalism resurrected as a legal fantasy.

To clear up the global financial system by checking the excesses of the offshore network, as the reformers suggest, is merely to wipe the shit off your shoe in the comfort of your own home, and to neglect the big mess where the stain came from, outside in the dark, where you cannot see and where you do not want to go. The pile of shit outside is too much to deal with, so you have to turn away. Yet that world outside is already the condition lived in by the majority of humanity. The reformers, for all their "global" vision, are really, when faced with the reality of the horrific conditions suffered by so many, quite myopic. No amount of effort to correct inadequate financial transparency, expose illicit transactions, stop money laundering, curtail tax evasion, and transform "rogue" banking can make any material difference to the world when those efforts are made merely to sustain the integrity of the financial system. Does not that financial system, offshore and detached as it is, already defy integrity?

Besides the naïveté of the reformist position, the multilateral hope of a clear-cut legal solution is only sustainable if it is judged to work in the interests of all states concerned. If it is not, its authority quickly ebbs away, and the states that are not content return ever more entrenched in their own sovereign positions. There is also a sense that global multilateral activity must be proportionate to the threat or problem it is trying to deal with. If one state, at least one powerful state, feels its interests are not represented sufficiently, the authority of the whole multilateral edifice crumbles in bellicose default to individual positions. Thus, what appears as a matter of cold, objective reason is quickly undercut and undermined by the hothouse emotions of national political sentiment.

This is what happened as soon as George Bush came to power in 2001. He swept aside the naive rhetoric of the global transparency reformers and replaced it with the sovereign exceptionalism of U.S. capitalism. If there was ever a promoter of the secret realm of capital, it was Bush. His chief economic adviser, Lawrence Lindsay, had long opposed even minimal anti–money laundering regulations on U.S. banks, declaring that "current money-laundering enforcement practices are the kind of blanket search that the writers of the Constitution sought to prohibit." The extension of such regulations was therefore clearly out of the question.

The Bush administration's first Treasury secretary, Paul O'Neill (previously the chairman and chief executive of Alcoa, the large U.S. aluminum multinational), had just two meetings in early 2001 with G7 counterparts on the various multilateral initiatives before withdrawing the formerly strong U.S. support. The initiatives and blacklists were to be put "under review" by the United States. In a letter to *The Washington Times*, O'Neill said that although he shared "many of the serious concerns that have been expressed recently about the direction of the OECD initiative [on harmful tax competition] . . . the project is too broad and it is not in line with this administration's tax and economic priorities." The specter of forced tax harmonization on the world's economic powers was too much for O'Neill to bear. He added, "We have no business telling any nation what their tax rates should be."

In response to Bush's turnaround, European finance ministers attacked the United States for disrupting international initiatives on tax havens and saw this as another example of the new administration undermining cooperation to tackle global problems. France's finance minister summed up the extent of European dismay with the United States: "Whether it concerns the struggle against the greenhouse effect or against money laundering and tax havens, the largest power in the world cannot disengage from the planet's problems." The Europeans were left wondering whether the United States was going to carry on with the initiatives with some watered-down, bilateral approach to tax havens, or none at all. "How far can it go?" asked a clearly frustrated OECD official. "Do we scrap all attempts to make people pay taxes? Do we scrap all attempts to combat money laundering?"

The more vexed the Europeans got, the more Bush's friends in the Senate and in the Texas bank fraternity came out in support of the administration's new antireformist line. There were a host of other voices too. No less than two hundred free market economists in the United States signed an open letter to Bush: "Dear Mr. President, we ask again that you stop the OECD's ill-conceived project. As the world's largest economy and single largest contributor to the OECD's budget, the United States has the ability to pull the plug on this unwise proposal." Heading the list of distinguished signatories was the patron saint of free market economics, Milton Friedman. Bush was feted as the man who could—and would—preserve the right of capital to protect itself from interference by government. And if that right was to be preserved by letting corporations and capital use the instruments of protected, secret freedom in offshore tax havens, then reform of those instruments was quite unnecessary.

Terror and the Secret Realm

Then came a reversal to beat all. In the days after the terrorist attacks on the World Trade Center and the Pentagon, the Bush administration—having just sharply reversed prior U.S. commitment to "clean up the dark side" of the international financial system—set up the most sweeping, comprehensive, and authoritarian legal and institutional measures ever taken by the United States (or any other state in all likelihood) to control global capitalism. "We have developed the international financial equivalent of law enforcement's 'Most Wanted' list," declared Bush. He told the financial world that it was now "on notice": "If you do business with terrorists, if you support or sponsor them, you will not do business with the United States of America." The conflict between reform of the financial system and its continued liberalization had now been subsumed, as a response to the terrorist attacks, into a situation where the United States sought control of all the bits and pieces of the system in order to accomplish two major goals: to enhance U.S. capital's offshore freedom, and to protect the physical, onshore security of the United States.

Thus the new situation combined, in seemingly contradictory terms, exaggerated versions of each of the previously conflicted positions: on the one hand, a measure of increased offshore freedom of capital (to keep the economy growing), and on the other a measure of increased onshore control of capital (to protect the economy from terror). In one stroke, there arose a need to markedly increase the control and the freedom of capital both at the same time. The reason for this development was that the most regressive, violent, and nihilistic recesses of the secret realm had expressed themselves in the form of terror directly and most visibly against the United States, and to a large extent had done so through the sinewy instruments of the global financial system. To raise funds for terrorism and to distribute them to his followers, Osama bin Laden had set up legal businesses and investment vehicles that crisscrossed the financial system with criminal schemes, individual donors, and Islamic charities, all of which moved money through onshore and offshore banks, front companies, and a range of formal, informal, and illegal cash transfer systems.

The future freedom of U.S. capitalism in the world now (in Bush's view) depended absolutely on the control of the financial system by which global capital operated, and with it the total eradication of the most exaggerated expression of the secret realm—terror—from it. These reactions formed U.S. policy in the aftermath of 9/11 and were based on a belief that Islamic terrorism could be routed quickly and sufficiently by taking direct action against it at the level of the global financial system.

"Money is the lifeblood of terrorist operations. We're asking the world to stop payment," said Bush, launching a new federal agency, the Foreign Terrorist Asset Tracking Center, to "expose, isolate and capacitate [terrorist] financial holdings." The Federal Reserve ordered all banks under its jurisdiction—domestic as well as foreign branches of U.S. banks—to search through their records for any accounts or transactions involving the nineteen people identified by the FBI as the 9/11 hijackers. Bush then announced what he called "draconian" measures in the fight against terrorism: twenty-seven alleged terrorist individuals and organizations, mostly Middle East–based and Islamic, were to have their assets frozen; foreign banks and institutions were to be targeted by the United States and have their assets frozen if they failed to assist the United States by passing over banking information related to the terrorist attacks; and transactions linked to bin Laden and his "Al-Qaeda network" were prohibited.

At home, a whole raft of anti–money laundering measures, well ex-

ceeding those that the Bush administration had dismissed out of hand
only months earlier, was introduced and put into effect immediately.
Banks and financial services companies were ordered to increase their
scrutiny of account holders, particularly those involving correspondent accounts opened in the United States through foreign banks. A
ban on carrying more than $10,000 in cash across U.S. borders was or-
dered. The Treasury secretary sought new powers from Congress to
penalize banks in countries determined to be of "primary money
laundering concern," and sought further powers to force such banks
to identify the ownership of once secret accounts and to bar holders
from correspondent relations with U.S. banks. Neoliberals screamed
betrayal and alarm at the new financial command being invested in
the Treasury secretary. "It represents the effective abolition of financial privacy and due process," the Center for Freedom and Prosperity
told Bush. "It is inappropriate in a country dedicated to the rule
of law."

The European states, introducing their own anti–money laundering measures to combat terrorist financing, welcomed the United
States's U-turn. Prompted by a tragedy of such unprecedented proportion, the United States was taking the lead once again and this time
pushing for far more stringent criteria to be imposed on the countries
of the "dark side." It wanted new international rules that required
banks anywhere to inform regulators even if they had only "reasonable
grounds" for suspecting that funds were to be used for terrorism. This
measure—more authoritarian than the reforms advocated by even the
most ardent aficionados of financial transparency—was entirely consistent with a post-9/11 approach that imagined total control as the
route to preserving freedom. With that end in mind, the United States
now gripped the throat of the global financial system in order to choke
Al-Qaeda out.

To be sure, the tragedy first of all involved a terrorist group piloting
planes into buildings and killing the occupants. Nevertheless, it was

the image of terrorism secretly—and freely—at home in the global financial realm that formed the United States's immediate response to 9/11 and gave it its shape, form, and structure. In that image, Bush's resolute psychology of will—that self-righteous, narcissistic concern for individual freedom that had been violated by the freedom of another—found what it needed: an adversary that appeared to be as sufficiently organized, capable, and coherent as the United States itself. Such an adversary could be made the object of reprisals proportionate to the calamity of 9/11. And because such an adversary was seen to manipulate the global financial system, the United States could take control of the system in order to "preemptively" protect its freedom.

Within forty-eight hours of the attacks on New York and Washington, the United States officially declared bin Laden and Al-Qaeda as the main subjects of their investigation. Bush's strategic line on Al-Qaeda was based on the view that it operated like a multinational business and organized its finances and operations accordingly through a network of offshore and onshore entities—banks, funds, companies—in the global financial system. Al-Qaeda was a "global" organization that existed "in some 60-plus countries." "One person"— Osama bin Laden—was at the top of the organization. He was the "guy at the head of this network"; "the chairman" of Islamic terrorism's "holding company." The task was to strike on the "financial foundation" of this network, uncover its "safe havens," and "identify the size of the organization's balance sheet." The way to expose Al-Qaeda would be to trace its money through the financial network, from the sources where the funds originated right through to the individual operatives on the ground—to follow the money and catch the perpetrators before they acted again.

The image of Al-Qaeda as a global company was easy to grasp. With bin Laden as CEO, CFO, and chairman, the journalist Peter Bergen called it Holy War Incorporated, a "veritable corporation that has exploited twenty-first century communications and weapons technologies in the service of a medieval reading of the Koran and holy war." In the image constructed, officially and in the media, it was a multinational engaged in the business of terrorism, with offices and associates represented across the world. So, like any business, it would need to make investments in property, shares, and other businesses, and to be invested in by others. Each element in the global business of terror was clearly linked to another in logical fashion—from the man on the margins who delivered a truck to a parking lot at the right place and time right up to those at the center planning strategy. There would be a modus operandi that, once identified, would help uncover all the inner workings of the business. Cut off the financing, and the business would wither and die.

The U.K. government's official document on the evidence relating bin Laden to the attacks on the United States portrayed Al-Qaeda clearly and soberly as a multinational business. "Since 1989, Osama bin Laden has established a series of businesses to provide income for Al-Qaeda, and to provide cover for the procurement of explosives, weapons and chemicals, and for the travel of Al-Qaeda operatives . . . the businesses have included a holding company . . . a construction business . . . an agricultural business, and investment companies." Al-Qaeda was "a terrorist organisation with ties to a global network," and like a business in the global economy, it worked through financial networks that paralleled and intertwined with networks used by respectable corporations, blurring a line between the legitimate and illegitimate. Yet the more the image of a large corporation was mobilized in the fight back against Al-Qaeda, the more its blind spot became apparent. Speaking of it as a global business didn't make its assets any easier to locate or its financial interior any easier to penetrate. If Al-Qaeda was a multinational, it was one that was as offshore—and hidden—as it was possible to get.

Osama bin Laden was immersed in the interior of the offshore network from an early age. He grew up as a privileged and cosmopolitan son in a wealthy family that had built a fortune earning millions of dollars from Saudi government contracts to restore the holy mosques of Mecca and Medina. The Bin Laden Corporation grew into one of the Middle East's largest conglomerates, with interests encompassing construction and investments in European and Islamic mutual funds specializing in telecommunications, electronics, shipping, and property. His father had laundered money for the House of Saud, the Saudi ruling family, in the 1970s, and would have known well the tricks and deceptions to be played with capital. To this day, the family company is believed to operate through subsidiary holding companies in the Bahamas, the Virgin Islands, and Cayman.

Trained in engineering and economics, bin Laden, of course, chose not to follow a career in the Bin Laden Corporation. Instead he sought refuge in radical Islam, which offered an alternative to the increasing commercialization of Saudi Arabia in the late 1970s. The turning point came with the Soviet invasion of Afghanistan in 1979. Using his own money and his knowledge of business, bin Laden became instrumental in recruiting Islamists to the cause of the Afghan mujahideen. In addition, his family background in construction prepared him to manage and finance infrastructure projects for the mujahideen in eastern Afghanistan, where he built roads, hospitals, tunnels, and storage depots. In the early 1980s, bin Laden returned to Saudi Arabia, where he organized financial support for the mujahideen, exploiting his contacts with the Saudi elite to obtain financial donations for the Afghan cause. Later, bin Laden joined the mujahideen directly on the ground in Afghanistan to fight the Soviet army, and he distributed to the mujahideen funds funneled through the Bank of Credit and Commerce International by the CIA. After the Soviet withdrawal in 1989, bin Laden returned to Saudi Arabia a hero, feted by the Saudi government as a positive role model for a country keen to stress its Islamist credentials.

Ironically, it was the collapse of BCCI in 1991, and not some new political or religious development, that saw bin Laden return to a central role in the growing international Islamic movement. BCCI had served as a front for a variety of Islamist causes, including the Afghan resistance. It had also been used by the governments of Pakistan and Saudi Arabia for "covert operations." Its collapse forced radical groups to find new ways to move funds to their operatives. Bin Laden stepped into the breach and offered the use of his own international accounts and companies as instruments for the transfer of Islamist funds. A network emerged of accounts and holdings in the Middle East, Africa, and Europe, crowned by the Shamal (North) Islamic Bank in Sudan, in which bin Laden invested $50 million of his own capital.

Within just a few years, bin Laden had succeeded in putting together a financial system that enabled the movement of hundreds of millions of dollars around the world for the support and funding of disparate groups of radical Islamists. Bin Laden had structured the system along offshore lines, so as to be completely watertight and sealed off from the outside world, and so that no traces connecting Islamic terrorists with sponsoring states could be discovered by Western security authorities. The only visible part of the system was a quasi-legal network of Islamic centers and charities that acted as fronts through which funds were transferred to individual terrorists on the ground. In the trial of four men convicted of the 1998 bombings of the U.S. embassies in Nairobi and Dar es Salaam, a former financier for bin Laden revealed that funds were channeled from Riyadh bank accounts to accounts in Holland, Malaysia, the City of London, and even a branch of Barclays Bank in the London suburb of Notting Hill Gate. Fifty million dollars were believed to have originated from Saudi businessmen and then passed into the bin Laden financial network. Bin Laden was quite explicit about his exploitation of the offshore system and its secret devices. His followers were as "aware of the cracks inside the Western financial system as they are of the lines in their hands," bin Laden told a Pakistani newspaper two weeks after 9/11, adding, "These are the very flaws of the Western financial system that are become a noose for it."

In the aftermath of 9/11, then, the image developed by Western intelligence of Al-Qaeda as a worldwide corporation, with a network plugged into the global financial system, seemed very convincing. The network simply had to be identified, turned inside out, and finally overcome. Yet the picture of Al-Qaeda as a coherent, integrated multinational business with global operations and sophisticated financial activities (that were even said to have included the shorting of millions of dollars of stocks in the foreknowledge that the attacks on the United States would send markets reeling) was an unsubstantiated, if politically convenient, construct. As soon as one tried to get a grip on it, its cohesiveness and identity melted away.

Post-9/11 scrutiny showed bin Laden to be, among other things, a grand master of offshore economics. His use of established offshore networks, with their protected freedoms and secrecy setups, had bewitched investigators and was still no less impenetrable. To this he had added private banks, in Africa and elsewhere, where supervision barely existed, and a network of charities, many with legal status in Western countries, that added further complexity to the overall picture. There was the hawala system, an international money transfer system that bypassed banks and allowed payments to be made in one place in return for cash being provided in another, with no record of the transaction made (and thus no traces by which to follow Al-Qaeda money through the system). There were the tens of thousands of "money service" businesses in the United States alone that offered easy and unsupervised check cashing, wire transfer, and currency exchange facilities, not to mention transfer points for gold, diamonds, and other precious commodities.

All these factors made the Bush administration's militarized approach to uncovering Al-Qaeda's finances a circus, one that was bound to fail. Nevertheless, the United States, lacking any real strategy, pressed for more control over the global financial system generally. Its Western allies followed suit, imposing stringent anti–money laundering reporting regulations not just on banks, but on accountants, lawyers, real estate agents, casino operators, auctioneers, car dealers, even jewelers, who faced imprisonment if suspected of failure to report money laundering to the authorities. The new security chiefs resumed naming and shaming tax havens, offshore finance centers, and states that permitted lax financial controls, declaring them global pariahs once more—this time for their role as conniving agents of international terrorism. Their days were numbered, we were told, this time for sure.

Yet the crackdown on terrorist financing didn't amount to much, for it soon became apparent that Al-Qaeda was not some accounting trick that could be uncovered and righted by regulators willing to spend a few weeks in Grand Cayman. Rather, it was not a centralized command and control operation with bin Laden as chief executive, but a disjointed, fragmentary organism operating at street level in the metropolitan centers of the West, where disillusioned young men banded together and engaged in small-scale financial fraud, stole identities and credit card data, communicated through the Internet and cell phones, and used multiple identities to evade capture and detection. These men were, in the main, petty criminals hiding from detection in the city crowd; in them the secret realm mind-set enthusiastically coupled with the totalizing ideology of annihilation and self-destruction.

It also became clear that there was no hard distinction between those willing to bomb aircraft carriers or fly hijacked planes into office buildings. If anything, flying into buildings made bombing ships look relatively easy. After all, how much money did a suicide bomber need? About $1,500, according to a captured Hamas bomber—about the cost of flight school and a one-way ticket from Boston to Los Angeles, the 9/11 hijackers showed us. The small amounts transferred among terrorists were much easier to hide than the billions of dollars drug traffickers dealt with.

Meanwhile, the Bush administration's keenness to crack down on offshore tactics began to work against the interests of its allies and corporate patrons, who were placed on money laundering blacklists just as the United States most needed their support in its "war on terror." As it grew obvious that multilateral action was a blunt and cumbersome instrument with which to intercept terrorist financing—and that it wouldn't bring about the collapse of Al-Qaeda any time soon—the United States resumed its original but less ambitious mission to clear up the vague "dark side" of the global financial system, putting pressure on target countries and tax havens only when doing so suited its immediate objectives. The image of "Holy War Incorporated"—a great adversary that conveniently measured up to the West in terms of its coherence and structure—fell away, leaving an exposed weakness in the United States and its allies. What exactly was the terrorist threat? How did it operate? Who were its perpetrators? In the absence of any clear identity of the nature of the threat and how it was to be overcome, the United States drew away from the international community and turned inward—a suffering soul gathering the strength needed to preserve itself—and considered what recompense it had to exact from the world for the injustice suffered, for its ideal of freedom so defiled. In effect, the U.S. government sought a secret realm of its own, free from obligation, scrutiny, or accountability—all of which (so the thinking went) would inhibit its freedom to fight the war on terror.

The Secret State

In the years immediately following 9/11, the Islamic extremist terror threat—seemingly global in its presence, but no more locally felt than in the actual horrors caused by it—pushed the Western industrial nations deeper into their own corners. The United States, in particular, moved toward a divisive and destructive unilateralism in international affairs, and escalated programs for national security and self-protection as a priority. This was the immediate psychological reflex to the fear of the unknown, to the uncontrollable and horrific nonidentity of adversaries out to murder innocent people.

Until the Western states can completely annihilate their hidden adversaries (whose own fanatic nihilism is a tragic journey to the salvation of total identity, promised in exchange for self-murder), they will seek refuge in their own secret realm in the name of sovereign protection, exercising authoritarian control over suspected enemies of the state, often citizens themselves.

We have already seen how the state asserts its onshore control to harness the dynamism of offshore capitalism and the market. This practice will not abate, for the state will need those free instruments of capital—and the wealth created by them—to buoy up flagging national spirits in the coming years. This is why multilateral action against tax havens and offshore centers will always be at best discretionary and ambiguous on the part of individual states, which can remain self-sufficient only by adapting to capital and riding skillfully on its back.

The new secret state will sponsor more corporate protectionism as the market economy and the fear-driven state grow more accustomed to their cohabitation and eventual union. Expect no dilution in the close relationship between capital and the state, especially now that national security and defense are the new fundamentals of onshore state control. Expect no mercy in the government of the secret realm.

8. Coda: The Ruins of Offshore

Myth will continue to exist as long as there is a single beggar.

—WALTER BENJAMIN

Proteus Moon

The music has ended on the eve of Cayman's five hundredth anniversary. The hard soca rhythms that bounced around George Town's walls and banks have stopped. The people make their way back to Walkers, south of George Town, or back up to West Bay at the top of the island. The streets are the nearest they get to being torn up (save for the hurricanes)—soft drink cans and plastic food containers from the home-cooking stalls strewn on the road, ordinarily unnoticed gutters now visible, bearing the remains of the evening.

The moon is high above the harbor, its beam highlighting the rigging and masts of the tall ships that have come to Cayman for the anniversary celebrations. Replicas of caravels, Boston schooners, brigantines, and blockade runners rock on their moorings, creaking.

Perhaps it is the moon of Proteus up above, for the planet Neptune does have a moon with this name. Everything is unusual about this moon. It was discovered only in 1982, by the *Voyager* 2 spacecraft. This was strange, as Neptune's smaller moon, Nereid, was discovered thirty-three years earlier. But Proteus' essential darkness (it is one of the darkest objects in the solar system) had hidden it from human scrutiny. It absorbs all but a fraction of the sunlight that strikes it, and so reflects only a fragment of light back to Earth. Remarkable too is the moon's strange shape. It is shaped more like a box than a sphere. Proteus is perpetually on the verge of its own transformation: if it were just slightly more massive, its own gravity would cause its irregular shape to change into a perfect sphere.

Proteus is the dark moon of the secret realm. The little light that shines from it explores the recesses and hidden spaces of Earth and probes holes that reach deep inside it, cutting it open. The precise constellation of the offshore world now suggested that one of Proteus' rare beams would break the surface of Cayman and reveal the world's dark interior.

Trouble in Paradise

After being named and shamed in the blacklists of 2000, the Cayman Islands moved faster and more comprehensively than any other offshore financial center to bring itself up to the international standards the G7 and other multilateral bodies required. Before the terror attacks of 9/11, and well before the United States gripped the throat of the international financial system, Cayman had been checked out of the offshore world's sin bin, officially approved and applauded by the wise counsel of global financial probity.

Cayman's atonement was historically unparalleled, and it consisted in the islands' regulatory authorities undoing its standards of secrecy, in open violation of its contracts. A private bank with a reputation for laundering South American drug money was closed down. US$33 million, allegedly stolen from the Peruvian government by its former head of intelligence and stashed in a Cayman bank, was frozen, and the money was returned to Lima. Shell banks that did not have a physical presence on the island were told to either open up a branch on Cayman or get lost. Bearer shares—held in secret by the beneficial owner—were abolished. Financial services companies were directed not to promise confidentiality and secrecy in their marketing material. Secrecy laws were changed to make it easier for outside financial authorities, like the Securities and Exchange Commission, to request "confidential" banking information. The coup de grâce was the impending trial on the island of four local bankers charged with money laundering, paraded as showpieces of Cayman's commitment to cleaning up.

But Cayman gave away too much too fast in its desperation not to fall afoul of the newly vigilant United States and its crusade against the dark side of the global financial system. This was perhaps understandable, as a declaration of anathema out of Washington would wreck the years of hard work that had made Cayman the globe's fifth-biggest banking center. It would wreck a domestic economy that in its dependence on offshore banking had brought wealth and an enviable standard of living to the island.

So Cayman gambled; it tightened up regulations and supervision in excess of what was required, in the hope that its practical commitment to banishing its dark side would bring rewards from the outside world: financial, in the form of mainstream, respectable capital relieved that Cayman was no more a sinner; political, in the approbation it would receive from the ruling powers. Rehabilitated, Cayman would finally take its place in the wider world on terms acceptable to the club of leading economies, and its competitive advantage as an offshore center, not a withheld secret but an open advantage, would be maintained, even enhanced.

It was not to be so. Post 9/11, Cayman would sleepwalk, exposed and defenseless, into a new era that would see no less targeting of tax havens by the industrial powers. Always at the forefront of any targeted action against the tax haven community (and even more so as the United States and its allies combed the offshore world in search of terrorist finances), and already demonstrating that it was quite prepared to act against offshore practices that had long been tolerated, Cayman became a liability, not only to dirty money that needed a safer haven but, worse, a liability to "respectable" capital, which perceived George Town as selling out its competitive advantage, effectively making it a much less attractive place to do business in. Capital is a fickle and frightened animal. It seeks out secrecy, advantage, and the smooth and easy flow of business, and if those could not be guaranteed or promised in Cayman, it would find refuge elsewhere. So Cayman began to change. Private banking on the island became a shadow of the glory days. Corporate registrations started to decline. There were fears of foreign investment declining, a stifled economy soon to fall asleep under the weight of regulation and multilateral directive.

Cayman, stripped of advantages and too much given away, had now to claw back what little it could—or face its demise as an offshore financial center. It was up against not only tax havens that would profit at its expense, but the industrial powers, who earlier had found that globalization moved a little too fast for comfort—and generally did so through the mysterious offshore structures of organized crime, terror, and multinational business alike. To exercise their authority over tax havens—to reclaim their stake in footloose capital gone offshore through corporate tax dodges, or to crack down on organized crime—

the industrial powers had wanted to impose global, multilateral standards on offshore tax havens. These standards, the industrial powers believed, were the only way to effectively police and regulate the offshore world. Begrudgingly, Cayman acquiesced to the global program of standardization. But every attempt to create a level playing field offshore was sabotaged, either by Cayman's tax haven competitors or by powerful nation-states breaking their multilateral promises, as was the case when Bush came into office. Cayman's position was dire: it had yielded to the policy of standardization in the hope that that policy would win out. In doing so, it had given much away, and left itself at the mercy of effective global governance of the offshore world. Now that this seemed no more than a pipe dream, Cayman had to preserve whatever advantage it could to survive.

When the smoke from the crackdown on the financial system cleared, a new force could be seen taking aim at the offshore tax havens. The European Union savings tax directive had been around for a while, but it was delayed and obscured following 9/11. It now moved out into the open, like a battleship appearing on Cayman's horizon.

The idea behind the EU initiative was clear enough: to tax the savings of EU citizens held in tax havens. Naturally, Britain, as a member of the European Union, insisted that Cayman, its dependent territory, sign up to the directive. This would mean that Cayman would exchange bank information with the United Kingdom and other EU member states. One of Cayman's last competitive advantages, its residual banking confidentiality, would be swept aside in a single stroke. Cayman resisted pressure from Britain. Signing up to the directive would cost Cayman up to US$40 million a year in lost business from EU residents, a local report said. The reporting costs alone for Cayman's banks would be astronomical. Hardest hit would be Cayman's nest egg: its tax-exempt mutual funds. And worst of all, U.S. investors would be deterred from Cayman, fearing their identities would be revealed inadvertently when banks screened European residents.

Very soon capital would bypass Cayman and head off to Hong Kong or Singapore, Bahamas or Bermuda (none of them dependents of Britain), where the savings tax directive would have no authority. "People won't want to do business with us anymore," said Kurt Tibbetts, an elected member of the Cayman legislature. "The world we helped to build is now crashing down on us."

The pressure from the United Kingdom continued. It said it would impose the directive on Cayman by direct legislation from Westminster if the island did not budge. Cayman said it would resist such force and would take the United Kingdom to court. It pointed to Austria, Belgium, and Luxembourg, which had won the right to apply withholding taxes on savings and turn them over to the EU instead of giving up their secret bank information to member states. That is what Switzerland was proposing. Though not an EU member, Switzerland was crucial to the implementation of the savings tax directive because of the large deposits of European money there, and it would not finalize a deal with the EU unless it could extract concessions on separate OECD negotiations to preserve its banking secrecy. This hardly looked like a level playing field, argued Cayman: if we signed up to the directive, all our clients seeking offshore tax advantage would move their money to Switzerland.

Cayman, having gambled away its competitive advantage on the back of a promise to impose general reform on the global financial system, now played hardball in order to get its own concessions from the British government. "It is not the 1800s where as a territory they can shove us around with laws and regulations," said McKeeva Bush, Cayman's leader of government business.

Cayman was fighting for its life as an offshore center. As a last resort, it sacrificed political progress in the hope of maintaining offshore financial freedom. In a gesture of defiance against its old colonial masters, it rejected any further discussions on a written constitution for the island. A constitution would have introduced a properly representative electoral system, with one person one vote, elected government ministers, and political parties. Such notions had already been regarded with suspicion on Cayman as underhanded attempts by Britain to divide and rule the island—to lure it onshore and out of the tax haven business. Now Britain wanted to sacrifice Cayman to its objectives of power in a unified Europe.

In the past four decades Cayman has changed beyond all recognition. It once supported itself through the sea; it now supports itself through global capital. It has seamlessly exchanged one type of relationship with globalization, one based on the export of labor, for another, based on the export of financial services. This exchange, which has brought income to Cayman, was possible only because Cayman's bankers "opened up" the island and offered it utterly and completely to outsiders whose interests have been at best respectably commercial and at worst downright criminal. Its law, its government, its land, and its people—its trust—have all been sacrificed to these ends. This is the deal that Cayman made forty years ago, and because of it, Cayman is as dependent financially on world capital as it is politically on the United Kingdom. Between these poles of detached freedom and remote control, Cayman has carved out its own peculiar realm of existence.

Caymanians are nostalgic for the era when they took on the world and looked after themselves. At the same time, they are proud of their wholesale deliverance to capital, for on this their existence depends, and so it is the only yardstick by which they measure their success.

Of the forty thousand people on the island, less than half are native Caymanians, the direct descendants of the Europeans and African slaves who settled on the island from the 1700s. The remainder of the population are those brought by Cayman's bitter fruits. Fifteen thousand U.S. and European citizens are the agents of global commerce on the island, living privileged and very well-rewarded lives. At the other end, there are thousands of immigrants of many nationalities, principally from Jamaica, the Philippines, and Honduras—all laborers, hotel workers, and domestics—who have come to physically build and service Cayman's expansion.

And here is the problem: "native" Caymanians see themselves as a minority stuck in the middle between the wealthy commercial class and the immigrants. They are resentful of the former, denying them citizenship and the right to vote, even though many have been on Cayman more than twenty years and are well integrated. They resent their mansions in South Sand too, yet consider a career in offshore banking and finance the only one worth following. So Caymanians who do not make it to the banks and trust companies in George Town are considered losers in the eyes of their own people. At the same time, they resent the Jamaicans and other immigrants, who, they fear, will take over their jobs and cause instability. "There are too many Jamaican domestics," they say. "Send them home—but not mine." So they restrict Jamaican entry into the country and rotate immigrants from other nations to meet the high demand for labor.

On the outside, Cayman's unexamined, offshore, detached society comes to resemble that of any other country struggling with the pressures of modernity. The churches have long ago ceased to act as a genuine compensating force against social anomie. Families do not function as they used to, and the global media culture of a "right now, right here" lifestyle lies in wait for an opportunity in every modest house on the island. Criminal cases are on the rise, as are drug offenses, robbery, and domestic violence. It is not unknown now for masked men carrying firearms to hold up George Town restaurants and bars frequented by tourists. Outsiders are routinely blamed: Hondurans for gambling, Jamaicans for gun violence. But it is mostly native Caymanians in the islands' prison.

The specter of poverty is once again a reality, with unemployment less uncommon and more than half of Caymanians just managing to scrape together enough to cover food, rent, and utility bills. "What happens if there is a leveling off in our financial services economy? What do we do then?" asks Kurt Tibbetts, one of the most prominent spokesmen for a new political and social settlement in Cayman. "We have paid a price for massive growth in the years gone by. There used to be none of this keeping up with the Joneses, having a BMW, or even a car at all. Now our whole world has turned topsy-turvy, and people are falling through the cracks. There are huge risks from social unrest. Like a domino effect, it could all fall down."

Offshore Wreckage, in Miniature

We are on the verge of the secret realm. At the extremities, offshore is so distorted and so detached from onshore norms that it begins to eat itself up and self-destruct. How far capital and the state have traveled offshore in the global economy; how implicated capital and the state are in each other's destructive offshore existence. We now see, in miniature, the secret, inverted pillars that hold up the roof of the global economy—and turn the whole world upside down.

Along Cardinal Avenue stands Cardinal Plaza, where the empty former offices of Euro Bank Corporation await new tenants. In May 1999 Euro Bank was closed down by the Cayman authorities. Charges followed accusing the bank's senior officers of running a systematic money laundering operation. Three years later the case came to trial in Cayman. Within a few months the trial was suspended and the defendants acquitted in a public scandal involving Britain's secret intelligence service, MI6. Cayman is still reeling from the repercussions of the Euro Bank scandal, a story that precisely illuminates the contradictions of our offshore world.

Euro Bank had been a fixture on the islands since the 1970s, serving onshore clients—generally private individuals looking for secrecy to evade taxes and hide assets from litigants, creditors, and wives. In this it was no different from any other private bank on the island. It operated in a fairly relaxed regulatory environment where the government was happy to just pick up revenue from bank licenses and let establishments like Euro Bank get on with it.

In 1996, private banking in Cayman received a modest shake-up when anti–money laundering legislation, in the form of the Proceeds of Criminal Conduct Law, was introduced onto the island for the first time. The shake-up was modest because Euro Bank and other private banks on Cayman were able to use the new law to acquire immunity from prosecution in money laundering cases in return for the occasional supply of information (known as Suspicious Activity Reports) about their clients to the islands' new Financial Reporting Unit (FRU). To the banks, the new law was a kind of quid pro quo arrangement specially devised for Cayman, where things could go on pretty much as before.

Edward Warwick was an assistant manager at Euro Bank. He became quite a regular source of intelligence to the FRU when the new law was introduced, but his relationship to the man who ran the unit went back further. Warwick was working at Finsbury Bank and Trust in the early 1990s when he first met Brian Gibbs, a former Metropolitan Police detective inspector from England, who had come over to Cayman to run the island's anti–drug trafficking unit. After Gibbs moved to the FRU and Warwick got a job at Euro Bank, the relationship continued.

Warwick became Gibbs's ears and eyes inside Euro Bank. Unbeknownst to his colleagues at Euro Bank, Warwick would meet Gibbs and supply him with intelligence on Euro Bank's clients and what they were up to. But it was not just Warwick who was leading a double life. Gibbs was too. He was working for Britain's secret intelligence service, MI6. Warwick didn't know this. Neither did he know that he was the service's key source in Euro Bank and had been given the code name Warlock. MI6's official name for its covert operation against Euro Bank was Operation Victory.

The MI6 plan with Euro Bank, like its other operations on Cayman's banks, was to wait, watch, and listen. If its sources on the island, unknowingly for the most part, provided intelligence on some suspicious character using Cayman's financial apparatus, local action by Gibbs would be undertaken on the approval of MI6. However, MI6's role needed to be completely concealed from the process, as Cayman's own politicians and officials had no knowledge of the agency's existence on the island. Furthermore, MI6 employed means of intelligence gathering that ran directly counter to Cayman's confidentiality law.

The patient watching and waiting in Operation Victory came to an abrupt end in May 1999. In a civil case brought by the U.S. Federal Trade Commission, Kenneth Taves, a U.S. citizen, was indicted for a massive credit card fraud. Taves had stolen US$37 million from 800,000 credit cards by signing their owners up to pornographic Web sites without their knowledge. Many of the cardholders did not even have computers, and some had not even used the credit cards in question.

Taves had arrived on the scene at Euro Bank in 1997. His father was already familiar with Cayman and had previously used Guardian Bank. Guardian was closed down in 1996 by the Cayman authorities after its owner was indicted in the United States on tax-evasion charges. Taves senior then moved his account to Euro Bank, and after that the first of the big $500,000 checks from his son came rolling in to the second floor of Cardinal Plaza. The Taveses had between them five accounts at Euro Bank, and Kenneth Taves was said to have transferred $25.3 million in illegal profits through his accounts over the course of two years, with his lawyers allegedly assisting him to move some of those funds into accounts in the South Pacific tax haven of Vanuatu, and to Vaduz in Liechtenstein.

With the news of Taves's arrest and his connection to Euro Bank made public in the press, Britain now pressed Cayman to go ahead and use its new anti–money laundering powers. In May 1999 things started to happen fast. Euro Bank was placed under the regulatory control of accountants, pending an investigation by Gibbs. The investigation was covertly controlled by MI6 in London in the interests of getting arrests and charges laid down as soon as possible. The next step was to close Euro Bank and put it into court-supervised voluntary liquidation. Then twelve arrests at the bank followed, including those of the chairman, the general manager, various owners of the bank, and the Taves account managers. By early 2000, five individuals were charged, and everything was readied for a prosecution that was going to prove nothing less than a systematic agreement to launder money at Euro Bank.

With the Euro Bank trial due to get under way in mid-2002, what became known as the London Plan was devised at MI6's Vauxhall Cross headquarters. Privy to the plan were the agency, Gibbs, the Cayman Islands attorney general David Ballantyne, and senior members of the prosecution team. The essence of the plan was that no copies of the MI6 intelligence material on Euro Bank were to be used in court in Cayman unless all references to MI6 were removed. The premise of the plan was clear, but its precise implementation was detailed and complex, revolving around two factors: first, to reproduce the material on the FRU computer back in Cayman, from where it would be disclosed to the defense in court. This was important because the material—much of it from Edward Warwick—had to appear as if it were completely generated in Cayman by Gibbs in the course of his FRU work, without any MI6 involvement.

The second key factor was more complicated, in that it involved certain analysis to be made of the material in order to decide whether disclosure should be made on the FRU computer in the first place. Material was to be disclosed only if it had not already been disclosed in any other form to the defense, such as in a Suspicious Activity Report. This was to avoid the defense getting suspicious about the duplication of disclosed material, which could lead to difficult questions about the material's provenance. And there was more. Material was not to be disclosed to the defense if it was judged that its sensitivity made it subject to Public Interest Immunity (PPI)—in which case an application would be made to the court to withhold disclosure from the defense and permit it to be shown just to the trial judge alone. The job of the prosecution therefore would be to keep a watch on developments in court to decide what material would best be used in the context of PPI.

The crux of the London Plan, and the contradiction that would cause it to backfire, was that the demand was being made in London to secretly control the use of material by the prosecution in open court, the precise use of which, in the case of PPI applications, could only be freely decided in Cayman as the trial proceeded. This fact did not pass MI6 by—they recognized the contradiction. To a certain extent, such a contradiction is inherent in any kind of activity where a particular goal being pursued openly in the public realm is being secretly influenced or manipulated by a process of deception that shares the same goal but uses means that conflict legally or morally with those used in public, and ultimately, if exposed, can jeopardize the common goal. The secret control of the public realm by means of deception in order to advance a particular interest was as applicable in MI6's scheme for the Euro Bank trial as it was for the clients that had used Euro Bank's offshore structures to hide their tax evasion and dirty money in the first place. Such were the distortions of state and capital in their offshore bid to outdo each other. In essence, the means used by dirty money and the state mirrored each other, even as their goals were in open conflict.

The way through their contradiction, as it now occurred to MI6, was the key role Gibbs was to play on the ground in Cayman. Gibbs's function, in effect, was to mediate between the controlling demands of MI6 and the prosecution's strategic use of the material as it became relevant in the trial. To fulfill this function properly—to use the MI6 material in reality but make it appear that it was not being used—Gibbs had to be detached as far as possible from the proceedings of the case. Indeed, this point was so crucial to the way the prosecution was to operate that it had been decided as far back as August 2000 to exclude Gibbs as a witness or from giving any evidence in the trial.

As the trial began in June 2002, the "in-court" element of the London Plan got off to a good start, with a successful Public Interest Immunity application granted the prosecution for material considered to be fairly sensitive, though not connected to Warwick. Nevertheless, the prosecution had to work hard to persuade MI6 to even let them apply for the PPI, as the agency was worried that the judge and court in Cayman would blurt out its contents in public.

However, it did not take long before the defense sensed something odd about the prosecution's case. The question they found themselves asking was: If Gibbs was the head of the FRU and the lead investigator for the prosecution, then how come he appeared to be so completely absent from the prosecution's case? What was perhaps stranger still was that Gibbs himself had not given a statement. Going one step further, the defense wondered whether there had been meetings between Gibbs and Euro Bank that had not been disclosed. In response to defense questions, Gibbs was ordered by the court to make a statement disclosing all his appointments and meetings with Euro Bank between 1995 and 1999. The London Plan's weakest link—the virtual but necessary invisibility of the man whom common sense would have judged to have been quite visible in the trial—was beginning to be exposed by the defense.

The defense, though, had not worked the problem out by themselves. They had got lucky. The loose mouths on Cayman that had so worried MI6 indeed proved to be a bonus. The defense team had been tipped off by someone on the island that Warwick had been an informer of the FRU while he was employed at Euro Bank. The defense had not let on in court earlier that they had this information. They just wanted to ruffle a few feathers to get Gibbs to produce a statement. Then, on July 2, the day before Gibbs's statement was due, the chief defense barrister, Michael Hill QC, declared in open court that Warwick had been an informer "formal or otherwise of the FRU." This was a fact the prosecution must have known about for some time, said Hill. The prosecution was now visibly on the defensive, with their lead barrister protesting that any relationship Warwick had with the FRU was entirely normal, and just standard practice for any bank employee across the world who was required to report suspicious activity to the authorities. Andrew Mitchell QC concluded for the prosecution, without any trace of irony, that "it would be a shame if anybody went away from here with the impression that there is some sort of informant issue that is being hidden from the defendants."

But of course there was. And in a controlled panic, Gibbs left George Town's law courts to think about what to do. He had the statement of all his contacts with Euro Bank to finish that day. If he was to conceal the truth, that statement would be more of a demanding deception to conceive in the light of what was beginning to come out into the open. He had another problem too: things had moved so fast and quickly in the trial that he had not finished editing and changing the material that his MI6 controller had brought back to him from London to replicate on the FRU computer. As it turned out, this was not a simple mechanical task; it involved Gibbs in lengthy analysis and study of the material. He simply had not finished. He took the material MI6 had given him out of a folder securely locked away in his office and shredded it. Then he sat down and finished off his statement, merely noting that he had spoken to Warwick a number of times prior to the introduction of the 1996 anti–money laundering law and since then in relation to a few Suspicious Activity Reports. Now that the material that would point to his lies was gone, the deception was less demanding to make. He was freer to deal with the ordeal at hand. Such distortion and denial of the truth showed how the secret state, at work offshore, corrupts the legal process.

The trial was put on hold while the defense prepared an application to the court allowing them to cross-examine Warwick about his relationship with Gibbs. The application was approved in early November 2002. A sequence of events would now unfold that would bring Warwick's relationship as an informant out into the open, as it would Gibbs's collaboration with MI6 and practically every detail of the London Plan.

The Warwick cross-examination in the absence of a jury quickly produced the results the defense was looking for: a relationship with Gibbs that was much more involved than had previously been disclosed. Gibbs's July 3 statement, written hours after he had shredded the MI6 material, was seriously contradicted by Warwick's latest evidence. Gibbs was again instructed to be interviewed by the prosecution for the presentation of a further statement on November 26, in which he was to give the definitive account of his dealings with Euro Bank and Warwick.

What the prosecution now needed to know from Gibbs, in order to prepare the statement, was the extent to which he had disclosed the MI6 material, suitably adapted, according to the London Plan, on the FRU computer. They were not prepared for Gibbs's answer. He had not disclosed it, because he had destroyed the material, he told them. Why? asked the prosecution. Because his MI6 controller had telephoned him and told him to destroy all material at his office and home that might connect him to MI6. Why? asked the prosecution. Because a search warrant for a raid on his home and office had been ordered, and the Cayman Islands police were about to carry it out. Why? Because he was suspected by the Cayman judiciary of bugging their telephones. So he destroyed everything, including material not related to the trial, to protect MI6. The story sounded unbelievable.

The next day, Gibbs told Andrew Mitchell and the attorney general that MI6 had re-sent the material overnight from London. It looked like there might be life left in the plan yet. To be perfectly sure of the situation, Mitchell asked Gibbs whether it would be possible for MI6 to resend the material to the prosecution direct. Gibbs doubted it. But it was possible, and MI6 sent the material over to Mitchell via secure fax. Then Gibbs told the attorney general that he had lied: he had not received the material overnight from MI6, but had discovered in his office a version of the material he had been editing, which he had hidden in a safe place and forgotten about. Gibbs was becoming ever more unbelievable. The lies, deceptions, and double-dealings he was forced to make were ruining the Euro Bank trial well before any of the defendants had even been called to the witness stand. Not long after, the London Plan was disclosed to the court in full and the case fell apart.

Six months after the trial started, at a cost of $14 million to Cayman, the defendants were acquitted, the judge ruling that there had been an abuse of process by the prosecution that had misled the court through the destruction of material relevant to the trial and the "extra-judicial alteration of the state of the evidence." Gibbs ran from the island with his family to Britain, because, the governor said, "of a potential risk to his safety." He was followed out later by David Ballantyne, the attorney general, after the islands' elected executive council refused to sit down in a room with him, fearing every word would find its way back to the spies in London.

The anger at their betrayal was felt deeply by Cayman's political elite. The colonial master they had served so well had plotted and schemed behind their backs, their relationship with Britain—once the bedrock of Cayman success as an offshore financial center—now fraying and falling apart. "A great wrong has been committed in this country," the islands' chief elected minister, McKeeva Bush, declared. But there was a tragic naïveté in Cayman's official response, for after all, this was not *their* country—their allegiance was to the Crown, on whom they depended. For all that they imagined they had broken free into the world, they were, in truth, mere offshore subjects, not their own people. That secret, strange dark space found in the endless struggle between freedom and control in the global economy—that was their jurisdiction. They had decided to inhabit that realm, to profit from it in order to survive. It had been their choice.

Around the coast of Cayman lie dotted the wrecks of ships run aground on the rocks—those of pirates, colonial powers, and global traders. On a map of Cayman's distorted contours they are marked in detail: the Wreck of the Ten Sail, 1794; the *Augustus Caesar*, "lost here in 1765"; the *Oro Vende*, 1983. But Cayman is as much marked by the wreckage on its shores: of BCCI, Enron, and countless scandals—none the more so than Euro Bank, Cayman's own ruin, the topographic sign of its going under.

With Euro Bank, Cayman had traveled deep into the offshore interior of the secret realm. Hidden, criminal capital tried to evade and manipulate onshore state authority so that it could be cheated to satisfy the impulse of an ever more rapacious freedom, spurred on by deceptions that could cut the path to ever greater wealth and power. And into the depths of that criminal interior had come the secret realm of the state, using deception too to catch what escaped its control. Together, capital and state found in their deception a natural fellowship of secrecy, both to preserve themselves and then to fight it out for mastery. This was the inverted, upside-down offshore world that Cayman had bred in its fat, prosperous belly and had spewed out, but to no relief. Cayman was neither free nor in control, but paralyzed and humiliated by the outside forces of the secret state and secret capital; both had nestled in its midst and brought Cayman to the brink of disaster. In this disaster was reflected, in miniature, the inverted image of a world turned offshore.

Into the Secret Realm

It is the morning after the fireworks and soca jump-up on Cardinal Avenue. Anniversary Day 2003: five hundred years exactly since Columbus first sighted the islands on his last voyage to the New World. George Town is still and quiet, the sun muted by the gathering of large black clouds, a few raindrops felt as I pass around the corner of Church Street into Fort Street. Still there is no sound, no sign of life. Is it over? I wonder, finished already? In Cayman, you have to get close up to see and hear, or else you might miss something and walk on by.

I passed the library, closed this Saturday morning. The young men usually studying there now marched by in white shirts, black trousers, striped neckerchiefs, and berets—stiff and regimental, holding the flags of Great Britain and Cayman. Behind them other young men paraded into Panton Street, boy soldiers in khaki uniforms and big black boots. They came to a rest in front of the law courts and lined up on one side of the street, opposite half a dozen rows of chairs, where Panama hat wearers with gray, thinning hair sat beside their wives, who wore floral dresses and clutched handbags.

The Police Band struck up a brassy tune, echoing off the walls of the offices and banks that dominated George Town's modest skyline. McKeeva Bush, the leader of government business, and Eric Crutchley, the managing director of Cayman National Bank, their wives beside them, rose to their feet as the fanfare began and Prince Edward, Earl of Wessex, arrived. Prayers were said and the national anthem sung.

"This is a sacred place," said McKeeva Bush, behind him the islands' quincentennial Wall of History, covered by a blue sheet, to be unveiled shortly by the prince. "It is about the preservation of the Caymanian way of life," he continued. "Cayman's history is not of war and conquering, but of rising from humble beginnings, and of the hardest-

working people in the world." Cayman was safe and clean and en-
dorsed by people in George W. Bush's administration, who'd recently
told McKeeva Bush that Cayman was one of the most important
countries in the world.

Prince Edward made his way over to the Perspex podium. His
mother, the queen, had sent a message wishing Cayman a peaceful
and prosperous future. There were some polite, restrained claps. The
prince paused, thought, and referred obliquely to the islands' current
troubles with the British government over Euro Bank and EU tax directives. It should not be forgotten, he pointed out, that there was a
distinction between Cayman's relationship with the Crown and its relationship with Britain. He wanted to stress the warm relationship that
Cayman had with the Crown. The guests laughed in relief, the ten-
sion briefly defused.

The prince unveiled the Wall of History, a twenty-foot-long wall of
shiny black marble tiles on which were painted a sequence of pictures
representing Cayman's history, from Columbus's sighting to an image
reflecting the unveiling itself. Cayman had never striven harder to
find its identity as it did at this moment. To do so made sense amid all
the uncertainty. This moment was Cayman's onshore epiphany.

> I'm coming, coming very soon,
> O beauteous isle to thee.
> Although I wandered far, my heart
> Enshrines thee yet
> Homeland fair Cayman Isle,
> I cannot thee forget.

The words of Cayman's national song, sung out solo without ac-
companiment, rang melancholy across the town. The guard of honor
stood to attention as the scouts removed the flags and the army cadets
prepared for the departure of the prince. The Police Band resumed,
and the royal party departed.

The black clouds hung over still, and light drops persisted. The gathering broke up, and local politicians and island bankers peeled off, stopping for a moment to greet one another in a casual, knowing kind of way. There was no sign of it given away, but in secret, the islands' elite were murmuring about independence, that forbidden fruit they had refused to taste in order to seek security and protection under the wing of their colonial master. That relationship had worked so well. Now the veil of global tax initiatives and the Euro Bank debacle floated over them; they were reminded that Britain's involvement in their affairs was no longer such a boon.

They now questioned their dependence on Britain. It spelled the ruin of their offshore financial freedom, and without that they would be tied to a master they resented, with nothing left to show for themselves. Perhaps independence was the way forward, to preserve and protect their livelihoods and economic sovereignty. Who knows, the islands' bankers confided to one another, who would be targeted by MI6 next? Were the spies at my bank? one would say. Quite possibly, the other would reply; hadn't several men convicted in the United States in the past year used your bank to launder millions of dollars?

If handled in a controlled way, the gentlemen of Cayman agreed, there could be a stable transition to independence within the next few years. This move would be entirely on the grounds of preserving their offshore freedom as a financial center. It was best to preserve the old government-business alliance and conserve autocratic rule. No constitution. No political reform. Independence could serve only the interests of commerce, not the people.

Cayman was not entirely on its own. It had a good friend in the United States, particularly with an administration that disliked multilateralism and dealt with Cayman on a one-to-one basis. Perhaps a U.S. alliance was the most profitable way to progress, the good burghers ruminated in the expat exclusivity of George Town's Cricket Square bar. "We love it when the Republicans are in power," said one. "Here, here," said all.

Back in town, at the water's edge, another memorial was being unveiled, this time to Cayman's seafarers and the generations of fathers
and sons who had gone out to sea to earn a living. An architect from
Madrid was in the small group that assembled around the memorial
statue. Diego Colon was in town, the twenty-first grandson of Christopher Columbus—the man who had journeyed across the Atlantic
with ancient sea stories in his head, of Odysseus, of Heracles finding
the golden apples of Hesperides at the end of the world, of Sinbad
the Sailor. The man who had discovered the Island of Paradise, from
where retrograde humanity could be reborn, and where, on the other
hand, there was gold beyond all belief to make adventurous men like
him rich forever.

George Town's streets and walls opened up passageways into a secret realm where the modern world had begun and where it pursued
its colonial conquest for trade and political power, using slavery and
savagery in the name of the Christian kingdom to come. The thresh-
olds came alive and opened up like nature: the sign on the front of a
run-down office block, BANK AUSTRIA CAYMAN ISLANDS LTD., led down
into the hidden interior. The pirate mannequins gawped outside the
duty-free shops and showed the way. Euro Bank drew you into its
beautiful layers of empty, contentless forms harboring secret, dirty
capital. And down deep in this protected realm where absolute control was held over the world, the wealthy, powerful, and criminal
could be seen crafting their deceptions to let them be free forever after, above all law but their own. The secret of the secret realm was
revealed, the source of its mystery encountered, the dark, distant light
of Proteus' moon twinkling in its depths.

In Cayman's history, and in the modern world's, is imprinted the
secret realm, the interior refuge that formed thousands of years ago in
man as he took possession of the outside, natural world. From this
refuge sprang the solid sense of his own individual identity, of man in
sovereign possession of himself. But as this great leap was made, all

possession came to be hidden away inside the shell of ownership, the fortress walls of protection erected, the distance from life and others secured. Undercover, from the vantage point inside the shell, perhaps as a consolation for the new liberty of detachment, an ideal beauty was imagined of a self back in league with nature, of reconciliation with what was thought of as lost.

Now out again, passing back into the world from the depths, Cayman's beautiful forms that promised freedom became instruments of ruin, never attaining the grandeur of the ideal they had promised, so far detached as they were from the labors of everyday life. But how could the ruins of that lost ideal, once created, just drift away forgotten, as if time were empty? No, these debased forms sensed their own naturelike utility as technological instruments of capital—their endlessly malleable, transforming, and changing nature used for progressive ownership and control of the world. Naturalized, illegitimate forms of offshore power hid inside modern capitalism as had the little hunchback inside the mechanical Turk, the eighteenth-century automaton that fooled everyone into believing it could play a winning game of chess; as the hunchback secretly manipulated the hands of the automaton to make a move, so the secret realm wins every move for capital.

Everywhere now, returning from the heart of the mystery, these offshore instruments appeared as allegories of a fallen, fossilized freedom, there to tell us the dismal truth of the offshore world to which we had been banished. For the abuse of nature's freedom, and our attempt to steal it away for our own ends, nature exacted its revenge. The mythic power of darkness enveloped us as a ceiling we could not pierce, except through the ferocity of our mad, loving intent to break the claustrophobic veil that holds us down.

Finally, back out again through the deceptions into the light of their evident fall in George Town, the passageways sealed up again to keep the world in darkness.

After this experience, there was a need to get away from George Town as quickly as possible. The drive around the Atlantic-facing edge of Grand Cayman, to Cayman Kai, on the north side, took over an hour. The terrain was sometimes sparse, rugged; on the land side there were thick woods. Waves crashed on the sea-facing side. Away from George Town at last, and through East End, an area to which freed slaves in the 1830s had first set out from town, to build their own houses and lives on the rougher, harder edges of Cayman's shores.

At the tip of land at the top of Cayman Kai, a wedding reception was under way. I stopped, parked the car, and took a look. It was an American affair—they'd landed just twenty-four hours before and would return the next morning. Everything was being crushed into the shortest available time. A single pan player did his best to the recorded background music. A weary, tired woman broke off from the party, comforting a friend who was upset and crying, her eyeliner smudged. No cares of the onshore world had been left behind in this supposed paradise isle.

As I looked into a pool of water by the shore, raindrops broke the surface, sending a crab running away. It brought back the time I was out swimming and noticed a bunch of playful, brightly colored fish swimming past my ankles. I had quite a shock when I realized that a bigger, uglier dark brown fish was hovering around my shoulders. Now it was getting darker. A mosquito buzzed by.

On the drive back to George Town, I saw the secluded seafront properties that lined the road. Tiled front drives. Buildings whipped by the dust of the concrete that had just built them, stirred up by the wind. Each unoccupied and empty. The occasional housemaid out in a side yard, watering plants, putting something out, sweeping. Domestic workers waiting for lifts on the country road south, young women sprung out of Jamaica, away from home in unfriendly Cayman, waiting in the rain.

The names of the villas flashed by. Golden Pond. The Lagoon. So

Serene. Sea Island. Legasea. Twin Palms. Tranquility. Detached, empty forms, monuments to their own offshore isolation.

Up and down George Town's Eastern Avenue the cars go. There seemed to be more now, perhaps the vehicles were just bigger, on the verge of turning into SUVs, with dark-tinted windows and impressive aluminum wheels. The music from the cars was distinctly louder. Out thumped the rhythm-and-blues tune of the moment, the mixed-up offshore/onshore world of total freedom and total control, expressed in the words of the song:

> Got somebody, she's a beauty
> Very special really and truly
> Take good care of me like it's her duty
> Won't you ride by my side night and day . . .
> No letting go. No holding back.

I stopped the car for the red lights at the intersection of Eastern Avenue and West Bay Road. The choice was to drive into the center of George Town or go back home. Home it was—for a life outside the offshore networks, a life lived out of the secret realm, where freedom must be brought up again from those protected depths that had stolen and corrupted it. To go back onshore, reattached to the body of society, in league with nature, where freedom must move people together, not push them apart.

Meanwhile, elsewhere in Grand Cayman, out of town, in the smart suburban mansions of South Sand and in the Yacht Club, the islands' elite would gather to plot Cayman's self-determination in the offshore world. Yes, they mused, the United States is our only friend now. Very soon the time will come when we will have to act to protect our offshore freedom.

And out of Dog City on the edge of George Town, the first beggar would appear, and people would wonder why.

Notes

1: Our Offshore World

5 "a small number of individuals . . .": *Caymanian Compass*, May 8, 2003, p. 4.

6 "there were cows wandering . . .": quoted in Anthony Sampson, *The Money Lenders* (London, Hodder and Stoughton, 1981), p. 225.

7 Thirty years ago: Benson Ebanks interview transcripts (September/October 1997), Cayman Islands National Archive.

9 By the end of the 1970s: Sampson, p. 228.

13 Talk in the 1960s: Sir Vassel Johnson, *As I See It: How Cayman Became a Leading Financial Centre* (Lewes, The Book Guild, 2001), p. 11.

16 From the time of the first permanent settlements: Consuelo Ebanks and Carol Winker, *The Southwell Years: Recollections of Caymanian Seamen and Those Who Served at Home* (Cayman Islands, Cayman National Cultural Foundation, 2003), p. 10.

16 Records show that Blackbeard: *Cayman Islands Colonial Report*, 1953.

17 By 1937, half of the islands': Ebanks and Winker, p. 102.

17 With most husbands and fathers: Ebanks and Winker, p. 98.

17 Yet the men sacrificed much: Ebanks and Winker, p. 11.

17 Captain John Hurlston: Hurlston interview transcript (November 14, 1990), Cayman Islands National Archive.

18   A Michigan shipping tycoon: Ebanks and Winker, pp. 13–14.

18   Homemade porridge: Ebanks and Winker, p. 98.

18   Benson Ebanks worked: Ebanks and Winker, pp. 95–97.

19   Men who had spent: Johnson, p. 109.

19   By the mid-1960s: *Cayman Islands Government Report*, 1961–65.

20   Others, like Thomas Jefferson: Jefferson interview transcripts (March/April 2002), Cayman Islands National Archive.

21   The Cayman company is a separate legal being: C. S. Gill, *Cayman: The Offshore Financial Capital* (Grand Cayman, C. S. Gill, 1997), p. 12.

22   It can enter into contracts: Gill, pp. 20–21.

22   "I have long dreamed . . .": quoted in Sampson, p. 223.

22   With its own private bank: Gill, p. 47.

23   From 1950 to 1975: R. A. Johns and Christopher Le Marchant, *Finance Centres: British Isles' Offshore Development since 1979* (London, Pinter, 1993), p. 2.

23   "an international corporation . . .": quoted in Sampson, p. 223.

23   Tax haven expert: Jim Hougan, *Spooks: The Private Use of Secret Agents* (London, W. H. Allen, 1979), pp. 205–206.

32   Trusts were common too: Johnson, p. 151.

33   "If you don't think . . .": quoted in *Nor'wester*, March 1973.

33   In 1976 Anthony Field: Johnson, p. 154.

33   The investigation: *Newsweek*, June 28, 1976.

33   "taxpayers have exploited . . .": IRS memo quoted in *Newsweek*.

33   Castle Bank was considered: *Washington Post*, May 3, 1977.

34   "No information relating . . .": quoted in Johnson, p. 155.

35   The IRS investigation: *Newsweek*, October 13, 1975.

35   California tax attorneys: *Newsweek*, June 28, 1976.

35   Organized crime groups: *Newsweek*, June 28, 1976.

2: The Offshore Corporation

41   A settlement was reached: Charles Lewis, Bill Allison, and the Center for Public Integrity, *The Cheating of America* (New York, HarperCollins, 2001), pp. 186–87.

43   At the turn of the millennium: Lewis et al., p. 138.

43   For 1999 as a whole: *Financial Times*, March 27/28, 2004.

46   U.S. multinationals are the undisputed: *Financial Times*, February 2, 2004.

46 The News Corporation corporate structure: *The Economist*, March 20, 1999.

46 according to an Australian parliamentary investigation: *The Independent*, February 4, 1998.

47 As a further government bonus: Sol Piciotto, *International Business Taxation* (London, Weidenfeld and Nicholson, 1992), p. 100.

48 According to the OECD: Lewis et al., p. 77.

49 Chevron and Mobil: *Transfer Pricing and Corporate Taxes*, www.itic net.org.

50 J. W. Smith details the mechanics: J. W. Smith, *The World's Wasted Wealth 2* (Institute for Economic Recovery, 1994), p. 138.

51 One company operating a transfer: Lewis et al., p. 76.

51 Apple did manufacture: Lewis et al., pp. 77–78.

52 A more recent case: Agence France-Presse, August 4, 2004.

53 In 1990 it was estimated: Sen. Byron Dorgan, *Global Shell Games: How Corporations Operate Tax Free* (www.washingtonmonthly.com/features/2000/0007.dorgan.html, July/August 2000).

53 British and U.S. tax authorities: Peter Dicken, *Global Shift* (London, Sage, 2001), p. 247.

53 "in the midst of general unfreedom . . .": Theodor W. Adorno, *Negative Dialectics* (London, Routledge, 2000), p. 283.

3: The Offshore Interior

55 Indeed, Enron had a special unit: *New York Times*, January 17, 2002.

55 It also received: *Financial Times*, February 4, 2002.

56 "I don't want a competitor to . . .": quoted in *Wall Street Journal*, August 6, 2002.

56 "windowless isolation": Theodor W. Adorno, *Negative Dialectics* (London, Routledge, 2000), p. 219.

57 Very occasionally Enron: *St. Petersburg Times*, February 4, 2002.

58 In 1998 Fastow: *Wall Street Journal*, November 8, 2001.

59 Lay and company were convinced: *Newsweek*, January 21, 2002.

59 Jeff Skilling told Wall Street: *Wall Street Journal*, November 8, 2001.

59 "They wanted to climb . . .": quoted in *Newsweek*, January 21, 2002.

60 "sporadic fashion": *U.S. Bankruptcy Court: Third Interim Report of Neal Batson, Court Approved Examiner* (June 30, 2003), p. 18.

61 In March 1998: the details of the Rhythms transaction in the sections that

follow are from the *Report of Investigation by the Special Investigative Committee of the Board of Directors of Enron*, February 1, 2002, and the *Third Interim Report of Neal Batson*.

64   Variously called a special purpose vehicle: C. S. Gill, *Cayman: The Offshore Financial Capital* (Grand Cayman, C. S. Gill, 1997), pp. 53–57.

65   Harford has said: *Miami Herald*, February 21, 2002.

65   "We must make sure . . .": Harford is quoted in *Miami Herald*, February 21, 2002.

69   However, this was just pocket change: *International Herald Tribune*, May 9, 2002.

70   Only a few months: the details of the LJM2 transactions are from the *Report of Investigation by the Special Investigative Committee of the Board of Directors of Enron*, February 1, 2002, and the *Third Interim Report of Neal Batson*.

70   More diverse investors: *Financial Times*, January 30, 2002.

72   "Raptor looks to be . . .": Sherron Watkins letter to Kenneth Lay, August 15, 2001.

72   An internal report: *Financial Times*, January 30, 2002.

75   "It is not that . . .": Testimony of Alan Greenspan before Senate Committee on Banking, July 16, 2002.

4: Offshore Freedom, Onshore Control

83   In 2000 Congress approved: *Financial Times*, February 9, 2002.

83   Coincidentally, of course: *Financial Times*, February 9, 2002.

84   Earlier, Lay is alleged: *The Guardian*, February 2, 2002.

84   All the while: *Financial Times*, January 29, 2002.

84   In August 1998: *The Scotsman*, January 29, 30, 2002.

85   "We [Enron] have many friends . . .": Karl Milner, a former aide to Gordon Brown, quoted in *Financial Times*, January 29, 2002.

85   John Wakeham: *The Guardian*, January 30, 2002.

85   Ralph Nader defines: Ralph Nader, *Cutting Corporate Welfare* (New York, Seven Stories Press, 2000), p. 13.

86   Despite the billion-dollar aid package: *Financial Times*, September 20, September 3, 2004.

87   "because private financial markets . . .": Nader, p. 70.

87   The savings and loan bailout: Nader, p. 15.

87   "freed the industry . . .": Nader, p. 15.

87 "In the end . . .": quoted in Nader, p. 16.

88 For the five-year period: Nader, p. 77.

88 in 1992, $32 billion: Sen. Byron Dorgan, *Global Shell Games: How Corporations Operate Tax Free* (www.washingtonmonthly.com/features/2000/0007. dorgan.html, July/August 2000).

92 it would be able to reduce: *International Herald Tribune*, May 14, 2002.

92 Meanwhile, banners held aloft: Associated Press, May 9, 2002.

95 Tyco held its shareholder meeting: *Financial Times*, March 9, 2004.

95 "Sorry, Stanley": *Wall Street Journal*, May 9, 2003.

95 "We are working through . . .": quoted in *New York Times*, February 18, 2002.

96 Over time, cross-border: *Financial Times*, February 2, 2004.

96 whose address: *Financial Times*, March 9, 2004.

96 "exquisite rootlessness": Charles Derber, *Corporation Nation* (New York, St. Martin's Griffin, 1998), p. 168.

101 A government spokeswoman: *The Times*, February 11, 2002.

103 His personal fortune: *The Guardian*, February 14, 2002.

103 putting him into: *The Times*, February 11, 2002.

103 LNM today: *Financial Times*, March 20/21, 2004.

103 producing sixty-five million tons: *Financial Times*, October 27, 2004.

103 "arguably the best . . .": quoted in *The Observer*, February 17, 2002.

103 he bought a house: *The Times*, February 11, 2002.

104 passing the donation: *Sunday Telegraph*, March 10, 2002.

104 Shortly after Labour was elected: *The Guardian*, February 23, 2002.

105 Apparently, one of the companies: *Sunday Telegraph*, March 10, 2002.

106 It was the prospect: *The Guardian*, February 14, 2002.

107 "Today's action . . .": quoted in *The Observer*, February 17, 2002.

111 the government now encourages: *Financial Times*, March 27, 2002.

111 this has led to a situation: *Financial Times*, November 20, 2001.

113 One example of such corruption: OECD, *Behind the Corporate Veil: Using Corporate Entities for Illicit Purposes* (Paris, OECD, 2001), p. 35.

113 A recent estimate: OECD, p. 21.

114 "tie national and local . . .": Peter Dicken, *Global Shift* (London, Sage, 2001), p. 276.

115 "The primary concern of . . .": *Financial Times*, January 31, 2002.

115 "It is perhaps most useful . . .": D. M. Gordon, quoted in Dicken, p. 243.

5: Interlude: The Secret Realm

119 "Authority has no strength . . .": Anonymous, Internet.

119 We meet Proteus: for the story of Proteus, see Homer, *The Odyssey* (London, Penguin, 1991), pp. 45–70.

120 The basic opposition: A. A. Long, "Thinking About the Cosmos: Greek Philosophy from Thales to Aristotle," in Robert Browning (ed.), *The Greek World* (London, Thames & Hudson, 1999), pp. 101–14.

122 what Marx had to say: Karl Marx, *Pre-Capitalist Economic Formations* (London, Lawrence & Wishart, 1975), p. 85.

123 "The natural element . . .": Hegel, "Philosophy of Right," in Frederick Weiss (ed.), *Hegel: The Essential Writings* (New York, Harper Torchbooks, 1974), p. 282.

124 "maritime networks . . .": Philip de Souza, *Seafaring and Civilization* (London, Profile, 2001), p. 5.

125 "the laboratory of his forces": Marx, p. 97.

126 Royal currencies and taxation: Fernand Braudel, *The Wheels of Commerce* (New York, Harper & Row, 1982), p. 519.

126 "*Tout est ici . . .*": quoted in Braudel, p. 526.

127 "For some time now . . .": quoted in Marx, p. 138.

127 "masters and possessors": quoted in Charles Taylor, *Sources of the Self: The Making of Modern Identity* (Cambridge, Cambridge University Press, 1992), p. 161.

128 "The vexations of art . . .": quoted in Caroline Merchant, *The Death of Nature: Women, Ecology and the Scientific Revolution* (San Francisco, Harper & Row, 1980), pp. 169, 171.

129 "Let us hope for . . .": quoted in Taylor, p. 330.

129 "submit in silence to . . .": quoted in Taylor, p. 326.

130 "speaks to us in . . .": quoted in Taylor, p. 357.

131 "Newton first saw order . . .": Alan Ritter and Julia Conaway Bondanella (eds.), *Rousseau's Political Writings* (New York, Norton, 1988), p. 108.

131 "Rousseau first discovered . . .": Ritter and Bondanella, p. 108.

132 "indifferent to humanity": Immanuel Kant, *Critique of Pure Reason* (London, Everyman, 1998), p. 4 [Aix].

132 "the moral use": Kant, p. 19 [Bxxiv].

133 nature was regarded: Ernst Cassirer, *Kant's Life and Thought* (New Haven, Yale University Press, 1981), pp. 165–206.

133 practically forced to be free: Bernard Williams, *Truth and Truthfulness* (Woodstock, Princeton University Press, 2002), p. 181.

135 "I must therefore abolish knowledge . . .": Kant, p. 21 [Bxxix].

135 "Only in a person . . .": Cassirer, p. 247.

136 "all might be well": Theodor W. Adorno, *Problems of Moral Philosophy* (Cambridge, Polity Press, 2000), n. 198.

136 "to the moral welfare . . .": Norman Hampson, *The Enlightenment* (Harmondsworth, Penguin, 1976), p. 213.

136 "degenerated into ideology . . .": Adorno, p. 172.

136 The Tragedy of Freedom: the critique of Kant's moral philosophy in this section is based on Adorno, *Problems of Moral Philosophy*.

138 "Laws in reality . . .": Adorno, p. 125.

139 "obsessive isolation": Williams, p. 122.

140 "deeply tragic . . .": from an interview with Berlin in the program "Isaiah Berlin—Historian of Ideas," broadcast on BBC Radio 3, December 1999.

141 politics and society in late nineteenth-century Vienna: see Carl E. Schorske, *Fin-de-Siecle Vienna* (New York, Vintage, 1981).

143 In his work on the arcades: see Walter Benjamin, *The Arcades Project* (Cambridge MA, Belknap Press, 1999).

143 "quest for order": Zygmunt Bauman, "The Quest for Order," in Peter Beilharz (ed.), *The Bauman Reader* (Oxford, Blackwell, 2001), pp. 281–87.

144 Balzac contemporaneously related: Ernest Mandel, *Delightful Murder: A Social History of the Crime Story* (London, Pluto Press, 1984), p. 5.

144 "Each morning . . .": quoted in Mandel, p. 5.

144 The bourgeois would cover up: Benjamin, p. 122.

144 "To live in . . .": Benjamin, p. 216.

145 In the bourgeois interior: Walter Benjamin, *Charles Baudelaire: A Lyric Poet in the Era of High Capitalism* (London, Verso, 1992), pp. 167–69.

145 "removed from the . . .": Benjamin, *Baudelaire*, p. 47.

145 "a criminal career is . . .": Benjamin, *Baudelaire*, p. 79.

6: Offshore Heaven, Offshore Hell

150 where a free port and tax benefits: Tony Doggart and Caroline Voute, *Tax Havens and Offshore Funds* (London, Economist Intelligence Unit, 1971), pp. 14, 41.

150 in 1936 the maximum individual rate: Charles Lewis, Bill Allison, and the Center for Public Integrity, *The Cheating of America* (New York, Harper Collins, 2001), p. 9.

150   A joint congressional committee: Sol Piciotto, *International Business Taxation* (London, Weidenfeld and Nicolson, 1992), p. 100.

150   the British 1866 Companies Act: Doggart and Voute, p. 43.

151   Beaverbrook's General Trust Company: Michael Pye, *The King over the Water* (London, Hutchinson, 1981), p. 8.

151   currency stolen by the Nazis: Pye, pp. 58–59.

151   "I began by spending . . .": quoted in David R. Legge, "The Visionary Who Saw Cayman's Future—and Then Helped Build It," *Cayman Executive*, vol. 1, no. 1 (1993), p. 59.

151   Milton Grundy: Anthony Sampson, *The Money Lenders* (London, Hodder and Stoughton, 1981), p. 225.

151   In that year: Sampson, p. 225.

152   "The timing was terrific . . .": quoted in Legge.

152   "These islands are . . .": *Cayman Islands Government Report*, 1970.

152   "Geometric shapes . . .": *Nor'wester*, June 1972.

153   "The moral foundation . . .": *Nor'wester*, February 1972.

153   "a kind of economic sanctuary . . .": *Nor'wester*, February 1973.

154   "It was like Switzerland . . .": Lem Hurlston interview transcripts (December 1996), Cayman Islands National Archive.

154   Doucet started out: the November 1972 edition of the *Nor'wester* provides some excellent background material on Jean Doucet.

156   "They were very futuristic . . .": Lem Hurlston interview transcripts.

156   "a charming array . . .": *Nor'wester*, November 1972.

157   Doucet celebrated the opening: *Nor'wester*, August 1974.

157   "That's rather odd . . .": Lem Hurlston interview transcripts.

158   Questions were being asked: Sir Vassel Johnson, *As I See It: How Cayman Became a Leading Financial Centre* (Lewes, The Book Guild, 2001), pp. 160–61.

158   Interbank shut its doors: *Nor'wester*, November 1974.

158   The Cayman government deliberated: Johnson, p. 163.

160   Suitcases arrived: Benson Ebanks interview transcripts (September/October 1997), Cayman Islands National Archive.

160   charged a 10 percent counting fee: this figure was quoted by a banker interviewed in Cayman.

160   "they used to boast . . .": Benson Ebanks interview with author, May 2003.

160   Learjets would arrive: Benson Ebanks interview with author, May 2003.

161   various other subsidiaries: *Financial Times*, January 14, 2004.

161   football: *Financial Times*, January 3, 2004.

164   Stefano Tanzi, son of the founder: *Cayman Net News*, January 16, 2004.

165 equal to the combined foreign debt: the comparisons are based on figures cited in *The Economist Pocket World in Figures* (London, Profile, 2001), pp. 38–39.

166 "I was in agreement with . . .": quoted in *Financial Times*, January 3, 2004.

167 when Parmalat announced: *Bloomberg*, April 26, 2004.

167 besides the forged Bonlat statement: *Cayman Net News*, January 16, 2004.

168 In the wake of Parmalat's downfall: *Cayman Net News*, January 6 and 16, 2004.

168 Elsewhere in the Parmalat offshore network: *Financial Times*, January 14, 2004.

168 The investigation into the offshore network: *Cayman Net News*, January 16, 2004.

169 "The unification of . . .": quoted in Bobbio's obituary, *Financial Times*, January 20, 2004.

7: The Politics of Offshore

171 The competition to get tax down: *Financial Times*, May 1, 2001.

173 the U.S. Justice Department: R. T. Naylor, *Hot Money and the Politics of Debt* (London, Unwin Hyman, 1987), pp. 302–304.

173 This was based on: Sir Vassel Johnson, *As I See It: How Cayman Became a Leading Financial Centre* (Lewes, The Book Guild, 2001), p. 300.

174 The time had come: Anthony Sampson, *The Money Lenders* (London, Hodder and Stoughton, 1981), p. 228.

174 Putting pressure on Cayman: Naylor, pp. 298–99.

174 "routinely indulged": Naylor, p. 298.

174 Although—in the early 1980s: Naylor, p. 298.

174 Sir Vassel Johnson: Johnson, p. 318.

175 Rather, they prospered: Norman Peagam, "Treasure Islands," *Euromoney* Supplement (May 1989), p. 11.

175 Deposits by U.S. citizens: Peagam, p. 12.

176 Here the world's economic diversity: Jonathan Winer, "The Coming Wave of Transparency Reform," *Vital Speeches*, vol. 66, no. 7 (January 15, 2000), p. 207.

176 BCCI grew faster: see Austin Mitchell, Prem Sikka, Patricia Arnold, Christine Cooper, and Hugh Willmott, *The BCCI Cover-Up* (Basildon, AABA, 2001).

177 The bank had a prominent: Sampson, p. 227.

177   openly publicized: interview with former Cayman police officer, April 2003.
177   But the hundreds of shell companies: Peter Truell and Larry Gurwin, *BCCI: The Inside Story of the World's Most Corrupt Financial Empire* (London, Bloomsbury, 1992), pp. 190–97.
177   A receiver was appointed: Truell and Gurwin, p. 311.
178   In fact there was no compulsion: see William Wechsler, "Follow the Money," *Foreign Affairs*, July/August (2001).
179   hedge funds were not required: *BusinessWeek*, October 12, 1998.
180   The firm quickly raised: Paul Blustein, *The Chastening: Inside the Crisis That Rocked the Global Financial System and Humbled the IMF* (New York, Public Affairs, 2001), p. 309.
180   LTCM's specialty: Blustein, pp. 308–10.
181   "More than twice . . .": see testimony of R. M. Morgenthau before U.S. Senate Permanent Subcommittee on Investigations, July 18, 2001.
181   LTCM earned investors: Blustein, p. 310.
181   And at its height: Blustein, p. 309.
182   To make the hedges pay off: Blustein, pp. 309–10.
182   thereafter its leverage rose: Winer, p. 207.
183   investors themselves: Blustein, p. 310.
183   "Losses of this . . .": quoted in Blustein, p. 312.
183   "Why should . . .": *New York Times*, September 25, 1998.
184   "Had the failure . . .": quoted in Blustein, p. 325.
184   The best the U.S. authorities: Winer, p. 207.
185   Greenspan maintains: *Financial Times*, February 19, 2004.
185   "serious deficiencies in supervision . . ." Caroline Doggart, *Tax Havens and Their Uses* (London, Economist Intelligence Unit, 2002), p. 250.
185   Along with twenty-five other: The "low quality" group comprised Anguilla, Antigua and Barbuda, Aruba, the Bahamas, Belize, the British Virgin Islands, the Cayman Islands, the Cook Islands, Costa Rica, Cyprus, Lebanon, Liechtenstein, the Marshall Islands, Mauritius, Nauru, the Netherlands Antilles, Niue, Panama, St. Kitts and Nevis, St. Lucia, St. Vincent and the Grenadines, Samoa, the Seychelles, Turks and Caicos, and Vanuatu. The "middle quality" jurisdictions were Andorra, Bahrain, Barbados, Bermuda, Gibraltar, Labuan (Malaysia), Macao, and Monaco. The "high quality" category included Dublin (Ireland), Guernsey, Hong Kong, the Isle of Man, Jersey, Luxembourg, Singapore, and Switzerland.
185   It kept itself off the OECD's blacklist: The OECD found the following

jurisdictions to be tax havens: Andorra, Anguilla, Antigua and Barbuda, Aruba, the Bahamas, Bahrain, Barbados, Belize, the British Virgin Islands, the Cook Islands, Dominica, Gibraltar, Grenada, Guernsey, the Isle of Man, Jersey, Liberia, Liechtenstein, the Maldives, the Marshall Islands, Monaco, Montserrat, Nauru, the Netherlands Antilles, Niue, Panama, Samoa, St. Lucia, St. Kitts and Nevis, St. Vincent and the Grenadines, the Seychelles, Tonga, Turks and Caicos, the U.S. Virgin Islands, and Vanuatu.

185 Suddenly it was open season: *The Guardian*, May 2, 2000, ran the article "Gangster States" by Jean Maillard, a French judge. The article "warns that global crime is exploding as offshore tax havens prostitute their legal systems."

186 "a dark day . . .": *OECD Observer*, June 22, 2000.

187 a great instrument for putting pressure: see OECD, *Improving Access to Bank Information for Tax Purposes* (Paris, OECD, 2000), p. 22: "One of the elements that has fuelled globalization in the last decade has been the liberalization of financial markets . . . This liberalization was in part a response to the threat to financial markets posed by offshore financial centres." See also M. Hampton and J. Abbot (eds.), *Offshore Finance Centres and Tax Havens: The Rise of Global Capital* (London, Macmillan, 1999), p. 15: "Banking authorities around the world attempted in the late 1960s and 1970s, to regulate the new international capital market . . . but they failed. There have always been some offshore centres which had few regulatory scruples and which therefore attracted the international financiers. Eventually instead of continuing their unequal struggle, the supervisors decided to repeal their own regulations and bring the financial markets back home."

187 At this time, in order to prevent: Winer, p. 207.

189 Foreign banks and investors: Blustein, pp. 245–46.

191 Yeltsin's oligarch cronies: "Moscow's Most Wanted Man," *The Guardian*, April 27, 2003.

191 For every dollar of inward investment: Prem Sikka, *The Role of Offshore Financial Centres in Globalization* (www.essex.ac.uk/AFM/research/ working papers/WP03-02.pdf).

191 The Russian Central Bank admitted: Wechsler, "Follow the Money," p. 40.

191 A subsequent review: Winer, p. 207.

193 Cayman and Nauru appeared: Wechsler, p. 40.

193 direct links to oligarchs: Jeffrey Robinson, *The Merger: The Conglomeration of International Organized Crime* (Woodstock, Overlook, 2000), pp. 152–69.

194 It was at this point: Wechsler, p. 40.

194 the $100 million that Raul Salinas: see minority staff report for the Permanent Subcommittee on Investigations, "Private Banking and Money Laundering: A Case Study of Opportunities and Vulnerabilities" (November 1999).

194 "There is a dark side to . . .": statement by Treasury Secretary Lawrence Summers, at the G7 press conference, July 8, 2000.

195 international rules and directives: Wechsler is explicit on this point.

195 "Coalitions of the willing . . .": see Wechsler.

196 Liechtenstein's police: *The Economist*, June 24, 2000.

196 Switzerland stepped up: *The Economist*, July 29, 2000.

197 G7 finance ministers: G7 finance ministers press release, Fukuoka, Japan, July 8, 2000.

198 "part of the broader . . .": Bradley Jensen of the Free Congress Foundation, quoted in *Financial Times*, June 1, 2001.

198 The Heritage Foundation: *Financial Times*, May 1, 2000. The Heritage Foundation's position was definitively stated by Daniel J. Mitchell in "An OECD Proposal to Eliminate Tax Competition Would Mean Higher Taxes and Less Privacy," *Heritage Foundation Report* (September 18, 2000). The report begins: "A specter haunts the world's governments. They fear that the combination of economic liberalization with modern information technology poses a threat to their capacity to raise taxes."

198 Senator Don Nickles: *The Observer*, May 6, 2001.

199 Toward the goal: for a good description of the protagonists involved in financial transparency issues, see Leslie Elliott Amijo, "The Political Geography of World Financial Reform: Who Wants What and Why?" *Global Governance*, October 1, 2001.

202 "current money-laundering practices . . .": Lindsay is quoted in Wechsler, p. 40.

202 In a letter to *The Washington Times*: O'Neill is quoted in *Financial Times*, May 1, 2001.

203 In response to Bush's turnaround: *Financial Times*, May 18, 2001.

203 "Whether it concerns . . .": Laurent Fabius, France's finance minister, quoted in *Financial Times*, May 18, 2001.

203 "How far . . .": quoted in *Financial Times*, June 1, 2001.

203 "Dear Mr. President . . .": Letter from economists to George W. Bush, May 31, 2001.

204 "We have developed . . .": George W. Bush, White House speech, September 24, 2001.

205   To raise funds for terrorism: William Wechsler, "Strangling the Hydra: Targeting Al Qaeda's Finances," in James F. Hoge and Gideon Rose (eds.), *How Did This Happen?* (New York, Public Affairs, 2001), pp. 130–35.

205   "Money is the lifeblood of . . .": George W. Bush, White House speech, September 24, 2001.

205   At home, a whole raft: *Financial Times*, October 6/7, 2001.

206   "It represents the effective abolition": quoted in *Financial Times*, October 6/7, 2001.

207   Bush's strategic line: George W. Bush, White House speech, September 24, 2001.

207   Holy War Incorporated: see Peter L. Bergen, *Holy War, Inc. — Inside the Secret World of Osama bin Laden* (New York, Free Press, 2001).

208   The U.K. government's: The document was released by Downing Street on October 4, 2001.

209   His father had laundered money: Yossef Bodansky, *Bin Laden: The Man Who Declared War on America* (California, Forum Prima, 2001), p. 3.

209   To this day: *The Guardian*, October 3, 2001.

209   Trained in engineering: the account of bin Laden's education and involvement with the mujahideen in Afghanistan is based on Bodansky, pp. 11–29.

209   it was the collapse: Bodansky, p. 40.

210   Within just a few years: Bodansky, pp. 40–44.

210   "aware of the cracks . . .": quoted in Wechsler, "Strangling the Hydra," p. 134.

212   About $1,500: *The Economist*, June 1, 2002.

212   The small amounts transferred: *Financial Times*, November 20, 2001.

8: Coda: The Ruins of Offshore

216   The little light that shines: "The moon rises at midnight" by the Finnish poet Eeva-Liisa Manner suggested the imagery used here.

218   There were fears: *Cayman Net News*, May 2, 2003.

219   The reporting costs alone: *International Money Marketing*, April 4, 2003.

220   Very soon capital: *Financial Times*, December 1, 2003.

220   "People won't want . . .": Kurt Tibbetts interview with author, May 2003.

220   Though not an EU member: *Financial Times*, March 9, 2004.

220   "It is not . . .": quoted in *Financial Times*, December 1, 2003.

222 they resent the Jamaicans: this observation about Caymanians was made by Kurt Tibbetts in interview.

222 Criminal cases: *Cayman Islands Annual Report*, 2001.

222 as are drug offenses: *Royal Cayman Islands Police Service Report*, 2000.

222 It is not unknown: the *Cayman Compass*, May 10, 2003, reported such an episode in George Town.

222 But it is mostly: Lem Hurlston interview with author, May 2003.

222 The specter of poverty: *Financial Times*, July 16, 2001.

223 "What happens if . . .": Kurt Tibbetts interview.

224 Edward Warwick was an assistant manager: the details about Euro Bank in this section (unless otherwise stated below) are based on interviews undertaken by the author in Cayman in May 2003, and on Hon. Chief Justice Anthony Smellie's *Findings of Fact on the Abuse of Process Application* concerning Criminal Indictment 6 of 2001 in the Grand Court of the Cayman Islands (see www.quinhampson.com.ky/pdf/LegalUpdateEuro Bank.pdf).

224 Warwick was working: *The Guardian*, January 18, 2003.

225 Taves had stolen: AP, July 16, 2003.

225 The Taveses had between them: *Los Angeles Times*, August 25, 1999.

235 Were the spies at my bank?: this concern was raised by a Cayman banker interviewed by the author.

235 "We love it . . .": this comment was made by a Cayman businessman interviewed by the author.

236 ancient sea stories: see Valerie Flint, *The Imaginative Landscape of Christopher Columbus* (Princeton, N.J., Princeton University Press, 1992).

Acknowledgments

The idea for a book on the offshore world grew out of a conversation in June 2001 with Dollan Cannell, with whom I had worked previously on a television documentary. At the time I was thinking about an idea for a film on money laundering. Dollan's suggestion that I might approach the subject better through a book led me, within a few weeks, to shift the focus onto the offshore tax-haven world itself, which seemed to lie not only behind the particular phenomenon of money laundering, but also various other secret goings-on within the global economy more generally.

The landscape of deception was already quite familiar from my work at Kroll, where I started in 1999 as an analyst, quickly learning that much of the intelligence and investigations work I undertook into businesses and companies—from the most respectable to the downright criminal—was back-routed to wealth and assets secured in the offshore world.

The final piece of the puzzle to kick-start the idea was a long interest in the work of the German critic and writer Walter Benjamin, who had written about the nineteenth-century bourgeois domestic interior—with its ornamental casings and coverings—as a space where the wealthy hid their valuable objects away from the outside world while leaving them on show, provocatively veiled. This mysterious act was a sign to the world that the owners of such wealth believed they were unique individuals, more so, at least, than those who possessed less, and a breed apart from those who possessed nothing.

That there might be a fruitful relationship linking Benjamin's ideas about ownership and personal identity with the modern offshore world was encouraged by a series of intensely productive conversations with the late Dominic Simpson of Kroll, a most perceptive and much missed reader of Benjamin, during the summer of 2001; by September 2001, I pretty much had the scope of my subject and the way I wanted to treat it worked out. Then, with the terrorist attacks of September 11, what had been an exciting period of pulling different strands together on a financial subject not quite in the headlines — and therefore seemingly containable — came to an end, with the offshore world under immediate scrutiny by the Bush administration as an area whose tough regulation was said to be critical to national security.

Suddenly, there was a kind of freezing over of the original terms of the subject, which now had a whole new heap of mythology poured over it, leaving so much more to come to terms with, decipher, and unpack. This, in part, is the reason for the long germination of the book before you.

I am very grateful to my former employers, Kroll Associates, who gave me time off from work in 2002 to begin researching the offshore world. I would particularly like to thank Richard Blaksley, who introduced me to the arts of corporate investigation and who responded generously to my requests for time out of the office to write.

I owe a great debt to my editor at FSG, Paul Elie, whose timely interventions kept me on track and showed me how the further reaches of my research could be profitably incorporated (or put to one side). As I finally sat down to put everything together and write in 2003–4, Paul's faith in the project and his practical guidance were at last able to express themselves on the page. For this, besides much else, I am grateful to Paul. I would like also to thank Kathryn Lewis and Kevin Doughten at FSG for their assistance.

I am grateful to Zoe Newman and Rachel Furness for research assistance.

Among the very many people who have given me help in writing this book, I should like to express my thanks particularly to the following: Nigel Acheson, Jennifer Balfour, Charlie Bell, John Boaden, Timothy Brittain-Catlin, Ishbel Bruce, Victoria and Mischa Bruce-Winkler, John Christenson, Justin Dukes, Omer Erginsoy, T. R. Fehrenbach, Paul Field, Dennis Fleary, Richard Gardner, Ben Hamilton, Tommy Helsby, Howard Jones, Dan Karson, Andrew Marshall, Dick Marston, Rayna Milkova, Alessandro Nürnberg, Colin Osborne, Liliana Pop, June Reid, Joscelyn Richards, Kirsten and Max Schou-Nicolaisen, Brian Stapleton, Anne Tiedemann, Frank Trentmann, and Louis and Maria Wonderly. I would like to thank everyone in the Cayman Islands who so generously gave up their time to talk to me.

I am grateful to Søren Lind and the Brecht House Society in Denmark for two peaceful writing weeks overlooking the Svendborg Sund in May 2004, and to Heather McLaughlin and the staff of the Cayman Islands National Archive for their assistance a year earlier.

I would like to thank my agent, Clare Alexander at Gillon Aitken Associates, for her sustained commitment to this book.

As always, I owe the greatest debt to my wife, Sukai, whose support, advice, and encouragement have been invaluable.

Index